Making Policy Work

Many tools are on offer to politicians and other policy-makers when they seek to change policy outcomes. Often they choose to concentrate on one set of tools, but fail to see the costs as well as the benefits – and may not consider the available evidence regarding their effectiveness. This innovative new textbook clearly sets out the main tools of government, and provides an analysis of their efficacy when applied to public problems.

Each chapter examines the relative benefits and costs of using a key tool that is available to improve policy outcomes, drawing on a diverse literature, a large number of empirical studies and a range of contexts. Areas covered include:

- Governments and policy outcomes
- Law and regulation
- Public spending and taxation
- Bureaucracy and public management
- Institutions
- Information, persuasion and deliberation
- Networks and governance.

Offering a clear and comprehensive evaluation, and highlighting the set of powerful tools commonly available, this text encourages students to consider the most effective combination in order to manage key issues successfully. Including a useful glossary of key terms, this book will be of great interest to all students of public policy, administration and management.

Peter John is the Hallsworth Chair of Governance, University of Manchester, where he is a co-director of the Institute of Political and Economic Governance. He is known for his work on public policy, in particular *Analysing Public Policy* (second edition forthcoming 2011, Routledge).

Routledge Textbooks in Policy Studies

This series provides high-quality textbooks and teaching materials for upper-level courses on all aspects of public policy as well as policy analysis, design, practice and evaluation. Each text is authored or edited by a leading scholar in the field and aims both to survey established areas and present the latest thinking on emerging topics.

The Public Policy Primer
Managing the policy process
Xun Wu, M Ramesh, Michael Howlett and Scott Fritzen

Designing Public Policies
Principles and instruments
Michael Howlett

Making Policy Work
Peter John

Making Policy Work

Peter John

Routledge
Taylor & Francis Group

LONDON AND NEW YORK

First published 2011 by Routledge
2 Park Square, Milton Park, Abingdon, Oxon, OX14 4RN

Simultaneously published in the USA and Canada
by Routledge
711 Third Avenue, New York, NY 10017

Routledge is an imprint of the Taylor & Francis Group, an informa business

Typeset in Times New Roman by Taylor & Francis Books
Printed and bound in Great Britain by CPI Antony Rowe, Chippenham,
Wiltshire

British Library Cataloguing in Publication Data
A catalogue record for this book is available from the British Library

Library of Congress Cataloging in Publication Data
John, Peter, 1960-
Making policy work / Peter John.
    p. cm. – (Routledge textbooks in policy studies)
Includes bibliographical references and index.
1. Policy sciences. I. Title.
H97.J659 2011
320.6 – dc22   2010034414

ISBN: 978-0-415-37544-3 (hbk)
ISBN: 978-0-415-38029-4 (pbk)
ISBN: 978-0-203-83078-9 (ebk)

Contents

Preface

When teaching public policy, I used to get asked a hard question, often from practitioners studying for a master's degree. Does the theory of public policy make a difference to what happens in the world? To these students' dismay, I found I could not answer their query very well. Rather lamely, I used to say it is important to understand causation in public policy to find out what policy makers can and cannot do. My other surprising lack of response was that I could not suggest a book that would help them answer the question either. I had to go back a long way, such as to Pressman and Wildavsky's classic *Implementation* (1973), to get close to a satisfactory recommendation. Rather than examine impact, much of the literature on implementation and delivery describes the introduction of policies and evaluates different models that explain public decision-making. Even the tools of government literature, which has greatly influenced my thinking, is also more interested in elaborating what are the main things governments can do rather than in assessing the effects of particular tools. I also found the policy evaluation literature to be disappointing as it tends to focus on particular fields of activity rather than deal with the big questions. Experts, such as economists, social policy researchers and subject specialists, carry out these kinds of studies on the particular public problems, such as in housing and the environment. Political scientists, with their attention to decision-making and institutions, have not ventured so much into this topic.

Without a ready answer to the students' question, I decided that I could write such a book, which is the one that follows. Its purpose is to set out the main tools of government, the main things that governments can do and the resources they can apply to public problems, either directly or indirectly. The book then assesses the evidence for the effectiveness of these tools, drawing on a diverse literature, a large number of empirical studies and a range of contexts – something no other text has tried to do. Without wanting to assume that governments can only do one thing, I wished to engage in an argument about the desirable balance of tools that are commonly available. I wanted to find out, were I a politician in charge of a government department or local council, where I would put my organisation's scarce energy and resources. I desired to have an argument about the relative benefits and costs of each choice using the best evidence I could find.

Driving the book is my optimistic conception of the possibilities of social science, which in my view has the independence and techniques to be able to answer the question the book poses, or at least to go a long way towards doing so. In this way, the book reaches back to the tradition of using scientific knowledge for the benefit of the public realm, something that inspired the founding thinkers of the study of public policy, such as Aaron Wildavsky. I hope that some indication of the limits to knowledge comes across too. For during the writing of this book, my awareness of the weakness of many quantitative evaluations of policy interventions came to the fore. I became convinced of the importance of randomised controlled trials and their superiority over other methods of policy evaluation and theory testing, even though I am aware of the difficulties of carrying out these experiments too. The reader will find some examples of experiments I have found useful and interesting whilst not losing sight of the benefits of other methods, such as quasi-experiments, case studies and good statistical analysis of panel and time-series data.

In partnership with colleagues from the Universities of Manchester and Southampton, I became interested in using field experiments to evaluate the non-standard tools of government, based on more light-touch and/or deliberative interventions (see www.civicbehaviour.org.uk, John *et al.*, 2011). Without wanting to give away the central message of the book, the reader can see a continuum that begins in the early chapters on the standard and well-tried instruments of the state – finance/taxation and law/regulation – then moves to the less standard ones presented toward the end. In the course of the book, the reader can get a sense of the direction in which I have travelled intellectually. Hopefully, having been on this journey, I can now answer the question the students posed to me, or at least refer them to a book.

Acknowledgements

Firstly, I thank my editor, Craig Fowlie, who encouraged me to write a book on policy analysis. We were trying to get permission to publish a second edition of my *Analysing Public Policy* (1998) and he suggested I could do a more applied piece while we were waiting for the rights to come through. In the end, in spite of my enthusiasm, the book took much longer to write than both he and I expected. So I also thank Craig for his patience.

I am very grateful to everyone who responded to the original proposal, in particular the attendees of Colloque International: Instruments d'Action Publique, 20 and 21 December 2004, Sciences Po, Salle Goguel, 56, rue des St Pères, Paris, France, where I presented the early ideas as a paper. The comments I received, in addition to those from the anonymous referees, helped me refine the concepts and intellectual framework. I also was intrigued by the rather Gallic amazement at the audacity of my project, which made me want to do it all the more.

Some of the work the book discusses draws on collaborations I have had the pleasure to participate in recently, as many of the references in the text attest. I thank my funders for allowing these projects to happen, in particular the Economic and Social Research Council. I very much appreciate the efforts and intellectual stimulation of my co-researchers, who have helped shape my ideas. In particular, I thank Rebecca Askew, Anthony Bertelli, Tessa Brannan, Sarah Cotterill, George Boyne, Keith Dowding, Ed Fieldhouse, Francesca Gains, Matthew Goodwin, Stephen Greasley, Alan Harding, David Halpern, Mark Johnson, Hanhua Liu, Helen Margetts, Hisako Nomura, Oliver James, Zoë Morris, Alice Moseley, Nicolai Petrovsky, Liz Richardson, Nirmala Rao, Graham Smith, Gerry Stoker, Corinne Wales, Hugh Ward and Hal Wolman.

Most of all, I appreciate the help of Francesca Gains, Helen Margetts and Mick Moran, who took the trouble to make detailed comments on the first draft of the book. Their insights and reactions were very useful in clarifying the ideas and helping me avoid some of the worst bear-traps of this tricky topic. I am also grateful to Shaun Bevan for his advice on the glossary. I very much appreciate the hard work of the editors at Routledge, particularly

Nicola Parkin, and of the copy-editor, Victoria Brown, who helped improve the quality of the manuscript.

Finally, I thank my partner, Mike Williams, for putting up with the excessive amounts of time I spent in front of a computer screen whilst researching and writing the book, and for indulging in my listening to a large amount of opera at the same time, the output of which dominates the acoustic of our small flat.

1 The tools of governments and policy outcomes

One of the enduring questions that students of public policy like to ask is: what difference does politics make to the outcomes citizens and politicians care about? In other words, do the decisions that governments arrive at have an impact on such desirable states of affairs as good public health, low levels of crime, balanced economic growth and better student performance? This question is important because many people believe that creating or fostering desired outcomes is what political institutions and policy programmes are there for. The point of voting, having political parties, procedures for decision-making in legislatures and rules in bureaucracies is to create effective public policies that lead to desirable changes in the conditions of the world. If the results of such public deliberations and the application of expert forms of knowledge are negative or indifferent, the political system can only give the appearance of effective public action, producing symbolic policies, which are of little use to anyone other than the elites and their clients. As Edelman (1964, 1988) highlighted in a series of volumes, these symbolic policies often only appear to solve the problems they address, perpetuating the illusion of action. Without some influence in the real world, the stuff of politics would be largely redundant, mainly about slicing up the public purse to distribute resources between entrenched interest groups. In more sinister fashion, some public choice theorists argue that policies benefit interest groups who aim to persuade politicians and bureaucrats to use the monopoly power of the state to protect their interests (Stigler, 1971). As a result of the lack of competitive pressures, the state expands its activities to reward these groups, but with little net benefit to public welfare.

But if politics is able to fulfil its purpose by influencing policy outcomes, it should be a task of political scientists and policy scholars to find out what key factors are at work within the political realm. In particular, what choices can public decision-makers make to get to a more desired state of affairs? What resources can they deploy and do those choices matter? The privileges of office should give leaders the power to encourage or impose change, applying the legitimacy, authority, power and capacity of the institutions of government to enhance public welfare. This task can be done in different ways, such as engaging in a programme of legal reform, increasing the level of public funding or reforming political institutions. With some wisdom, leaders might be able to get the best from the limited time, capacity and organisational ability present in the societies they govern by making the right choices about which resources to deploy and by how much.

An understanding of the consequences of these choices should be part of the behavioural agenda in the study of politics – to find out what causes what. But its more typical application stops at the study of voting behaviour, party competition, cabinet composition and legislative decisions. Such an approach would use the same sophisticated methodological tools as contemporary political science to see what is the impact of the state and public decisions on the wider society and economy. For policy-makers want to know what actually works, using the best social science evidence on offer.

In this way, the policy-orientated study of politics can serve an underlying normative mission, which is to make recommendations about which political arrangements, laws, sets of organisations, levels of funding and types of intervention work best, using scientific evidence to weigh up the efficacy of each choice. In that sense the study of policy outcomes is a branch of policy analysis, which seeks out solutions to maximise human welfare. Indeed, this book is inspired by work in the utilitarian tradition, similar in underlying approach to the classic texts of policy analysis, such as Dror's *Public Policy-making Reexamined* (1968), which seeks to improve the rational bases upon which public decisions are made, and to assess the quality of public decision-making and its ability to provide informed and critical answers to the problems of the day. It is also possible to add the large amount of research in public policy studies about where policy comes from, and what causes variations in public policy across time and place (see John, 1998, 2011 for a review), or the many public policy studies that add knowledge by describing recent reforms, problems of implementation, the relative influence of institutions and the institutional processing of policies, to name just a few topics in recent studies. But this book is mainly interested in what happens down the line, outside the so-called black box of policy-making once a decision to prioritise has been made, seeking to find what particular resources policy-makers can best use to realise their and society's aims. The book suggests that these implementation choices are constrained by institutions and the practice of politics, which limit decision-makers' room for manoeuvre. This book is concerned as much with the political constraints on government effectiveness as with the practical question of how to improve policy outcomes. In that sense, it seeks to bring together understandings of the effectiveness of policy choices with knowledge about the operation of political systems.

The six central chapters of this book aim to assess the current state of the evidence which shows the impact of how governments choose to implement their policies. It might be thought this task had already been done in other works of social science, especially with such an emphasis on evidence-based policy in recent years. Moreover, there have been research initiatives, such as the Centre for Evidence Based Policy (www.evidencenetwork.org), the

United Kingdom Cabinet Office's strategy unit (http://www.cabinetoffice.gov.
uk/strategy.aspx) dedicated to collecting research-based evidence, publications
like the Magenta book (Cabinet Office, 2003), and a series of speeches and
exhortations (for example, Davies, 2004). Added to these explicit declarations
are swathes of evaluation research across the world on every policy initiative
possible.

So why have a book summing up the evidence if there is so much already
out there? There are three main reasons. The first is that much of the research
is done at the micro-level, say about what surgical procedures work well and
how best to implement them, which produces practical knowledge, but it does
not tell governments which instruments overall work best, nor does it provide
a perspective from the study of politics. Yet even the implementation of a
surgical procedure expands to the bigger questions about the right way to
achieve the best result (communicating information, regulating, funding the
changes, reforming the bureaucracy and so on), which tend not to be discussed so much in evaluation studies. The second reason is that evidence-
based research often focuses more on particular initiatives, using examples of
what works, and much less on the mechanisms needed to achieve the outcomes. Indeed, a lack of attention to the causal impacts of policy instruments
is one reason why many policy innovations tend not to get implemented
properly or are implemented too quickly. Policy-makers get surprised that
pilot schemes do not turn into effectively implemented policies rather than
consider the deeper issues about how the tools governments deploy achieve
their objectives. The third reason is that the literature from the study of public
policy on the tools of government does not greatly consider the evidence from
across a range of disciplines and uses examples rather than reviewing the
systematic analysis of quantitative or other data. In short, there is a gap
caused by the diverse nature of the research on this topic, which appears in
the literature of different disciplines rather than in one place. So much of this
book is taken up with discussions of this evidence, which appears right across
social science, with the aim of bringing some of it together. One finding
comes out almost at the start: how difficult it is to substantiate claims about
the impact of what government does. Not that this book is inherently pessimistic, but it does say that finding out about policy effectiveness is sometimes
near impossible. Not only is it difficult to carry out a policy change, it is hard
to conclude from extant studies about what it was about what government did
that worked or not. The book hopes to make some progress in summarising
what the knowledge out there says about the effectiveness of government
decisions. To do so it uses a range of studies not usually citied in the policy
analysis literature.

Before launching into a discussion of the evidence for the effectiveness of
the use of different kinds of political resources, the rest of this chapter discusses the nature of policy performance and policy outcomes. It summarises
the different kinds of resources and tools open to governments and other
public agencies with a view to categorising them and to understanding their

nature. Finally, the chapter reviews the methodological issues that arise from evaluating their impact. In this way some of the key issues and topics of the book are addressed.

The importance of policy performance

The most important place to start is with what this book seeks to explain. This is the policy outcomes that governments or public agencies want to improve. Some think they are part of the real world, far away from the artificial and fraught environment of policy-making, such as at Westminster, in Congress, in the Mayor's office or at Berlaymont. Policy outcomes are what decision-makers should be concentrating on and responding to. They might seem to be a straightforward thing to define, but it is not entirely clear, at least in the literature on public policy, what they are. For one, in the study of public policy, a messy distinction appears between policy outputs and policy outcomes, which are sometimes understandably confused in the statements of politicians and other policy-makers.

Policy outputs are what political systems produce in the forms of laws, financial decisions, organisational changes, new rules and so on, which are designed to achieve an objective. Policy outcomes are the consequences of these intended – and sometimes unintended – decisions, which are desirable states of affairs, such as a clean environment, lower crime and so on, though these outcomes may worsen, sometimes because of what governments do. In conventional wisdom policy-makers find it easy to do the former, but harder to do the latter – even though achieving better outcomes is what policy programmes are all about. Bureaucrats and politicians often find it more satisfying to focus on outputs because they are easier to achieve in a short timescale and reflect the capacity of current decision-making systems to implement a policy. States conventionally have powers to make laws and raise taxes, so politicians and bureaucrats can make decisions to change them, which can be recognised as such by media commentators, political rivals, interest groups and the electorate as valid and legitimate decisions. Groups may wish to lobby politicians for public spending changes; bureaucrats may want them because they serve their careers and expand or reshape their bureaus. So the very instruments and tools of government may be labelled as the objectives and outcomes of policy.

In contrast to outputs, policy outcomes are harder to change because political systems have less control over them than policy outputs, which come under the direct authority of the state or other bodies. Societies and economies are multi-causal complex systems so it is hard to predict exactly what a policy change and the application of the tools of government can achieve. As Pressman and Wildavsky (1973) say in their famous study of implementation, the successful implementation of policy relies on the correct causal inference between sets of actions. But social science tells us that it is rare that researchers can predict how the various elements of social and organisational life relate together in a law-like fashion over time and space. Governments have to make a considerable effort to monitor social changes, to respond to the feedback effects of their actions and to try to avoid generalising from any Hawthorne-like or study effects that may come about from what they do, especially at the initial stages of experimentation. There are many accounts of policy outcomes, evaluation and implementation (for example, Pawson and Tilly, 1997) that seek to increase the understanding about what makes policies succeed or fail. Often these accounts are cautious about what may be claimed, or they consider that factors may be specific to a particular place and point in time.

It is also hard thinking about performance in general terms. The kinds of outcome that governments want to achieve are very diverse. Some are incentive based, which are about human motivation in response to institutional arrangements, such as tax regimes or welfare systems that help people get into work. Other sorts of policy outcomes derive from individuals' norms of behaviour, which require a longer-term change in human beliefs and values to effect a change, such as belief in the benefits of a healthy diet. Other outcomes are about government changing the conditions that affect human behaviour, such as stimulating technological development through investment in higher education. Governments need to address some if not all of these various aspects of human motivation that either individually or collectively affect policy outcomes. They also need to be aware that there are feedback and interaction effects at work, which mean that attempts to change behaviour may have knock-on effects to other actions, or unintended consequences, and that getting to a successful policy outcome, such as a productive economy, may require combination of and linkage between different factors, some of which may not be under the direct control of government or public agency.

Much of the argument about policy outcomes assumes that they need to be maximised for public welfare to improve. This claim may be true in a limited sense that each policy – in a democracy at least – has been drawn up as a result of legitimate procedures, and that research and bureaucratic knowledge have to a certain extent sorted out what the purpose is of each policy programme and has sought to minimise the costs and maximise the benefits. But quite clearly there are moral choices about what are the best forms of social change that public policies are supposed to foster. Libertarians, radicals and others may disagree about what the good life is, and some would say these preferences are not compatible with each other no matter how much is known about the effects of government decisions on policy outcomes. The free marketeer is not going to like more public expenditure on welfare no matter how much the benefits have been shown to exist from deploying extra resources. Even if politicians could agree on preferred outcomes, there are trade-offs between different kinds, which need to be agreed upon, and which may reflect wider social values. At its most strong, some writers on public policy (for example, Yanow, 1996; Stone, 2001) think that the very problems policy-makers seek to solve are defined by their approach to understanding the world, meaning they identify different causal relationships needing public attention depending on their prior position. In that sense policy outcomes are conceived in the minds of publics and elites, and shift in time depending on these preconceptions.

In spite of these problems of agreement, the book claims that in practice many basic social goals are quite consensual. The kinds of outcomes this book discusses are generally uncontroversial, such as lower crime, higher educational achievement, better conditions in cities, a healthier population and an improved environment. Of course, there are moral issues in all policy decisions and some involve hard choices (Calabresi and Bobbitt, 1978). But this book assumes that no one can disagree that – in general – cities should have clean air, that street crime is bad, that reducing the number of heart attacks is good, that getting people back into work is generally a good thing and that something should be done about global warming.

The key policy outcome that is often assumed to be a good, but is controversial, is the economy, which may negatively trade off with other objectives, such as the environment, because of the way in which private economic actions may have collective costs. On the other hand, the economy can positively trade off with other objectives, such as combating poverty, as a prosperous economy improves the standard of living and creates more public finance. So a growing economy can make some outcomes harder to achieve and others much easier. This book is not primarily about trade-offs, however. Nor is it much about who benefits – it assumes in general that most benefit, which is a strong assumption, but a whole book could be taken up with a discussion of inequality. The book seeks to clear the ground to examine the causal mechanisms behind how the instruments affect outcomes mainly independent of equity and equality, though these issues do enter into the discussions from time to time, partly because greater equality may be a way to achieve more consensual objectives, such as a healthy society, because inequality may affect the life chances of a significant portion of society (Wilkinson, 1996).

The tools of government

In part, the answer to what drives policy performance would appear to depend on a number of practical issues and particular ideas embodied in each policy initiative, the summation of a series of recommendations of what works. It may be about the application of the knowledge, practices and intuitions of policy-makers as they implement a policy choice. There are many kinds of lesson that can be found, each with slightly different results, which vary over time, from place to place and between sectors of activity. What policy-makers can do is add together the experiences of these experiments and past practices, and use their judgements about which policies to follow, whether the policy can transfer to a different context, and the appropriate means to achieve their aims. If that were the case, then understanding the context of policy interventions is the key to policy success, which amounts to a series of case-by-case lessons. There can be no real progress in seeking a general explanation of policy successes and failures that this book attempts. But the book seeks to persuade the sceptic that there are wider sets of processes that may be generalisable from many of these cases, which reflect the need for clear conceptualisation of the main choices governments make about how to implement their policies.

The concept of the tools of government is one way of raising the debate above the consideration of local kinds of evidence. This approach categorises the resources of government into a small number of discrete types, each of which is based on a different account of cause and effect. Salamon and Lund (1989: 4) sum up what underlies this concept: 'the notion that the multitude of government programmes actually embody a limited array of mechanisms or arrangements that define how the programmes work'. Analysts thus should not be dazzled by the variety of different labels governments use for what they do – they usually reduce to a much smaller set of categories based on distinct causal claims. That these claims differ for the type of resource being considered generates the contrasts within the book. The question then arises about which causal claim is the more plausible given the context.

Particularly influential has been the work of Hood (1983) and Hood and Margetts (2007), who set out the four tools of nodality, authority, treasure (public finance) and organisation, which generates a memorable acronym from the first letters of each word. Government and other public authorities may use these different kinds of levers to try to achieve the ends they want. It is possible to set out such tools more elaborately and with greater differentiation (see Salamon, 2002). Then there are more complex schemes with a higher degree of theorisation (for example, Peters and Van Nispen, 1998; Howlett, 2005; Lascoumes and Le Galès, 2007). What these works have in common is the idea that governments or other public organisations, like local authorities, have at their disposal a toolbox that allows them to deploy different instruments in various combinations for the circumstances they face. The state or public authority gives those in office a set of facilities other actors do not have. For example, they can command others who may have no choice but to obey or to appeal to a higher authority, such as to a written constitution; or they can raise taxes or spend on one thing and not another. It is the capacity of the state or public authority that offers so much opportunity for influence, either in the human resources that are contained within public bureaucracies, or in the position of the state at the centre of knowledge-producing networks. The latter is what Hood (1983) and Hood and Margetts (2007) call nodality, which means that the state or other public authority can use its position to manipulate what outcomes it prefers. The argument is subtle: it is not just what governments or agencies do that matters, nor how much they pull the various levers they command; it is how they organise themselves and the way the institutions of government are configured that give the potential for extra leverage. The argument moves from the relative efficacy of combinations of resources to the management of capacity. For example, governments may allocate money to address problems and pass laws all they like, but if the organisation – or its networks with other agencies – is dysfunctional, nothing much will happen. So the analysis becomes less directed to the tools that governments directly control than to ways of organising, facilitating and thinking that help governments become more effective and get the most from limited resources, time, and cognitive capacity of both elites and masses.

There is much that follows in this book that draws on the valuable work that Hood, Margetts and others have carried out. Like others, this book offers its own typology of instruments, which resembles others, but has some important variations too. One innovation is the inclusion of institutional reform as a tool of government, which often tends not to be elaborated in existing accounts, where institutions are taken to be synonymous with organisational design, as in the Hood-Margetts scheme, and may be seen as an indirect and long-term means of affecting policy outcomes. It is included because of the attraction of institutional innovations to policy-makers in recent decades as governments have delegated responsibilities, devolved powers and reformed national institutions, often as part of a general programme of modernisation. The advantage is that it brings to the fore the political system as whole, or different parts of it, as an instrument itself. Politicians have to reconfigure the institutions they occupy – and, by implication, themselves and their power – to achieve effective outcomes. Making policy effectively is not just about the use of the tried and tested resources, but about reforming the political system itself and getting the incentives right for politicians and bureaucrats. This requires considerable reflexivity on the part of political actors that tend to be trapped within the operating assumptions of the institutions they occupy or from simplistic critiques of those assumptions. It also moves the book to consider – in part – what affects the choice of tools, a topic of academic interest of recent years (Lascoumes and Le Galès, 2007; Kassim and Le Galès, 2010).

The other distinctive aspect of this book is its greater attention to the factors that governments do not fully have under their control, which are the softer instruments, such as provision of information, the fostering of deliberation and the application of policy networks. These tools are often directed to altering the social processes that are hard to command because they are highly embedded and often resist change. Much of the critique the book offers of the more familiar tools of money and laws is that they find it hard to dig down deep into the structures of society that governments wish to influence, partly from the resistance that people and organisations have to incentives and direct commands. Instead – or in addition – more indirect ways of influencing citizen and organisational behaviour might have a better chance of changing their incentives and their norms. Non-standard instruments appeal to the capacity of reason and seek to encourage more active involvement on the part of those who are regulated. In spite of the loss of control they imply for the state, they might create deeper, more long-lasting changes than commands or incentives. In this way, the book partly replicates other accounts of instruments that distinguish between compulsory and voluntary instruments, say between laws on the one hand and networks on the other (see Howlett and Ramesh, 2003: 82–91), as well as mixed instruments. The book stresses the distinction between standard and non-standard instruments rather than the hard–soft continuum. This book, however, is not primarily interested in developing the typologies, which other authors have ably done already (for example, Howlett, 2005). Rather it seeks a better understanding of the different nature of the tools, partly from reviewing evidence about how they work in practice. This is the contribution the book hopes to make, to find out what the evidence says about the impact of the tools of government.

The argument the book presents is that there needs to be a further development of the underlying causal claims and a consequent assessment of the evidence base to assess how far authoritative statements can be made about the tools of government. Understanding government effectiveness needs a precise conceptualisation of the tool and a specification of the underlying theoretical claim about cause and effect, in particular how the individual or organisation responds to the instrument. It is related to classic divisions about thinking about society and politics: between those who think parties of government can create the conditions to improve social well-being from the top down, which contrasts with the faith in self-organising processes that governments can stimulate but not directly control. Unlike many of the social goals they pursue, the tools of government are not entirely neutral – which is a reverse of the normal principles of liberalism that leaves the moral choices to politicians, but the mechanics of implementing them to independent bodies, such as courts, bureaucracies and agencies. Partly because the choice of instruments raises such fundamental issues, policy-makers have often seized on one pathway because it offers a self-contained vision of the future as well as a simple set of claims, sometimes summarised by the term silver bullet. In spite of governments mixing the tools, hoping to have the best of all worlds, in practice they tend to concentrate on one principal way of going about their business, partly from simplicity and to economise their energy. They want to distinguish themselves from their predecessors and not to react to the problems with the previous approach. Some governments may reform in a top-down kind of way, like with the United Kingdom Labour governments elected from 1997–2010, which 6 *et al.* (2010) find had an authoritarian approach to introducing social policies. This policy style was supposed to be superseded by softer, more bottom-up policies, something the Conservative Party, with its Liberal Democrat coalition partner, is keen to follow in government.

Even though the packages of interventions a government produces will have most of the tools of government in them, the form of finance to fund them, laws to put them in place, organisational chains of command that have to be thought through, and information to be transmitted about the reforms, they will often use one instrument more than others as a way of focusing a policy or of characterising the intervention (see Linder and Peters, 1998). Not only do programmes use one tool more than others, over time some jurisdictions and places use the tools more, such as countries that spend more public funds than others, or select a particular voting system. The existence of interventions to study and variations across place and time help create the evidence the book draws on.

Different kinds of tools

So what are the different kinds of tools and their assumptions? Each chapter goes into some detail about each one, so here is a brief summary of what is to be assessed. Though there are various ways of counting them, the book outlines six broad levers, which express themselves as resources that governments have available to manipulate, in varying degrees, so as to influence public-policy outcomes – even if they contain different variants within them and there is some crossover between them too. As well as being determinants of policy performance, they may also be thought of as being subject to other government decisions, which also adds a further dimension of complexity because policy-makers do not just need to think about the influence on the outcome, but also the factors that influence or limit the lever or process. These may include internal obstacles to using the tool of government, the extent of information and intelligence available to policy-makers, but also the relative ease or stickiness in using the tool itself.

The six sets of resources are these (see Table 1.1 for a representation of the three pairs). The first pair is direct or top-down – reaching from the state or public authority directly to the individuals or groups that are needed to change to achieve the policy outcome or to buy in the capacity and technology to get things done. The first direct tool is through changing the incentive structure facing individuals and organisations by altering the law and reformulating the regulatory framework, something many western states often

Table 1.1 The tools of government

Top-down
1 Law and regulation
2 Public spending and taxation

Internal to the state
3 Bureaucracy and public management
4 Institutions

Non-standard
5 Information, persuasion and deliberation
6 Networks and governance

---

have the capacity to do providing they do not face obstacles from within the state, such as from another branch of government or a veto player.

The second is through increasing or altering the level of public finance directed to a public problem, whether it is about direct government services or transfer payments or affecting the different kinds and levels of taxation. This tool appears as the word treasure in Hood–Margetts tools of government scheme. The state or public authority can deploy more money to release capacity, buy in people dedicated to the tasks at hand and invest in technology to overcome human problems. The same effect may be generated indirectly by taxes, which in effect create a line of expenditure for a group of citizens, or impose costs or benefits depending on their activities.

The next pair of resources is more indirect, seeking to attend to the internal workings of the state or public authority that may have positive spin-off effects, perhaps helping the efficacy of tools number one and two. So the third tool is the organisation of bureaucracies and delivery agencies, which may be reconfigured by incentives for good performance, contracting out of public services, creating quasi-markets and improving regulation – what may be called the new public management. As a result, the public authority becomes more efficient in the way it carries out its actions, and there is a more effective chain of command from top to bottom. So in some ways this tool is part of the hierarchical approach implied by simple conceptions of tools one and two. Though in practice reforms of the public sector can involve decentralisation and the handing over of responsibilities to private enterprises and other non-state organisations.

The fourth resource is similar, but is deeper in requiring more radical change. It is the reform of the structure of the state or public authority through the redesign of formal and informal political institutions. This change can be a simple transfer of an institution from one context to another or a recalibration of an existing institution. For it to work it needs some thinking about the purpose of an institution, what principles it is based on and the causal mechanisms that can create desired behaviour among the decision-makers of a political system and at large in the wider society.

The next pair of tools is softer, and even more indirect, where there is less of a command and control mechanism but more of a reliance on cooperation, persuasion and social interaction. These tools are newer and less familiar to policy-makers, so are called non-standard in this scheme. The fifth tool out of the six is about the knowledge base of government, through communicating and persuading, using the ability of the state to communicate messages and to engage in acts of persuasion. This technique is also about creating more equal forms of dialogue between the citizen and the state through participation in local decision-making, and the co-production of public services by citizens working alongside the professionals. The sixth and final lever is similar: using the soft levers of networks and the system of governance to effect changes, such as through partnerships between the private and public sectors. These networks can connect to stocks of social capital, partly from using these soft linkages and ensuring the state is responsive and cognate with these social factors. Networks may create virtuous circles of cooperative activity that then radiate into more effective policy outcomes. The last factor is almost beyond the capacity of the state or other public actors, and can only be encouraged by other tools of government, such as public finance and delegations (Salamon and Lund, 1989). The tools of government may be seen as an infinite regress: tools needing to implement the tools, meta tools to introduce these guiding tools, meta-meta tools and so on.

It would be possible to conceive of elaborate typologies, and this book is at the low end of the number of tools it denotes. It is not as low as Hood and Margetts' (2007) four, but at six it is a long way below the thirteen that appear in Salamon's account (2002: 21). The decision is about taste and priority. The preference here is for simplicity. As Hood (2007: 138) writes, defending his scheme, 'After all, if all else is equal, scientists conventionally prefer simpler explanations, representations, and analytic approaches to more complex ones'. The attraction of six is that it creates three pairs of similar kinds of instruments: the classic tools of finance and law/regulation; the organisation and process tools of organisations and institutions, internal to the state; and then the softness and indirectness of information and networks.

The effectiveness of the tools

It is apparent from this brief discussion that each approach to the tools of government depends on a particular interpretation of what are the significant forms of action in politics and society. There is not just a description of the tool, but an account of the actions that result from it – the character of the tool and of the people and/or organisations affected by it are equal parts. At one end there is the apparently top-down approach embodied in some kinds of laws and from the provision of public finance. This perspective has the advantage that the objectives of the reform are clearly specified in advance and there is a clear plan of how to get to the desired outcome. The problem is that legislators may not foresee all the situations a law is designed to cover and a legal framework cannot adapt to fast-changing circumstances. Most of all, the very attractiveness of the top-down approach may lead to its downfall, for by specifying in advance the objectives, it can create resistance on the part of the general population, who may resent the application of levers designed for a particular purpose, especially if they feel they have not participated in the decision. The other types of action may be more powerful by affecting the behaviour of participants over the long term. Institutions have this quality, being long-term arrangements that affect the incentives of actors. They may embed certain social values, so leading to long-term social cooperation. The other set of actions tend to work less overtly and involve the incorporation of groups and citizens in common objectives. This approach gets over the problem of the top-down tools, and has the potential to create virtuous circles, based on trust and cooperation and mutual learning. But it may be the case that such tools may end up replicating the very behaviours and social practices that led to negative social outcomes in the first place. In the end their very weakness undermines them. That is the paradox that this book explores and seeks to confront.

Of course, such an account is an oversimplification. Each of these levers operates in complex ways, both controlling and encouraging. All the tools have to confront the problem of coordination, getting the balance between the ability to command and control, but at the same time ensuring they hand over some responsibility to other parties without compromising the objectives of a policy. The argument is that each approach is essentialist: each tool will default to its essential characteristic, especially when the circumstances behind a public policy get tough, such as in a war or an economic crisis. This is not necessarily a bad thing: focusing, getting the best out of a limited set of objectives can be good. Trying to be all things to all people can get a worse outcome if nobody is clear what the rationale or approach is. The ordinary citizen may find it hard to make sense of government action; there is ammunition for the critics and nobody is satisfied. Governments are often dithering somewhere between the two, emphasising some things but not others, such as appearing tough to one group yet conciliatory to another. But just doing one thing has its dangers too, missing out on obvious wins and links between the tools.

With the aim of simplicity, chapters aim to assess the costs and benefits of each type of government action. The approach is to use the method of the best social science: isolating the variable in question and assessing what influence it has. The case studies and examples discussed in the chapters do just this by looking at one set of instruments, or a particularly focused policy that has been subjected to a thorough and rigorous evaluation or where researchers are able to make tests of the assumptions. It remains for the discussion and then the conclusion to make a statement about the relative strengths and weakness of each tool and outline what is the best mix.

Acquiring knowledge about what works

The central chapters of this book review the evidence for the effectiveness of the tools of government. Each chapter first sets out the approach. It tries to get to its essence by making sense of the causal claims and finding out how they might work, as well as outlining some possible weaknesses. The outline takes up the first few pages. The main sections of the chapters review groups of studies that relate to particular aspects of each instrument or sum up particular interventions. It examines examples or evaluations of where the use of a particular resource, such as a new spending programme, worked in delivering policy outcomes. It reviews studies that suggest that some places or countries that tend to use a tool of government more than others tend to get better results than places that do not, which is where comparative research comes into its own. There is inevitably a process of selection: it is not possible to present all the evidence about different ways of intervening. What this book does is to select studies that have a particular take, in particular those that try to isolate the impact of a tool of government or a particular type of intervention. The aim is to understand the causal mechanism behind the use of each tool. Once this becomes the criterion, a large number of studies fall away, usually by being either too particular or too general for the purpose here.

One assumption of this book is that qualitative studies often find it harder to isolate the impact of one aspect of an intervention. This is because quantitative evaluations analyse a large number of observations of inputs and outcomes, either over time or across space, from which it is possible to make a generalisation. The natural variation in selecting observations reduces from having large numbers, so the researcher observes reliable estimates of the inputs and outputs of a policy. Statistical techniques can then evaluate the relationships to estimate the impact of one variable, in this case the tool of government, allowing for any other influences. This is not to say that qualitative studies do not successfully identify the impact of a causal process, or that most quantitative studies never fail – they often do. Moreover, qualitative methods are sometimes better at teasing out the interaction of different kinds of approaches in different places, and at assessing the importance of particular contexts that influence why a particular instrument works or not. But they are not so good at generalising with such certainty in the form of a hypothesis test and in ascertaining the strength of the effect with precision. The exception is where there is a particularly robust design, such as a natural experiment where one area or region gets something quite different, perhaps by accident. Then it is possible to make robust comparisons from qualitative methods.

But this book is not a paean to quantitative methods. The chapters take the trouble to explain the methods to see how a researcher tries to examine the impact of a particular factor so the reader can see what is going on. This approach leads to some elaboration of the details of these studies, which may need a little familiarity with the methods to understand the text. The book tries to make these as accessible as possible – which is as it should be because there is already too much mystification of these techniques. There is also a glossary of technical and other terms, which is at the end of the book. The idea is to help the reader if the text does not do enough to explain – or it is there just to browse through. The reason for this level of detail is to get across the design of much research to see whether it has the ability to get at the truth. Social science finds this task very hard because of the challenge of disentangling the relative influences on a policy outcome. Most of all, the units of a new policy, which is usually the object of most evaluations, are usually selected in some way, making inference not representative of what happens over the long term when the policy applies to all. Often the inputs researchers are interested in are not independent, sometimes determined by other factors in the analysis (what is called endogeneity), which leads to biased results. Many of the examples – both qualitative and quantitative – the book discusses face this problem, even the best studies published in the most reputable academic journals.

In spite of a belief in the virtues of scientific investigation, parts of this book veer toward a pessimistic account of knowledge acquisition. The more social scientists examine a problem, the harder it is for them to ascertain whether governments make a difference or not with the resources at their disposal. They may do so, but much current research finds it hard to conclude there is impact with a degree of certainty. Often the results seem inconclusive. Or it is not possible to separate out the influence of the use of a resource of government from all the other factors that influence policy success and failure. But not all is gloom, however. Some studies are smarter than others, and can overcome some of the core problems of making an inference about whether government intervention worked or not. Sometimes it comes from a fortuitous circumstance, like the natural experiment example mentioned above, or measuring change over time that gets interrupted by the intervention compared to an area that does not, what is called interrupted time series. In some contexts researchers can use the design of the study to their advantage, such as different groups getting interventions at different times. There is no one superior method. Instead the secret is to use the leverage in a piece of research that researchers can access if they are clever enough (see Shadish *et al.*, 2002 for a review of the different strategies).

The other possibility is randomised controlled trials. This is where the government agency evaluates its decisions by randomising who get it, such as one set of individuals and another, or one community and another. What is important is that one of the groups does not get a treatment or receives a different treatment. Because the differences between the groups have been removed from random allocation, the level of outcomes in the treatment group can only be attributed to the intervention and not to any other factor that might influence success. As result, researchers and policy-makers can compare outcomes between the treatment and control groups to find out how much the intervention affected the outcomes (see Torgerson and Torgerson, 2008 for a review of the method and its applications). For example, if a government randomly allocates a job-training scheme between treatment and control areas and measures the number of jobs created after the intervention, it is in a position to know whether the intervention worked and by how much. All it needs to do is to compare the average number of jobs created per area between the treatment and control groups, which is the effect of the intervention, and then to check whether the difference is more than would be expected by chance.

The reader would be right in detecting an enthusiasm for trials in this book and there are some excellent ones to report, but they do not open up the door of knowledge quite as much as expected. One reason is that they are still quite rare – outside health policy – as a form of evaluation, particularly for general public policies. This is because they are expensive and need special conditions to prevail, such as the ability to randomise into treated and control groups, which can be hard to do, especially if it is an institutional or organisational change being carried out. It may be hard to justify a randomised controlled trial to the politicians and bureaucrats as it may appear to deny one group a benefit. A trial may appear to be paternalistic, reducing the role of citizens to participation in an experiment, which may be unpopular compared to the relatively worthless experiment of piloting a policy. It may be the case that policy-makers want to move too quickly rather than wait for a trial to produce results.

In spite of some robust forms of evaluation out there, there is relatively little evidence upon which to draw about the tools of government once the limitations of most studies are taken on board. The record is fragmentary and dispersed, often hiding in specialist journals. But there are some gems of studies, some of which appear in this book. Often those done by economists have the edge. This is not because of the necessary superiority of the discipline, but because issues of causation and the specification of models are often at the heart of economists' attempts to explain things, especially when there is no experiment available. Economists tend to carry out a large number of robustness checks on their statistical models and seek to identify and model the endogeneity or selection in the studies they carry out. Moreover, there has been a revival of applied economics in which economists use their methodological skills to tackle practical and policy problems, as a series of popular books using the findings of recent economic studies attest (for example, Harford, 2005; Levitt and Dubner, 2005, 2009; Thaler and Sunstein, 2008). Alongside economists, the book reviews useful work by criminologists, lawyers, political scientists, psychologists, sociologists, social policy experts, urbanists and many others.

Conclusions

This chapter has set out the nature of the task of the book, which is about the evidence for the impact of the different kinds of public decisions of politicians and other key policy-makers. Familiar in the study of public policy, the concern moves away from the inputs of the political systems, such as elections, parties and public opinion and legislative deliberation, to the impact of the decisions on the ground, the policy outcomes. The aim is to understand how governments make best use of the resources under their control to get to desired states of the world, taking into account the feedback from politics to the selection of the instruments themselves. The idea is that the creation of policy outcomes is not just the result of effort or a clever idea, it involves setting into motion chains of cause and effect, whereby the different instruments that policy-makers choose have an impact depending on how much they are used and in what context.

The chapter has outlined what these instruments are without detailing too much of what will follow in subsequent chapters. More important has been the task of setting out some of the intellectual baggage that accompanies these instruments, assumptions about the way the world works and claims about the prime sources of leverage on social and economic action. Many of the instruments imply assumptions that are made by policy-makers and experts who use them. Advocates believe that one tool of government is more important because it contains a critique about how the world works and offers a particular solution to the problem.

This chapter has elaborated the key causes of difference between the instruments, between those that seek to control, direct and manage, and those that are more subtle in their impact through manipulating, encouraging and facilitating. It suggests that both have advantages – clarity and drive on the one hand versus adaptability and acceptability on the other. But both have different disadvantages: resistance and lack of intelligence for the former, drift and colonisation by powerful interests for the latter. The final chapter of the book considers whether this difference can be resolved, or whether it is possible to have a meta-analysis of what factors can determine when and how such tools should be used.

2   Law and regulation

The main reason for the existence of a public authority is to have a legitimate means of arriving at authoritative decisions. In most societies and jurisdictions people find it necessary to have procedures to ensure they come to binding agreements and decisions apply to whom they are intended to. These decisions might be reviewed and changed, but citizens expect some certainty of action from a public authority so they know some things are permitted and others are not. These are laws and other formal rules – often bundled together under the term regulation. These rules have authority and force because they are decided within or on behalf of the institutional structures of the state, which conventionally has a monopoly of legitimate force in a given territory. If the monopoly word is relaxed somewhat – as probably it should be even for states – then the capacity and legitimacy to make and enforce binding decisions is also the core feature or function of many regional, supranational and other public institutions.

To a certain extent, the authority that derives from the power and legitimacy of states and other political organisations applies to all the tools of government, such as public finance and taxation, discussed in the next chapter. There is, for example, a qualitative difference between finance coming from a public authority, with its legitimacy and accountability and the money private bodies deploy, even if it is for public and charitable activities. But the authority character applies much more to the capacity of states and other authorities to produce binding rules and laws that apply to citizens and to bodies within a territory. Law implies command. It may require an action, forbid another, set a target or regulate a private contract. If one party does not comply with the law or questions the meaning of the statute, another party, such as the government, can go to a court and get the law enforced and have penalties imposed if necessary. Agencies then have considerable backup to enforce the law and to apply sanctions and fines when carrying out their business and implementing public policies. They have both the sanctions of the core institutions of the state as well as the legitimate use of force on their side.

There are limitations to the extent to which law may be used. For example, when there is a breach of human rights, constitutional courts or their equivalents may rule on and apply the provisions of constitutional documents and agreements which may be applicable in a territory. For most acts of government, however, the law appears as the most powerful tool a public agency can have. It can be unequivocal in its command. There is no doubt – at least in principle – that it should be obeyed. Moreover, it does not take vast resources to pass and enact a law if there is consensus within the political system. The other attraction is that once the legislation has been accepted by the group or person regulated by it, then a self-enforcing system can emerge. The formal rules set up a framework to help someone to comply in the intended direction, and once others also see the advantage of doing so, the legal rule becomes the norm. The result is that individuals do not need to think greatly before complying and they end up following the law automatically. These sets of reinforcing factors help policy-makers get to desired outcomes. Generally, it is not the period immediately after enactment that shows how successful a law is. More important is the long term, which can reveal whether it beds down and gets accepted.

The surprising claim of this chapter is – for all the potential of law and other formal forms of regulation to guide behaviour and to shape policy outcomes – the evidence suggests it cannot be relied upon to implement policies effectively, or at least not in a simple way. There are some familiar challenges that apply to all the tools. Like other instruments, the use of law/regulation needs to be based on a valid theory of cause and effect. If the theory a policy is based on does not hold logically or the core putative empirical relationships it is based on have a weak empirical backing, then it is very unlikely a law can have the intended effect even if people obey its provisions. In the classic account of parliamentary sovereignty, parliament can pass any law, but it does not have a chance of achieving the desired effect if no one fully obeys or enforces it. Like with other tools, there is the cost effectiveness of the law in question. It is possible for the state to throw all its resources at a problem but to find the marginal benefits are much less than the marginal costs. However, if the law is based on a valid theory, the costs are not too high compared to the benefits and it is operating within the jurisdiction in question, given its legitimacy it seems reasonable to expect – other things being equal – positive consequences for the implementation of government policies. But this view does not take into account the special character of the law/regulation tool.

In spite of their potential power, laws often fail. There are five main reasons. Firstly, they are often never fully implemented and enforced – agencies often choose the laws they wish to enforce. This is because there are two steps involved: one is the passing of the law; the second is enforcement. While some laws get automatically enforced, most require some effort on the part of bureaucracies and other public agencies. It seems almost as soon as a law gets on the statute book it loses its special character and turns into more of an organisational tool of government, where what matters is the chain of command within bureaucracies (see Chapter 4). There is no way round differential implementation given the large number of laws and regulations and the limited capacity of the state and other public authorities to enforce them. As the number of laws and regulations expands, so this problem grows. In the end, the task of achieving effective regulation is a meta-problem. It is about prioritising which laws to implement, which is a political and societal choice.

This chapter does not suggest regulation is doomed. There are various ways to improve regulation, where legal and regulatory incentives may work in favour of successful implementation. An attention to the micro-level incentives and the means of encouraging positive feedback from the law to the desired behaviours can ensure the success of a legally regulated policy. When used too much, law may lose its effectiveness, especially if not fully applied. People can get used to not complying if there is no effective sanction. The loss of potency does not just affect observance of a new law, it can weaken obedience to the existing ones as well.

The second reason for the failure of regulation comes from the nature of politics itself. There will always be a temptation for the politicians to deviate from full implementation of a regulatory regime even if they know the benefits of it. The reasons are partly to do with corruption and lobbying by interest groups, but more likely it is because politicians prioritise short over long-term objectives. These limitations have been highlighted in the public choice account of regulation, which tends to assume an effective policy regime can become undermined by self-interest and the abuse of power (Stigler, 1971). For these reasons, policy-makers sometimes hand over responsibility for regulation to independent bodies to take the decisions on their behalf. This may be called an act of credible commitment, an attempt to try to steady their hand and to save politicians from following their short-run self-interests. In the end, the regulated groups may seek to take control of the decisions of the independent regulatory agency instead. Moreover, politicians cannot resist interfering with these schemes of delegation (Bertelli and John, 2010). So in spite of attempts to improve the transparency and independence of regulation, the exigencies of politics reduce its impact and effectiveness. Politicians can use the apparent impartiality of the law as a cover to follow their private interests.

The third reason law often fails is because it can move the onus of responsibility for action or inaction away from the individual to the state, which encourages passivity or resistance. When individuals learn to internalise norms from instruments that promote individual self-government, this can encourage them to observe a set of desired behaviours. In contrast, strong forms of regulation can encourage them to think compliance is something they have to rather than ought to do. The willingness to comply gets replaced with unwilling conformity to the law, where the individual obeys but inwardly does not agree with the measure. In this circumstance, there is less chance the policy gets implemented fully. Effective laws – even those with powerful sanctions – are usually introduced when there is public opinion behind them, when the direction of change is in their favour, so this is not a necessary tension. When there is a desire for a change, a law can help society move to a tipping point, to get to where people want to go collectively, but where their day-to-day individual desires do not get them. But it may also be the case a government introduces laws without this form of popular consent and capacity to persuade. Then passive – or even active – resistance is the consequence of the use – or overuse – of this tool. In this case, it is likely the objectives of the law, especially if it requires behaviour change of the citizens, will not be realised.

The fourth problem is similar to passivity, but works in another way. Top-down regulation can make the complier clever and more active in seeking to avoid the aims of the regulator. Individuals or organisations, when faced by formal controls, may invent complex strategies to avoid being successfully regulated. They may have information to hand the principal needs to implement the law. The consequence of regulation is that people start to think more strategically. If the rules are made more precise, they think of the kinds of action that are not covered by the rules. The more the regulator tries to catch out the regulated person, the worse the problem is, so regulation can end in a downward spiral of non-compliance. The effort at compulsion, particularly if it is replacing forms of self-regulation, may reduce or crowd out the willingness to comply as it appears to reward the opportunist and punish the virtuous. As with the other limitations of regulation, it is not entirely clear when this happens and when it does not because there are examples of successful regulation as well as the well-known failures. This patchy experience will be taken up later in this chapter.

The fifth reason is that implementation of the law may also require co-operation in the wider society at large. There are two steps involved. One requires compliance, which may be a relatively passive act; the other requires cooperation, which may involve negotiation and a more active outlook on the part of regulated groups. In short, effective policy implementation may need an active citizen or organisation. An example is in crime prevention: if the population are just compliant it may be still hard for the police to deal with crime because they need the cooperation of citizens to provide information about the location of criminals and to come forward to ensure criminal prosecutions are successful. How to get a more active civic society takes government a long way beyond the use of the law/regulation tool of government and into the softer tools the book considers in Chapters 6 and 7.

To assess both the positive aspect of law and regulation – as well as the costs and limitations – this chapter starts by reviewing examples from the top-down, punishment–reward model of regulation, and then moves on to assess less direct and more complex forms of control to find out if there are ways around the top-down regulatory trap. The chapter does not consider more informal, market and social forms of control, which may also be called regulation (see Jordana and Levi-Faur, 2004: 2–5 for a discussion of the meanings of the term), though the more recent work, such as on responsive regulation (reviewed below), does incorporate many of these processes and does not make a hard-and-fast distinction between legal and other forms of control.

Simple regulation

There is a simple model of regulation. The regulator designs an incentive structure that takes into account individual costs and benefits. If the new rule ensures the benefits exceed the cost, it is possible to get a desired kind of behaviour. This approach was popularised by Becker (1968), who wondered why enforcement was so varied for different kinds of legislation. He argues that the state could alter these costs and benefits. If the state can work out what kinds of activity it is better to encourage and prevent, it can then put resources into influencing behaviour for the kinds of people who carry out either desired or non-desired activities. The result would be an optimal allocation of resources to get enforcement. The effectiveness of law in Becker's scheme then is the result of careful calculations about the costs and benefits, which implies a pragmatic realisation of the limits to the reach of the law, but also offers solutions about how to improve its effectiveness if the agents of the state think carefully enough about the actions the law is designed to affect.

There is a fierce debate about whether it is possible to alter human actions on the basis of these calculations (see, for example, Sunstein *et al.*, 2000). This extends beyond the law/regulation tool to all the actions of government and the extent it is correct for governments to assume individuals are rational calculators in response to incentives and penalties, or whether or they should be treated more as boundedly rational so not so likely to take into account the costs and benefits (see debate over nudge in Chapter 6). So the debate is important for the success of all the instruments, including law/regulation. If economic incentives prevail, then it is possible to design a mechanism through regulation to ensure someone or some organisation complies; if not, then other kinds of message or framing are more appropriate. Both predict less than full compliance, but in different ways and for different reasons.

To what extent do the costs of breaking the law and the assessment of the chances of being caught affect the probability of compliance? For example, the existence of a deterrent has an impact on crime, but most criminological studies show the degree of punishment does not have an impact in terms of the severity of sentence (for example, von Hirsch *et al.*, 1999). There is empirical support for the economic perspective that the costs and benefits matter for property crime. For example, a study of the minimum wage in England (Hansen and Machin, 2002) shows that it reduces crime because potential criminals have more money so do not feel the need to commit crimes to supplement their income. The authors examined a pilot area before the policy was introduced to examine the impact of the wage on crime. They find the minimum wage reduced crime because it maintained the income of those most likely to commit it and affected their incentive to commit offences at the margin.

Levitt's (1998) research lends support to the claim that enforcement works. He examines the impact of arrests on crime using data on 59 of the largest cities in the United States from 1970–92. The argument is that if arresting works, then rational criminals should transfer their activities to another type of crime, one that is easily substitutable in terms of their skills. If incarceration works, arrests should reduce crime overall. Seeking to explain the level of crime, and controlling for a range factors – years, city population, black people, female resident households, unemployment and local spending, along with arrest rates in other types of crime (both substitutable and non-substitutable) – he shows arrests reduce the type of crime being targeted which is the impact of incarceration. The police's arrests of substitutable crimes also reduce the crime rate, which comes from criminals transferring their activities. This might not be an optimal outcome, but at least it shows the power of the legal instrument, both in terms of deterrence by shifting criminal behaviour and also taking criminals out of society by imprisonment.

A similar line of attack is in his paper on incarceration (Levitt, 1996). The argument is that the use of law in the form of enforcement of the criminal law should lead to a reduction in crime. But it is hard to show this relationship from just observing data about crime and prisons as both could vary together, say because the economy is affecting the number of crimes being committed. What Levitt does is to use prison releases from overcrowding in 12 US states to examine the impact of the level of imprisonment on crime for the period 1973–93. This means there is a part of the data that is affected by these releases that should turn into lower crimes – if it is assumed that those releases are random shocks. This means it is a natural experiment, not a randomised controlled trial, but where the world approximates to it. Levitt justifies this assumption because after the releases the level of the prison population returns to its normal path. Levitt finds these prisoners commit crimes – up to 5 per cent for property and 10 per cent for violent crime. For each prisoner released by prison overcrowding litigation, the total number of crimes per year increases by about 15 per cent. Levitt calculates this by a two-step method – two-stage least squares – whereby these releases are used to predict the level of prison population independent of crime, which can then estimate the effects of imprisonment on crime. The main analysis controls for the year in question, economic factors, police staffing, racial composition and age distribution. What Levitt is doing is cleaning up his model so it gives an accurate estimate of legal enforcement on crime. The problem, as Levitt admits, is the releases are not random because they are triggered by lawsuits, and these states are a small selection from the total.

In spite of the power of the state in affecting citizen behaviour, there are limits to how much the state can do. For example, when public authorities seek to deal with tax evasion, one review of the evidence suggests punitive strategies do not work (Leviner, 2008; see discussion below). Even enforcement activities – if costly – may not be economic. In the end the cost-benefit equation applies to the public authority as much to the individual. An example illustrates the point. Cornelius and Salehan (2007) examine whether tougher controls on immigration across the United States–Mexico border had an impact on the flows of migrants. What these authors did was to survey 603 migrants and potential migrants in rural Mexico. They reasoned that migration would depend on their information about enhanced security measures, perceptions of risk and actual experiences during past crossings. If the authorities increased the level of risk, there would be a disincentive to make an illegal crossing. In the study, the authors seek to explain intentions to migrate during 2005. Only 55 people were deterred from crossing because of the direct or indirect effects of border controls. A mere 6 per cent said it was more difficult to cross even though 72 per cent were aware of stronger border controls. Sixty-four per cent of those who answered the question said they knew someone who died while trying to cross. So people know about the increased penalty and the risks, but this does not affect their behaviour. Of those who had previously migrated, 13 per cent indicated they had been caught. Twenty-two per cent indicated the experience was harder than they had expected. The statistical analysis, controlling for all the likely factors to influence migration – education, sex and income – finds the perceived difficulty and danger does not have an effect on migration. Individuals who are more informed about border controls are more likely to cross (though there may be a bias in these findings because if the migrant is willing to cross – or has had more experience – they are likely to get information – as the authors acknowledge). Finally, they examine those who had crossed before: being caught does have a negative impact, but perception of difficulty does not. Being caught reduces the probability of crossing the border by about 8 per cent. Overall, this study shows economic interest trumps perceptions of personal safety and/or border controls are not strong enough to deter people. There are some flaws in the study, however, because the sample was limited to respondents in Mexico. There is no before and after measure to discover whether the change in regulation impacts on the perception of risk and hence compliance. But the paper effectively shows a basic point about how individuals respond to a regulatory regime.

The Mexico example reveals there are examples of behaviours that it is hard for top-down regulation to alter, in this case because of the powerful forces that impel people to cross national borders. It is also the case that low risk of detection is such that people feel they can take a risk. This speaks to a larger number of behaviours that people want to carry on doing which the state and other public authorities find very hard to detect. The classic example was the prohibition of alcohol – its sale, manufacture and transportation – in the United States from 1913–33, which only had a short-term effect on consumption (Miron and Zwiebel, 1991, who calculate this from health statistics). As the law was largely flouted, it had to be repealed.

One of the clearest examples is the consumption of illegal drugs, which has a powerful demand as a result of chemical addiction, lifestyle choice and peer-group pressure. Supply is very hard to regulate – drugs get through any border despite attempts to stop their supply in other countries and the large number of drugs enforcement strategies. Weatherburn and Lind (1997) examine the impact of regulation on drug consumption. They reason that it is impossible to prevent the use of drugs, but it might be possible for the authorities to reduce the consumption and increase their price. The researchers collected information on heroin seizures in Cabramatta, New South Wales, Australia from February 1993 to January 1995. To find out the price police officers in disguise purchased heroin on the drug market and noted the price they got before arresting the seller. They created a dataset containing over-time information on seizures, prices, admission rates in treatment clinics and arrests. They found that seizures of heroin in Australia had no impact on the price and purity of the drugs on the market. Nor was there any impact on people admitting themselves for treatment. This would appear to show the difficulties of a command and control enforcement strategy. Meier (1994), in a review of drugs policy, describes the cycles agencies go through in dealing with this problem, which includes bursts of intensive enforcement, followed by a revision of their plans. The implication is that policy-making reacts against the hopeless task of trying to control the use of drugs, but is ultimately not effective.

Experiments can show the limited gains to be had from tough enforcement strategies with drugs. Sherman *et al.* (1995) carried out a randomised controlled trial with the Kansas police department to evaluate the impact of enforcement crack houses – residences where dealers and purchasers of crack cocaine do business, generally regarded as a threat to the control of drugs, even more than the open selling of drugs on the street, and a source of violent crime. A raid is the arrival of a considerable police presence, the rounding up of those involved, followed by prosecutions and the closure of the house, a good example of a strong legal tool at work. The researchers hypothesised that these raids would reduce block level crime and disorder. So how well did these raids do? From November 1991 to May 1992 the police department cooperated in a randomised controlled trial. The researchers randomly allocated 207 public calls (when above five) to the police department that would precede a raid (a police officer would attempt to make a purchase from the crack house). One group (104) got the treatment – a raid – and the other locations (103) were left alone. The researchers then measured crime in these locations. The results are modest: an 8 per cent reduction in the level of crime in the places that got the raids and a reduction of disorder of 14 per cent. So the strong application of law tends to produce weak effects. That is not to say tough enforcement does not work, but it needs to be targeted at behaviour that can be controlled, which is very difficult with the use of drugs and their impact on crime.

Another target of intervention is the attempt to prevent people drinking alcohol and driving. This is a persistent and common form of behaviour, combining drinking with an activity that needs care and attention, driving a motor vehicle. It might be thought a relatively visible activity, such as driving a motorcar on a public road, and stiff penalties might work. But as ever it is not simple, partly because of the large number of drivers and limited numbers of police. It is hard to know how much behaviour changes without random breathalyser tests, which in some jurisdictions are illegal for the police to administer. It is not possible to evaluate the changes by looking at the alcohol levels of those who are breathalysed as those figures are affected by the regulatory regime. A study by Bertelli and Richardson (2008) gets round this problem by estimating the propensity to drink and drive from a national survey and seeks to find out whether these estimates correlate with the legal regime in each state. But there is no relationship between the score and the number of arrests for drink driving. Overall, the enforcement regime in the United States does not seem to have an impact on drinking and driving. The paper is an ingenious solution to trying to measure the effectiveness of a legal regime when there is no clear measure of behaviour, such as with drinking and driving. The problem is that it is hard to know whether the propensity score measures the behaviour, which is plausible, but is still an assumption.

It is possible for law-making authorities to keep on redesigning regimes so they get compliance in the end. This works well when the object of the regulation is visible and cannot move. In the case of English local government, for example, Parliament is controlled by central government, the executive, so if central government does not like the strategic behaviour local authorities sometimes use to avoid control, it can keep on legislating until it designs out the problem. Thus in the 1980s, local government accountants used a series of loopholes in hastily drafted local government finance legislation to run rings round central government and avoid spending controls, with central and local government running to the courts in an ever more complicated set of legal wrangles (Loughlin, 1986). But, in the end, central government kept on closing the loopholes until it eventually won because there were no more loopholes left, and local government had to keep within strict spending limits. This example shows a lot depends on the extent to which the principal – in this case the government – has access to legal rules, can get efficient information about what the agent is doing, and then has staying power and determination to keep going until the regulated party complies and effectively gives up resistance. The keep-going approach has its costs too, however, as it is always possible for any public agency to decide to outlaw something and put all its effort into ensuring it happens, but this can divert its energy from other activities the public agency needs to pay attention to – something Chapter 4 considers on performance management. The costs of compliance might not be worth it when run alongside the opportunity costs.

In some circumstances, bans can work. One clear example is where industries have to use certain kinds of chemical in their processes that are licensed. The government can change the licence and thereby enforce a change. One of the best examples was the protection of the ozone layer, which protects life on earth from the negative effects of ultraviolet radiation. Once governments had realised the effects of certain industrial chemicals on reducing the layer they banned their manufacture, even though they were produced for use in a wide variety of goods, such as fridges and aerosol cans. In 1978, Canada, the United States and Norway banned the production of chlorofluorocarbons (CFCs). There followed a world-wide ban in 1986 agreed by international treaty. From the manufacturers' point of view, once a country had banned the use of the chemical, there was nothing else they could have done except obey the regulation or else they could not have stayed in business. The only way in which business may have evaded regulation is through transferring production overseas, and even then government could have banned the import of products manufactured with the technology. In the case of ozone, international agreements can ensure global compliance. As a result, the depletion of the ozone layer had reduced by the 1990s, though not yet back to the levels before 1980 when depletion was first observed and still subject to natural variation (Weatherhead and Andersen, 2006). But the success of the ban needs to be seen in context. As Ahuja and Srinivasan (2009) point out, successful regulation depended on public opinion in the major polluting country of the United States of America being so strong that it affected the sales of aerosols. As a result, Congress supported the ban and a treaty was easier to implement. There was a clear smoking gun because the scientists had proven the case conclusively; and then there was a manufactured product that clearly did the damage. An identifiable culprit gave advocates and public opinion something to seize upon, something that is much harder to do with the science of climate change, for example, where there are many contributing factors and the evidence is not derived from one single cause or process.

Other examples are the banning of consumption of meat or providing for clean water as in the Clean Water Act 1972. Tax changes are in the same category, though there may be possibilities for evasion (see below). It may be easy to change some aspects of behaviour, but not to address the core problems the regulation is trying to address. Or it may encourage evasion or other kinds of activity. In spite of the consensus about the desirability of market-style or decentralised solutions, Cole and Grossman (1999) show top-down environmental regulation can work. Context and the stage in the evolution of an environmental regulatory regime can determine the efficiency of either a market or a command-and-control approach. In the end, much hangs on the case study, federal air pollution regulation in the United States from 1970–90. This is about the Clean Air Act 1970, a highly complex top-down regulation. It is the story about how the interests did try to capture the regulator, but the law did not impose the costs the critics predicted, and delivered improvements in air quality. This may have been the case, but the authors do not present evidence that it was the act that changed air quality as opposed to other causes, such as changes in industry practices. But they do look at the causal mechanism whereby the act focused on the technology needed to drive the improvements. They show that command and control are not inevitably inefficient.

Using the law to change social behaviour

More often in recent times, law and regulation are directed to change a particular behaviour to promote public welfare. This is not the criminal behaviour discussed above, but social acts that governments have come to think are undesirable, such as anti-social behaviour in young people, or people not separating out their household waste into recyclable and non-recyclable components. Policy-makers need to think carefully about how people are motivated to support such a measure. This is because it is almost impossible for public authorities, such as local government or the police, to enforce a law people do not wish to obey and where such behaviour is wide-spread, largely occurring in private. Public authorities need to link the change in the law with other kinds of incentives to change behaviour. The secret is the movement – and manipulation – of public opinion over a long period of time in the direction of the top-down measure, so that when the law is passed and implemented, it is not seen as an illegitimate imposition, but something that is probably right in the eyes of the general population, that the majority is behind, is supported by a number of arguments and comes with examples of successful implementation in other parts of the world. Once a majority of people are behind the measure, obeying it becomes the norm. Then it is not so easy for potential non-compliers to resist.

An example is workplace smoking bans. In England, for example, smoking cigarettes in bars and clubs was routine and hardly ever questioned. Places of work varied as to the extent they tolerated smoking. Workplace smoking bans were pioneered elsewhere, in New York, then Scotland and in other European countries (see Cairney, 2009). Partly influenced by these experiences, a long campaign largely won over public opinion, and there was a change in the law, which came into effect on 1 July 2007. What helped was the appearance of decisive evidence to swing public and political opinion. It was the increased awareness of the finding that secondary smoking harmed the health of employees, such as those working in clubs and bars. This meant trades unions supported the ban because it upholds one of their core values, that is, promoting the health of their members, despite the fact that many of their members like to smoke, such as those who go to working men's clubs. Hence many trades-union sponsored Members of Parliament spoke in favour of the ban when it was debated in the House of Commons. Now it seems a surprise to see working-class pubs with huddles of smokers outside, kept warm by environmentally unfriendly outdoor heaters, while there is clean air inside the warm but empty pub. This begs the question of how much the ban impacts on other health issues. But there is evidence of a reduction of smoking and other health benefits (see Allwright *et al.*, 2005 for a study of the effect of the ban in Ireland, which shows positive results, if from a small sample of 249 bar staff; and see Khuder *et al.*, 2007 for a study of the impact on heart disease on two matched areas in Ohio). With all this positive feedback, the regulatory clampdown appears to be a good thing rather than an example of authoritarian government.

Usually, however, examples of compulsion are not as clear-cut or so successful as the smoking ban, where there is a definite set of arguments in favour, a majority of the public who do not smoke, a specific outcome to achieve and benefits to seize. Other changes are much harder to achieve. One example is welfare reform, which changes entitlement to benefits, requiring claimants to work, what are called welfare-to-work reforms. These have been introduced in United States as well as appearing in the United Kingdom since the 1980s, and in particular with the Labour governments, 1997–2010. The main instrument is legal: there is compulsion designed to change behaviour. Usually other instruments apply, such as some modest funding and persuasion, and the organisation of bureaucracies to help provide opportunities and support to the people in the programme; but legal command is at the heart of the reform, so it is a good example of the tool at work, even if it needs to be looked at alongside others.

It is important to guard against tautology in the use of this tool: if the state compels people to work, and they end up working, this does not show that the programme worked. This is a bit like if you aim a gun and fire it at point-blank range and someone dies, then you have proved guns can kill people. A more sensible way of evaluating the impact question is to see what other consequences emerged from the programme, such as long-term employment or a better lifestyle, as might be indicated by lower fertility, for example. There are many evaluations of these kinds of programme, so this chapter presents just three. The first is a study by Kaushal and Kaestner (2001), which shows that welfare reform in the United States increased the employment opportunities of women. The national legislation was the Personal Responsibility and Work Opportunities Reconciliation Act 1996, which appeared to lead to a reduction in the number of people on welfare, as 1.8 million families left the welfare rolls, almost double the number moving off during the previous three years. In 1994, 5.5 per cent of the United States population was on welfare; after the reforms and five years later, this had reduced to 2.3 per cent. As ever with these evaluations, it is the method of capturing the effectiveness of the policy instruments that is crucial, and this study seeks to observe the difference between two groups, one of which has varying levels of intervention, the other which does not, so it is possible to observe the changes in the differences in the groups, and to perform statistical analysis controlling for the known predictors. This is a quasi-experimental method, not quite a randomised controlled trial, but getting close. The analysis uses data from the Census Bureau from March 1995–99, a nation-wide sample of about 62,500 cases, and then looks at the impact of time limits on benefits and family cap provisions. The finding is that employment changes did affect the target populations, which varied with the intensity of the reform. Unmarried women benefited. There are similar effects for hours of work. There are reasonable effect sizes in this study – the policy was effective, not just that it had an effect. But there are only a few significant differences in fertility as a result of these reforms. It is a good study, especially as it lags the reform by two years to see the down-stream effects. But there is the worry of selection – even with the differencing methods – as those who are most likely to be employed are selected into the reform or those states with programmes tend to be in places where employment is high.

Many studies use sophisticated methods to understand the causes. Kaestner, Korenman and O'Neill (2003) wanted to find out whether teenagers' behaviour changed, examining educational attainment, welfare use, fertility rate and marriage rate among teenagers in the years before and after welfare reform. The study uses a cross-cohort approach, which compares young people in particular cohorts who spent their teen years before welfare reform in 1979–85 with those who spent a substantial portion of these years after welfare reform in 1997–99. It analyses the United States National Longitudinal Surveys of Youth in 1979 and 1997. The results show that among the high-risk groups, welfare use declined, as did fertility and drop-out rates – and also marriage declined, which might suggest changes over the period. There was no change in non-marital births. Among low-risk women there was a decline in marriage and an increase in non-marital birth. The descriptive results are confirmed by the statistical analysis. This is an attrac-tive study, particularly with the time element, using the same survey. But it is not able to find out – nor does it discuss – whether other factors affect the cohorts which are not connected to the programme. These could be lifestyle changes or changes in the economy happening at the same time.

To evaluate effectively the impact of legal changes, as with other instru-ments, there are experiments – randomised controlled trials in the field – that can make accurate measurements of the impact of interventions. Here, who or what place gets welfare is randomised, which public authorities are often reluctant to do. Fortunately, welfare is one area where experiments have been tried out. Bloom, Hill and Riccio (2003) report results from a series of studies, pooling the estimates so they show a more generalisable impact. This amounts to experiments done in fifty-nine locations so there is no element of chance findings or cherry picking. They allow for comparisons, which show the importance of implementation in the process. They focus on the manage-ment of the programmes, such as the caseload, the attention to the clients and the degree of agreement in the bureaucracy (the organisational tools discussed in the next chapter) and how success varies according to the client group, the economic environment and the particular kinds of take-up by the clients. So the law does not usually act alone, but it involves a wide range of other tools. The programmes they looked at were job search assistance, basic education and vocational training. For this study, they pooled the data from three evaluations, which yields a large sample of participants and control group members (69,399) from 59 offices. Then there were follow-up surveys. The key outcome measure was earnings. They use a particular kind of statistical model that can take into account the variation at the office and at the individual level – a multi-level model. They can then allow for all the differences between the offices, such as caseloads and economic differences, as well as the treatment effects within the districts. They show the emphasis on quick client employment has the largest and most statistically significant impact, which shows the importance of this intervention. There are powerful effects for personal client attention (see Chapter 6, which reviews personalised interventions). From the perspective of legal regulation, the offices which tried to monitor strongly the progress of the clients were the least successful (though there is a danger of reverse causation as offices in areas where there are difficult clients might try to monitor them more closely – though they do allow for client characteristics). The level of intensity matters as caseloads reduce the impact of the programme. Education is also important, but not vocational education – which might reflect the wider liberal aims of education. Overall, it seems the softer side of the intervention matters.

The regulatory state and overregulation

The difficulties of using legal tools also emerge when government considers using regulation more generally as a way to steer public policy. This is the idea that government can stand back from using bureaucracies and the organisations of the state or market mechanisms, but set up a legally supervised system of regulation, whereby individual and group behaviour is governed by precisely calibrated instruments as set out in legislation and rules decided by the courts. The law may be enforced by a dedicated body, such as a commission, set at arm's length from the politicians, and used to regulate relationships that were previously delegated to professional institutions or associations, which ran policy matters according to a set of informal rules or professional codes. When informal regulation had become discredited, governments became tempted to set out clear legal rules and to enforce them as a way of bringing order to a private market and to the conduct of professionals, such as medical doctors. As Moran (2002) discusses, the concept of the regulatory state had its origins in studies of public policy in the US, such as the work of Vogel (1986). It has also been influential in understanding the European Union, which lacks powers of policy implementation except through national bureaucracies, so it has to rely on regulation to implement its policies (Majone, 1994).

The re-discovery of the power of the regulation led to an audit explosion from the 1980s and many new regulatory bodies were set up, both outside and inside government (Hood *et al.*, 1999). Moran (2003) outlines and discusses the expansion of the regulatory state in Britain since this period, characterised by extensive privatisation and the introduction of new regulatory bodies to control these industries. Whereas many activities, such as medicine, were largely self-regulated, the regulatory state sees it as its business to regulate them. The state had become uncomfortable with informal and decentralised traditions of regulation; now it wanted performance to be assessed in a public way. The version that emerged in the United Kingdom Moran calls hyper-modernism, so called because of its ambition to transform older forms of regulation. Moran believes excessive faith in the virtues of sub-government was replaced with a similarly held belief in regulation as a solution. It is the overreliance on the formal aspect of the law/regulation tool of government which is the concern here, which reflects hierarchical forms of thinking and tends to crowd out learning. It limits adaptation in response to information and effectively uses the insider knowledge of the regulated groups. In turn, hyper-modernism encourages strategic behaviour from the regulated groups that start to seek advantage from the rules and regulation. Added to this is the sheer speed and lack of deliberation about the policy choices, which lead to poor implementation of the reforms, and a series of policy disasters as a result. Behind Moran's argument is a claim from systems theory that argues command and control systems cannot cope with complexity: there is a need to return or recreate a self-learning system. Moran then recounts some powerful case studies of the failure of this system, such as over food regulation. The BSE ('mad cow disease') crisis in Britain occurred because the regulatory regime encouraged the disastrous spread of bovine spongiform encephalo-pathy, which then spread to the human population. It is possible to extend Moran's critique to the crisis of financial regulation during 2008, and of the argument for more traditional tools, such as bureaucracy, and the reinstate-ment of norms that could be used to regulate the banks (see Moran, 2010). Moran draws attention to the costs of regulation, which are to do with the problems of specifying the correct regulated relationship.

It is possible to overstate the problem, however. Moran draws attention to the United Kingdom's attraction to policy disasters, where it appears an adversarial and centralised political system led to ill thought-out and costly policies, such as the Child Support Agency, the poll tax and computerisation (Dunleavy, 1995). These policy errors appear to owe much to the breakdown of existing forms of regulation through professional norms, being replaced by swift legal changes designed to effect rapid change, what Dunleavy calls the fastest law in the west. The overuse of legal forms of regulation appears to lead to miscalculations and a loss of capacity of the state, and a series of policy errors as a result. What this literature tends to leave out is the near inevitable implementation difficulties that emerge with new projects, and it does not discuss the longer period of bedding down the policies or the capa-city of decision-makers to learn from mistakes and reverse their policies. For example, one of the greatest policy disasters in the United Kingdom was the single person local tax, the poll tax, which replaced the long-standard rating system, a local property tax. The poll tax was impossible to implement due to public resistance and administrative difficulties (Butler *et al.*, 1994). Sections of the public refused to obey the law, by not registering for the tax or paying it. But a mere three years after its introduction in 1990, central government had replaced it with a property tax (John, 1999). It seems the lack of potency of the law, when misapplied, can be remedied by retreats and rethinks without large losses in legitimacy. The influence of legal instruments needs to be seen dynamically, as part of a learning process whereby the regulators can correct their mistakes and get the policy right, a point highlighted by the school of responsive regulation discussed below.

Overall, Moran's and other scholars' work draws attention to the problem of regulation and to the dangers of over regulation, which impose costs on government and limit its capacity. It links to the literature that examines alternative forms of regulation. This reveals a reaction against overregulation and a realisation of the complexity of the task at hand when the law is used to regulate public policy.

Alternative forms of regulation

It might be thought the negative results this chapter has discussed in the form of limits to control and the dangers of overregulation show that law is not the most effective tool for policy-makers to use, or at least it might be important in some situations, and when run alongside other tools, perhaps as a stick behind the carrot and when public authorities have made careful calculations of the costs and benefits. But it may be the case that such an analysis mis-understands the nature of law. For there is a body of work that argues that persuasion and dialogue are at the heart of its effectiveness. For what matters is not just the passing of a statute and the application of sanctions, but how the law is understood by those whom it is intended to affect. For example, Bardach and Kagan (1982) argue that really tough regulatory regimes do not necessarily work. Studying the environmental enforcement in the United States, they find too tough an approach to enforcement undermines the cooperative relationships needed to implement policies effectively. A more flexible approach has a better chance of working.

The classic work in this tradition is by Braithwaite (1985), who studied the enforcement of safety regulations for mines in 39 disasters across the world. He discovered that most accidents could be avoided if the law was obeyed and the best way of getting there is better communication between the owners and the unions, perhaps through deliberative arrangements (linking to Chapter 6). Criminal sanctions would not work. This study looked at quantitative data as well as case studies. Braithwaite also reports the selection of pits each year for training and shows how this affected safety (though this was a non-random selection and may have involved some self-selection on the part of the pits – the ones already well disposed to the reform). Legal penalties remain important. But sanctions should build up gradually after cooperation fails. Toughness should be followed by forgiveness. With its strong results and passion of its author, this study helped to energise a research programme on restorative justice (see the review in Braithwaite, 2002).

There is a line of work in criminology that tests the efficacy of restorative justice ideas and measures. This is about seeking to provide an alternative to conventional forms of punishment in the criminal justice system. The argument is that conventional forms of legal regulation through sentences and fines tend not to lead to individual behaviour change and people carry on offending as before. Getting the perpetrators of crime to meet their victims may have a better effect. Note this is still a form of legal regulation as offenders have to take these actions, but it works in a different way, which allows for more responsiveness. It can take place in different formats, such as through the offender and victim meeting each other when mediated by an expert facilitator, or it can be in a wider group involving families and other people affected – even communities. It has been adopted in a wide range of contexts, in the United States, United Kingdom, Israel and South Africa.

The claim is that restorative justice will increase the satisfaction of victors and reduce recidivism (alongside other benefits such as reducing the costs of the criminal justice system, though it has a cost). But it is hard to prove it works. It is a challenge to set up a counterfactual of what would have happened without the intervention, particularly as victims are likely to select into restorative justice, which makes it hard to find a comparable population to study. Fortunately, this topic of research in criminal justice contains a lot of experimental and quasi-experimental studies. A meta-analysis – a systematic review of all the research – carried out by Latimer *et al.* (2005) only included studies that had a comparison or control group. For satisfaction it found a mean effect size for 13 tests of +.19 and positive effects in all bar one of the programmes. It found 32 studies that examined recidivism, with an overall effect size of +.07 (2005: 137), with two-thirds of the studies finding positive results. However, it is probably not right to put together the experimental and non-experimental work. As Strang and Sherman argue, the effects may not be so uniform when just the experimental studies are reviewed, having 'a significant crime reduction effect for violent offenders but apparently not for property offenders, at least in the short to medium term' (2006: 159).

Sherman *et al.* (2005) report on four randomised controlled trials – one on property crime (249 subjects), the other on violent crime (121) – carried out in Canberra, Australia, where restorative justice was seen as a substitute for prosecution, and then two in London on burglary and robbery (216 subjects), where the restorative justice could be used as mitigation for the offence. The interventions were very similar, being face-to-face meetings for about one-and-a-half to two hours. The courts dealt with those people in the control group. Fairly unsurprisingly, the results show the victims were more likely to receive an apology in the restorative justice group, and also there is a sense of forgiveness among the victims. To test for the stronger claim of an impact of recidivism, Tyler *et al.* (2007) report on the Australian Reintegrative Shaming Experiments, which randomly assigned 900 cases of drink driving to treatment and control groups. The treatment was a conference where the charges were dropped. The offender attended with five other friends or family members. The conferences were intended to ensure the offenders entered into an agreement to repair the harm caused by the offence, such as donating money to charity or doing community work. The treatment had no effect on re-offending, but it appeared to have influenced attitudes as recorded in a survey. Whether attitude change is enough to justify the policy in place of an impact on recidivism is a judgement policy-makers may wish to make.

Responsive regulation

The move to examine alternatives or complements to top-down hierarchical approaches to regulation is called responsive regulation (Ayres and Braithwaite, 1992), which involves adjusting the regulatory regime and using a balance of approaches to get to the right result. This is sometimes called smart regulation (Gunningham and Grabosky, 1998), which involves a careful assessment of the strategies open to regulators rather than jumping in with too strong an intervention. It may involve a regulation pyramid where self-regulation is tried first and then replaced with tougher forms of regulation. It may be associated with what is called risk regulation, where the authority seeks to calculate the risk of different interventions (see Hood *et al.*, 2003).

These new accounts of regulation have moved the debate forward. Rather than assuming top-down control works or leaving alone is best, it examines the different ways in which legal incentives can act upon a policy problem. As well as compulsion, it involves other kinds of incentives running alongside the law, or the regulatory framework being set up in a complex way, which is sensitive to the governance arrangements (and in many ways crosses over with the networks/governance tool the book discusses in Chapter 7, as well as crossing into finance and the bureaucracy – the topics of subsequent chapters). This may be called the hybridisation of regulation, or the term really responsive regulation (Baldwin and Black, 2008; Black and Baldwin, 2010), where regulation is not a one-off command but involves responsiveness to a changing situation. They write, 'once regulators have established their objectives, they should consider how any given regulatory approach comes to grips with the five fundamental tasks involved in implementing regulation so as to further those objectives. The tasks are as follows: (1) detecting undesirable or noncompliant behaviour; (2) responding to that behaviour by developing tools and strategies; (3) enforcing those tools and strategies on the ground; (4) assessing their success or failure; and (5) modifying approaches accordingly' (2010: 183). Black and Baldwin (2010) indicate the regulatory framework could be more responsive than even responsive regulation, involving a super-effort to adjust to the context, which then feeds into the risk assessment.

These kinds of regulation are increasingly popular, especially amongst policy-makers. The idea is that it is possible to move away from using economic forms of incentives to broader kinds of motivation, which draw on the more complicated reasons why people obey laws. Leviner (2008) uses the example of tax regulation and argues that simple utility theory will not explain why people pay taxes. As with crime more generally, making the punishment more severe does not affect evasion of taxes. It is more complicated than that. Being highly punitive can be counterproductive and creates resentment among normally compliant taxpayers. This can even turn people into the rational calculators as envisaged by economic theory, with a devaluing of the public good and unleashing short-term self-interest. This is rather like Frey's (1997) crowding-out effect, whereby altruistic behaviours become increasingly undermined by the availability of short-run economic incentives, often supplied by an external party. Leviner argues that tax regulators can think about these kinds of issues when they are designing their regulatory system. He set out five kinds of response: (i) commitment, (ii) capitulation, (iii) resistance, (iv) disengagement and (v) game playing, which can influence the regime and tackle different aspects. There may also be different kinds of taxpayers, and different rules can apply to each, providing they can be identified. In particular, legal regulators need to be sensitive to the citizens' sense of legitimacy. Citizens adhere to a sense of procedural justice, which needs to be respected when making legal changes, such as to the tax system. Leviner argues that there is no definitive programme to enact or a single best way to regulate. Leviner then sets out a case study of the Australian tax system, which was previously based on an authoritarian top-down model, where the authorities took on board the responsive regulation approach. Leviner describes the emergence of the tit-for-tat scenarios, which is where the regulator reacts to the situation in a dynamic fashion, which involves encouragement and persuasion but does not neglect the more punitive instruments either.

The movement toward really responsive regulation alerts analysts to the implementation difficulties of a hybrid regulatory system. Dorbeck-Jung *et al.* (2010) study the problems in such a system to protect minors from exposure to harmful forms of media in Holland. In spite of the law, it was very easy for a minor to buy or rent a video or to buy a cinema ticket. Most of the stores were unclear about the legal rules and did not think the law was serious in its intent, thinking it was mainly there for information. There was relatively little oversight and enforcement. Basically the Dutch government did not have an active interventionist approach to the problem. The observation that can be made about this case study is that it is an example of where the government was not particularly interested in enforcement and so perhaps is not a very good example of regulation – or perhaps it shows that legal regimes tend toward a lack of effectiveness if there is not the political will to enforce them. It would have been a better case study if the government was more interested in changing behaviour, but perhaps this is an example of where the difficulties of implementation feed back into the apathy of policy-makers. The paper does not discuss the meta-politics of regulation, but concludes with a reflection on the limits of really responsive regulation.

Conclusions

Law and regulation is a powerful tool – or set of tools – of government, which no state or rule-making public authority could imagine being without. It defines the political realm, forming a key part of the essential toolkit of states. As with the other tools, it is important to know what is its contribution to achieving effective policy outcomes, and what are the costs and benefits of relying on it. There is a significant amount of evidence, in particular good case studies of interventions based on compulsion and legal regulation. As ever, it is not easy to come up with a clear answer. Legal regulation can work – banning something when there is public opinion behind it. But there are costs to this form of governance in the lack of responsiveness of the regulator and a negative or strategic reaction from the regulated, even if they formally comply. History reveals examples of strong laws that fail. The tool works well as part of a package of different kinds of instruments, when the costs and benefits have been carefully thought about, and when it is relied upon as a last resort rather than on its own.

The failure of top-down and strong forms of control does not mean law and regulation are necessarily ineffective. Studies of restorative justice and responsive regulation show that some forms of legal control have a better chance of compliance and provide enforcement choices that can be appropriate for each situation. In the end, as with many tools, the reliance on law and regulation is a balancing act, and interacts with many other aspects of the resources of governments.

3 Public spending and taxation

Money buys actions of all sorts. With funds, an individual can satisfy hunger, have better living conditions, get a better education and achieve an improved quality of life. As so often with public policy, it is easy to move from the personal to the political and to assume that what the person can do individually translates into collective benefits. By spending more societies can solve public policy problems, like poor education standards, bad health, transport bottlenecks, the environment and security from terrorist attacks. It is a familiar claim. For across the world, there appears to be evidence that even small amounts of spending can have large impacts on outcomes. For example, it has been calculated that a significant proportion of deaths of under-fives in Sub-Saharan Africa and South Asia could be avoided by the expenditure of as little as $8 on immunisation (for each disability life-adjusted life year – see Jamison *et al.*, 2006: 54).

If only it were that simple. Spending money on policy problems involves coordinating bureaucracies (see Chapter 4) and setting into place chains of cause and effect in the wider society at large. These are the topics of other chapters, but it is the effect of the allocation of public finance to a problem that is of interest in this chapter, and how this may interact with other factors, such as the responsiveness of the bureaucracy and the information capacity of citizens. So it is possible spending increases may be authorised, but may not yield much in terms of benefit to those who need the services and may not fully address the problems that require attention. In many cases, the effect depends on how the money reaches the outside world. In some cases it may be possible to hand the money directly to a client group, such as pensioners or single parent families. But even if the group receives the resources, they may not get a long-term benefit from them. Such income changes may not translate into a better quality of life because of the decisions of the individuals who receive the funds, such as spending money on unhealthy lifestyles, or the money could get spent within bureaucracies rather than on the client group. The stimulating effect of money might get wasted on poor investment decisions and/or higher salaries for those working in the bureaucracy.

So public spending increases may not necessarily yield benefits or enough benefit to justify the cost. On the personal level income is fixed, so individuals face the problem of allocating income to different spending priorities so their overall welfare is maximised. Governments have the advantage they may vary the amount of spending by increasing or reducing taxes, but in practice they are limited in the extent they can do this because of the political pressures to keep the balance the same and limitations on how much debt they can sustain in the long term. The existing balance between government and private spending may represent trade-offs of welfare between different groups, and the political costs of changing that balance are high. If there are welfare gains of increased expenditure these need to be compared with welfare losses among groups that have higher taxes. Those taxation decisions may reflect decisions to incentivise certain groups to do things, such as volunteering for the public good, which may be disrupted by increasing taxation. Reducing taxation may be seen as an expenditure, a form of publicly directed spending to achieve a policy outcome.

There are also costs of increasing expenditure to very high levels because of the negative effect on the private economy. This is a form of crowding-out whereby extra expenditure reduces economic activity by increasing the costs of borrowing, which then reduces investment and in turn depresses economic growth. If there is no growth in tax receipts, public expenditure cannot keep up with the rise in spending need over time caused by socio-demographic changes like ageing and the rising costs of public-sector provision. Thus there may be costs in increasing public-sector expenditure that are not outweighed by its economic and social benefits. So the question becomes: do marginal increases in public expenditure have beneficial outcomes taking into account the costs of such activity in terms of taxes and incentives and other opportunities forgone?

This strategy does not rule out switching expenditure to gain benefits. But again, as with the private consumer, it is possible to assume governments have sought to reach equilibrium point given their best judgements about the costs and benefits. Switching expenditure may be about a different calculation of the costs and benefits or new information about the benefits of a particular line of expenditure. The most plausible way to look at the general issue as to whether increasing expenditure delivers benefits is when a government or administration enters power with the policy option available of increasing public expenditure, such as when a previous administration has kept spending artificially low. Then it is possible to think through the costs and benefits of that decision. It so happens in the United Kingdom there is such an example. In 1997, the Labour government entered power after 17 years of Conservative governments, which had kept public spending low and had sought to reduce it where possible. After two years where the new government had promised to keep within the previous administration's spending limits, it decided to increase public spending greatly, especially on the services of education and health. This is an instructive case study, which appears at the end of this chapter. The question is whether the Labour governments (1997–2010) achieved sufficient return on their investment and what special conditions operated in these circumstances. By looking at the general literature and this special case, it is possible to evaluate the contribution of public funding to generating better policy outcomes when there is a change in political preferences.

The welfare state

The impact of public expenditure is probably curvilinear: there are very high impacts from small amounts of expenditure if the initial level of expenditure is low. These progressively reduce at higher levels, and may end up being negative because the opportunity costs of spending may become very high. The high impact from an initial low level comes from the role of the state in providing public goods like safety, defence, transport infrastructure and street lights, which people cannot contribute to privately because they are indivisible and there are too many costs in deciding to subscribe to them. A state that did not provide public goods, but then decides to spend on them will get a great uplift in benefit. This explanation may help explain why states got established in the first place and populations accepted unpopular state activities such as taxes. But deciding to provide public goods is not the normal practice of modern states in developed economies as they are normally provided at some minimum level already. It might be possible to provide these public goods in a better fashion, but this is largely about management issues, discussed in Chapter 4.

The more familiar case is where the government wishes to spend more on welfare services. These are mainly private goods because they can be bought and sold for individual benefit even if the market does not provide them normally. In the absence of state provision they tend to be underprovided or only purchased by people who have high incomes. As well as the direct benefits to less well-off groups, there are knock-on benefits from higher welfare spending, such as greater social cohesion and a better functioning labour market. There is also the direct impact of the reduction of income inequality on outcomes, such as economic growth through a whole series of indirect effects through social cohesion. Later the chapter considers the possible negative impacts of the welfare state on the economy.

One thing to note from the start is that spending is only one aspect of the welfare state. It involves policies and procedures that help apply specialist knowledge to public problems. It is also about harnessing the capacity of bureaucracies, which forms the topic of Chapter 4. For that reason, Esping-Anderson (1990) proposes qualitative measures of welfare state development, for what matters is the type of citizenship these states embody and fulfil. But public spending is crucial to achieving these outcomes, however, as welfare programmes cost significant amounts of money.

It is a very hard question to answer whether the public spending on welfare states – and by implication changes in public spending – is effective, largely for the reasons this chapter opened with. If there are preferences for certain kinds of outcomes, then it is likely the spending can be directed to improve needs, such as poverty (Kenworthy, 1999). This might not be seen as an impact on outcomes, more the result of a change of priorities. It may be the case that – partially at least – if the state decides to give money to the less-well-off in society, then almost by definition there is a positive impact, because their income has been altered. What is being assessed is the preference for a certain type of policy or a pattern of distribution rather than the effectiveness of a policy instrument. It also may be the case that the outcome of poverty reduction might be more difficult to achieve than improving personal incomes, such as the benefits to the individual of long-term employment or better health.

The other factor affecting the assessment of the potency of the public spending instrument is the ability of states to fund anti-poverty schemes, which depends on national income. So it would not be surprising that countries with higher levels of income would be able to fund better schemes to relieve poverty. As a result, researchers are not measuring marginal schemes to improve the welfare state but the impact of higher overall income, which both affects welfare and lowers poverty through the spread of employment. As ever in this book, it is difficult to attribute a causal relationship between the tools or instrument and the policy outcome once the complex pattern of relationships is taken into account.

Qualifications aside, it is possible to review the large literature that suggests states that have allocated large amounts of public spending to welfare gain significant benefits. This is about the political decisions at crucial historical moments to create a welfare-enhancing state, which involves the institutionalisation of policy preferences at a particular point in time (Rothstein, 1998). The state embodies a collective positive effort on the part of society to raise the welfare of the less well-off. This is the argument for social democracy, which seeks to set in place a set of self-reinforcing outcomes. This is what Korpi (1985) calls an irrigation system, providing benefit to the target groups and to the wider society. Against this is the critical view that suggests welfare states allocate too few benefits to needy groups because of the ability of more wealthy groups to access these funds by virtue of their power in society and in their skill in dealing with the bureaucracy – the allocation of public finance gets skewed (Goodin and Le Grand, 1987). There is much evidence to this effect, but universal welfare systems also ensure resources get to those who need them. There is the counter argument that it does not matter if the middle classes benefit from the welfare system because their benefits may be counterbalanced by progressive taxation. These benefits buy them politically into the welfare state and avoid the negative outcomes from means testing benefits (Korpi and Palme, 1998). An alternative argument is that the welfare state weakens economic growth by reducing incentives to work and inhibiting a fully functioning labour market, arguments reviewed in a section below.

The key studies that relate to the use of public spending are about particular programmes. Core to these are those that evaluate one of the central objectives of the welfare state: the reduction of poverty, where there have been many studies, which are largely quantitative, so there is a little bit of technical discussion.

Firstly, Korpi and Palme (1998) test to see if the type of welfare regime affects the level of poverty. They examine data from eighteen countries, and mainly use descriptive statistics to compare countries according to type of regime and different sorts of outcome, such as inequality among the elderly. In spite of some promising links between welfare generosity and positive outcomes, it ends up being a weak test of the spending thesis, partly because of the difficulty of making an inference with a small number of country cases and limited allowance for the economic factors that affect the same outcomes. Much better is Kenworthy's (1999) study, which looks at 15 countries from 1960–91. This finds evidence of the effectiveness of using measures of poverty at a later time period than the intervention. It measures the extent of welfare state intensiveness as it impacts on different measures of poverty – by the percentage of transfers as a proportion of Gross Domestic Product (GDP), then the extent of de-commodification – the extent to which people can live independently measured according to the rules. This concept taps into the more qualitative definitions of the welfare state as indicated by Esping-Anderson. The third factor is the extent of social wage someone receives if they are not working. The statistical model controls for the level of economic wealth as well as the numbers in low-wage occupations. It finds that each of the measures of welfare state intensiveness does impact significantly on poverty. It is a carefully implemented research design, but overall it is not entirely convincing because what is being explained is not fully distinguished from what is doing the explaining. In spite of careful analysis of the influence of different cases on the results, it does not have many observations at 15 countries so is below what is normally acceptable in a statistical analysis even with its careful analysis of the outlier cases. He excludes the important cases of Japan, New Zealand and Austria because of lack of data for these countries.

Moller *et al.*'s (2003) study is superior because it uses panel data that measure changes over time and by place at the same time with 14 counties from 1967–97. They test a range of hypotheses that affect poverty, such as trade union density, left governments and constitutional structure (which relate to other topics in this book). But they also test for the generosity of the welfare state measured by the share of total spending and of social security transfers as shares of GDP. The results for pre-tax poverty show, when controlling for a variety of factors, that public spending matters, but in the opposite direction by increasing poverty, although the results are non-significant in later models. So here is a correction to the positive view of the earlier study. Poverty is a function of industrial unemployment, unemployment and wage coordination, which do not clearly link to state policy. But there are more encouraging results for poverty reduction, which is influenced by welfare state generosity and child and family allowances. If governments really want to reduce poverty, they can do it. In this view, the financial transfers are effective even if the overall relationship between spending and poverty is not positive.

Brady (2005) investigated poverty in 18 nations from 1967–97. The impressive feature of this paper is that it tests for both anti-poverty and the effect of economic growth on poverty. Previous studies, like Moller's, only control for economic development. This study tests for the impact of a large range of spending decisions increasing the range of inferences – and seeks to allow for the differential institutionalisation of the welfare state taking into account various traditions – and for a larger number of countries. It also studies the crucial period of the 1990s, which is when a period of retrenchment started to be felt. This generates a further hypothesis – that there should be a turnaround in that period. It uses, like other papers, the Luxembourg Income study to measure poverty. In many ways, the welfare state variables are similar to Kenworthy's – social security transfers as a percentage of the GDP. But it also includes some new measures: public health spending as a percentage of total health spending, non-military public employment and military spending as a percentage of the GDP. The findings are that public spending, both on transfers and on public health, matters for poverty, which is a similar finding to other studies, but economic growth matters too. Transfers does not come out as statistically significant – it is public spending that matters. The paper partially confirms that economic growth determines the level of poverty, but many other economic variables associated with poverty reduction also have an impact.

So there is strong evidence to show that public spending matters for the key welfare state outcome of poverty. But methodological problems make it difficult to assess the impact of public spending overall. As Atkinson (1999) points out, the impact of the welfare state is endogenous to economic growth. So the wealthier countries are better able to afford more generous welfare states. This may in turn moderate or disguise the costs of the welfare state – and so public spending – on the economy. As long as the economy does not tip into recession, then the correlation between high spending, good outcomes and economic growth can be maintained as a virtuous circle.

Finally, it should be added there are what are called micro-data studies that look at the income of target groups before and after an intervention, by using survey data, which show certain groups' poverty does reduce, such as among women, children and the elderly (Casper *et al.*, 1994; Christopher *et al.*, 2002; Jäntti and Danziger, 2000). The problem with these studies is that they do not look at the opportunity costs of expenditure as in the macro-level studies. But it is reassuring to know the targeted groups get the money. Probably spending is the best way to meet new needs if the opportunity cost is low.

The welfare state and the economy

Increasing public spending has costs that may even affect the efficacy of poverty-reduction policies. The size of national income devoted to the welfare state is supposed to affect the economy, which can influence the level of economic growth from the crowding out of private sector activity and investment. The other argument is increased spending may not have a long-term effect on poverty. An example is Murray's (1984) work that tried to show welfare benefits introduced in the 1960s increased poverty by the 1970s. But there is little evidence that welfare reduces work incentives and dries up the labour supply (Atkinson and Morgensen, 1993). Nor is there evidence about the impact of policy on overall levels of poverty: poverty in the United States in the 1970s went down in spite of adverse demographic changes, but then went up in a later period (Blackburn, 1990).

The state of academic knowledge about the impact of the welfare state on the economy is summarised by Atkinson (1999), who reviews evidence to show that there is little impact of the welfare state on the economy. There is a difference in results, with the welfare state thinkers such as Korpi and Castles thinking there is a positive impact, others showing a negative impact and other studies being neutral. One early study is by Korpi (1985). This analysis takes the economic growth of 18 of the Organisation for Economic Co-operation and Development (OECD) countries from 1950–73 and examines the impact of the change in the welfare state size – measured as the size of the social security transfer as a proportion of GDP – on growth, which ends up being a positive. This relationship continues for the 1973–79 period of economic turbulence as well. The problem is economic growth can affect spending as much as the other way round, which makes inference very hard. But what is more convincing is this study also tests other kinds of expenditure and finds little effect, which suggest measures to reduce inequality promote economic growth.

Weede (1986) studies 19 of the OECD nations with data from 1960–82, which includes Japan (which makes a big difference to the results). He uses social security transfers as a proportion of GDP. He shows welfare state expenditure decreases economic growth, which is a different finding from other studies using the same or similar data. The advantage is the use of pooled data – that is, data varying over time and place – but there are no tests for how wealth may affect public expenditure on poverty.

Castles and Dowrick (1990) examine the 18 OECD countries from 1960–85, seeking to explain the annual trend rate of growth of GDP, testing also Olson's thesis that institutional clogging slows down economic growth, and controlling for the variables of population growth, growth in employment and capital stock. They add government spending as a determinant, dis-aggregated into health, education and transfers. Their analysis is cross-sectional for the whole period, but it breaks down the data into time periods as well. They carry out a series of diagnostic tests and use a two-stage least squares model with government consumption at the beginning of the period as the instrumental variable. This tries to get round the finding that government expenditure is partially determined by economic growth. Overall, they find a positive effect on economic growth of the expenditure on transfers, though this effect is weaker than Korpi's, largely because of the inclusion of more independent variables. Even though the instability in the findings and the influence of single countries are important, the authors reject the hypothesis that the relationship between social spending and economic growth is negative.

But the negative effect is what one study shows. Persson and Tabellini (1994) evaluate the negative relationship between inequality and per capita growth across several periods. This is an evaluation of the impact of equality on growth, which shows a negative impact. Their work presents many tests of validity and alternative specifications of the data. They evaluate the role of state transfers in this process, finding a negative effect in an analysis of 15 countries. This shows instruments to create poverty reduce economic growth. These findings remain controversial, and the authors accept later data overturn this analysis (1997: 81, n. 61).

Atkinson's (1999) review of these and other papers concludes the welfare state and the economy studies are limited in what they can claim. One limitation is the small number of country cases, which means the analysis is sensitive to data from particular places, such as Japan. There are different definitions of the welfare state variable, which may or may not include tax expenditures – particular benefits in the tax system – and different measures of growth all generate different results. The key limitation is the account of causation as mentioned above, where it is almost impossible to disentangle economic growth from spending. What should be borne in mind is Saunders' (1986) critique, which suggests cross-national regressions are rarely able to sustain the weight of inference placed upon them, partly because they are carried out in particular time periods and with groups of countries. It is striking that after Atkinson's intervention this macro-level debate runs into the sand.

The main effect of public expenditures is through some selective spending, such as in education (Barro, 1991), through investment in human capital, which in turn generates economic growth. Barro's study increases the range of cases – 90 – to outside OECD countries using data from 1960–85. Again, like the other economic studies, the growth rate is inversely related to the share of the public sector of GDP. Crucially the size of the public sector is related to the amount of private investment, which in turn contributes to growth. It should also be noted this study measures the school enrolment rate, not the expenditure. Barro separately tests whether public investment expenditure influences growth, which it does not. This result, along with the other negative findings in the economics literature, remains unchallenged.

Overall, using the important case of the spending on the welfare state, a range of studies show positive impacts, either at the aggregate level or for the welfare of specific groups in the population. There remains the fear the overuse of this tool of government will crowd out other activities, such as economic growth or other beneficial self-organising activities. But no study gives conclusive evidence about these negative effects.

Selective taxation

It is not possible to separate out the effects of taxation and expenditure from each other. This works at the general level, as with the welfare-state studies, where both affect unemployment and the reduction of poverty, but it also operates with respect to specific activities where the state wants to increase or reduce the amount of private expenditure on an activity that is respectively beneficial or harmful. This is because individuals and organisations alter their behaviour in response to these financial incentives from the state. While taxes in general are aimed at producing the resources necessary to generate public spending increases, the exact shape of the taxation system can be part of the overall financial tool of government. An example is unemployment and poverty. If marginal tax rates for the low paid are set at too high a rate compared to welfare payments, there will be an incentive to stay out of work. If one of the aims of welfare is to prepare people for work, then this will lead to worse outcomes because of the benefits of people being in work, such as higher income and better health. It has a particular mechanism to effect change, different from giving resources to bureaucrats to hand to people as in the classic public-expenditure decisions discussed earlier in the chapter, even though it is really a form of public expenditure and some economists refer to these selective benefits as tax expenditures (Surrey, 1973). It works through altering individual or organisational incentives as they respond to the tax system. This is the source of its efficiency as it relies on directly affecting the individual/organisation rather than on indirect measures, such as information on its own (see Chapter 6) or laws that might be ignored or unenforceable (Chapter 2). Nor does it rely on putting the spending through a bureaucracy and risk the objectives of the policy being compromised (see Chapter 4). The other advantage is that taxation may be economically efficient because if the desired action is priced properly, then it allows other decision-makers, such as consumers and firms, to organise themselves in response to the new set of costs. If a non-desired activity, such as a short-hop plane ride, is priced to include the social cost, somebody who really needs to do it for personal or business reasons still can – it is just that the cost has been allowed for. This would be more efficient than banning internal flights in the United Kingdom, for example. The idea is that the economy and personal welfare do not lose out disproportionately from environmental regulation.

The problem with taxes is that it is not easy to control exactly what happens as a result. It is up to the individual or organisation to respond to the incentive, which is hard to tie to a preferred form of behaviour or to ensure the response is not just strategically designed to do the minimum to get the tax benefit (though this is not just a problem with taxes). Also individuals may be inattentive to the incentives of the tax system. Much work in economics shows the lack of knowledge individuals have of their marginal tax rates (Lewis, 1982). If individuals do not know what their tax rates are, this would effectively nullify the effects of this instrument. In fact, people are aware of some tax rates. Research shows that tax rules tend to have an effect. For example, the timing of marriages has been found to be based on changes in marginal tax rates, as a study comparing changes in tax policy in Canada and England and Wales shows (Gelardi, 1996). But individuals often respond as much to how the message is framed as the tax itself (McCaffery and Baron, 2004). The response depends on the presentation of taxes, in particular whether they are visible or not, which relates to the debate in Chapter 6 on information. For example, Chetty *et al.* (2009) carried out a field experiment in the United States on the impact of sales taxes on supermarket purchases. For a three-week period in early 2006 they put prices posted on the shelf excluding the sales tax of 7.375 per cent. At other times consumers were shown the taxes at the checkout. The result of showing the tax in the price tag reduced consumption by 8 per cent. To avoid the result being thought of as an impact of the study rather than the intervention, the authors examined changes in policies for sales (non-visible) and excise (visible) taxes in two states, which mirror the change in demand between 1970 and 2003.

The other problem is that it can be hard to show the impact of a policy when compared to a counterfactual of giving the money directly. This is because incentives exist when they give the individual a benefit from what they would otherwise have had – which is the tax expenditure concept. Consider tax incentives to charitable giving, for example. Here the state gives an incentive to give money by subsidising it, which arguably allocates more money to charities. But it depends on individuals giving more than they otherwise would have, and by implication the tax money is diverted from a likely expenditure the government could have made. So the benefit is not the money, but the effect of individual contributions on the behaviour of the voluntary sector in contrast to just getting a government grant. The end result is that the state spends money on tax rebates for society to get a more vibrant and dynamic voluntary sector than it would have got had it given the money to the charities directly. It is another kind of crowding out, but where the state uses taxation to avoid it.

The main example of the use of taxation to yield a policy outcome is the environment. The problem most societies face is that private consumption may damage the welfare of all, such as through pollution or more generally through producing too much carbon, a major cause of global warming. So taxation may reduce these externalities of private consumption and helps a country meet targets for combating climate change. In the United Kingdom, for example, there is a landfill tax, a climate change levy on business and industry, differential taxes on different kinds of petrol, and a congestion charge in London based on vehicles' use of a zone in the central city. Such taxes appear to have worked, such as reducing landfill, reducing congestion in central London and changing consumers' use of different kinds of petrol fuels by manipulating responses to prices (Fullerton *et al.*, 2008).

Commentators have criticised the top-down form of regulation as bureau-cratic and influenced inappropriately or captured by the group being regulated (see the review in Cropper and Oates, 1992). In contrast, taxation is thought to be efficient because it targets the polluter without a costly search strategy and is hard to evade. The taxation system may encourage innovation. Companies develop new products because they will increase their profits more than in the absence of a green tax. The revenue may then be used for further environmental schemes (or to reduce taxes elsewhere to ensure neutrality across the balance of taxation and spending overall).

But there is a considerable debate as to whether such taxes are the right instrument. As Chapter 2 argues, there are examples of where top-down regulation can work (Cole and Grossman, 1999). In part the effectiveness of taxes depends on knowing in advance the exact response of consumers to the incentive (Bovenberg and Mooij, 1994). Green taxes incur what is called deadweight costs, which is when the loss of consumer benefit and reduction in profitability for those industries are not offset by the benefits of expenditure from the tax. Economists argue green taxes need to be set at a low rate to avoid inefficiencies (Bovenberg and Goulder, 1996).

When not considering these costs and benefits, most studies show a positive effect of green taxes. For example, Hayashi *et al.* (2001) devise a model to estimate the effects of vehicle and fuel taxes on car ownership and use, looking at the impact on the replacement of cars and on the distance driven. This showed a significant change in Japan from 1980 to 1994. Andersen *et al.* (2001) review 40 studies of green taxes on pesticides in Denmark, Sweden, Norway, Iceland and Finland. Most of them show a reduction in CO_2, such as 15 per cent in Denmark from 1966–92 (2001: 19). Most official studies of environmental problems, such as the Stern Review (Stern, 2007), usually include taxes as an essential part of the armoury of policy-makers, and this is based on the amount of solid evidence that has built up over the years about their effects. The big problem is how much change in behaviour varying taxes can achieve, something that is partially dependent on the public acceptability of large tax changes. Also, for efficiency reasons, it is not possible to have green taxes too high, because of their distorting effect. In Europe, environmental taxes tend to be low, and have even reduced as a proportion of total taxes in recent years (Albrecht, 2006). In the Stern report, the tax proposals run alongside a wide-ranging set of changes needed to change the economy to make it friendlier to the climate. Nonetheless, the environmental examples show the power of this aspect of the financial tool of government.

The environment may be a special case, however. It affects activities where people are very price conscious, such as what fuel they buy for their car; and this incentivises business to produce more efficiently. It is also clear that behaviour change does have desirable consequences. As Fullerton *et al.* write, 'The considerations above imply that environmental taxes are likely to be particularly valuable where wide-ranging changes in behaviour are needed across a large number of production and consumption activities. The costs of direct regulation in these cases are large, and in some cases prohibitive. In addition, where the activities to be regulated are highly diverse, society may gain substantially from changing these damaging activities in the most cost-effective manner. In other areas, market instruments may work less well' (2008: 12).

Taxes directed at other kinds of behaviour may have less impact, such as between welfare and work, for example. In the United Kingdom, the government created the Working Families' Tax Credit, succeeded by the Child Tax and Working Tax Credit. This was designed to ensure families on welfare would have an incentive to work. This was paid retrospectively and was not to be reassessed for six months to reduce the compliance costs of the scheme. Critics thought the scheme was hard for the claimants to understand and it operated like a traditional welfare payment, with little impact on behaviour. Nonetheless, the scheme did increase the number of people in work (Brewer *et al.*, 2006). When combined with other policy changes, the supply of lone women in the labour force increased by 5.1 percentage points, though it reduced the participation of couples by a small amount. Research on the US tax credit, the Earned Income Tax Credit, shows it stimulates work even though individuals only have an approximate understanding of its provisions and do not understand the marginal impact. Taxation is a powerful instrument of behaviour change. But much depends on the way in which citizens receive the signals from the tax system (Congdon *et al.*, 2009). Going back to the Earned Income Tax Credit (EITC), Chetty and Saez (2009) carried out an experiment that shows better information affects the take-up of the scheme. The experiment was on 43,000 tax filers from a major company in Chicago. Half were randomly allocated to a treatment group. The treatment was a two-minute explanation about how the Earned Income Tax Credit works from a tax professional, which was aimed at changing the understanding of the marginal incentives. The researchers found a higher take-up of the advice at the poorer end of the income distribution. The advice led to increases of the credit by $67 and the treatment group was 2.9 percentage points more likely to report EITC amounts than the control group. Though the results were modest, the intervention was very cheap. The book discusses the information tool in Chapter 8, but it seems that taxes plus framing is a powerful combination of the instruments of government.

Spatially targeted expenditure

One way to examine the economic and other impacts of expenditures is to examine the way in which states target expenditure to particular localities as a way of overcoming particular socio-economic problems. These programmes have always been in existence, but they became more popular in the 1960s as a result of public awareness about deprived neighbourhoods and the way in which social and economic problems reinforce each other to create long-run problems for these places and for the people who live there. A typical way in which the funding for these places works is through allocating specific pockets of funds to address problems of these places. For example, in England

and Wales, the government in 1966 created the Urban Programme, which targeted funds to 56 deprived neighbourhoods. There are many such schemes, such as Empowerment Zones in the United States and United Kingdom. They may involve a variety of types of spending, such as direct support for businesses, infrastructure development, training programmes and special incentives to employ people. The theory is there needs to be an extra effort to get people out of poverty and to help neighbourhoods become self-sustaining economically, which can get them out of a negative equilibrium trap. The argument against this is that such expenditure is likely to be wasted, given the potency of current economic and social structures that cause some places to be prosperous and others not. So the gains are likely to be short-lived because the long-term factors that determine spatial inequality start to impact again once the intervention has been completed. This path dependence applies both to enterprises that may not wish to stay long in the area and to households who may find it hard to overcome their social problems. There is an even stronger argument that suggests these programmes may reinforce deprivation through creating dependency. Either they crowd out economic enterprises or they create extra welfare dependencies rather than encourage long-term growth and employment in these areas. Added to these criticisms is the comment made by critics (Imrie and Thomas, 1999) who suggest the emergence of spatially targeted schemes parallels a more general relaxation of spending effort through the welfare state so these programmes may be accompanied by a reduction of living standards and economic conditions right across the board, both in the targeted areas and outside them. This suggests it is hard to evaluate these programmes when they are linked with other public spending changes affecting the same areas.

As with other aspects of public spending, it is hard to evaluate just the impact of spending as opposed to the instruments of the bureaucracy and the means of implementing the programme. Nonetheless they do represent a spending effort, which is at the core of these policies, so they are a good test of the effectiveness of public spending as a tool of government. The other problem is there are a vast number of evaluation studies of this phenomenon, mainly tied to governments and quite short-term in their horizon. One example of this was a study of England's Single Regeneration Budget programme, which was a competitive funding scheme that allocated benefits in annual rounds to target areas 1994–2000. The study sought to claim these areas benefited from extra funds (Brennan *et al.*, 1999) by rewarding needy areas. However, the authors also show about 20 per cent of expenditure went to non-deprived local authority areas, a change in the distribution of funds. They assume rather than demonstrate the most needy wards actually are in the bid areas and ignore the possibility that money would have been spent outside deprived wards, even if they were included in the bid area. Later evaluation work concentrates on looking at changes within the programme's target areas, which again does not yield an inference (Rhodes *et al.*, 2005). The positive aspect of this review is it is very sensitive to the contexts of the intervention, and looks at changes over a long period of time in contrast to the short horizons of many studies. But comparing over time statistics with survey evidence of the rest of England does not show the impact of the programme.

Many studies are based on statistical analysis of impacts comparing the amount and existence of funding with the improvement over time. This needs to address the potential problem that areas get the extra public spending precisely because they may have the potential for improvement. The sponsors of a programme have an interest in its success; moreover, wealthier areas are usually better at lobbying for resources (John *et al.*, 2004). The results can bias the findings upwards because areas that find it hard to improve are not part of the analysis. In part this can be corrected by allowing for deprivation in the statistical models, but studies need to model the determinants of spending itself, say through a selection model. But few do this, presenting statistical analysis with no discussion of selection.

An example of this problem is a study by Galster *et al.* (2004). They evaluate Community Development Block Grant spending in 17 United States cities between 1994 and 1996. This programme was for neighbourhood interventions, distributing about $4 bn dollars annually. The study seeks to predict indicators of neighbourhood conditions: the home purchase mortgage approval rate, the median amount of the home purchase loans originated and the number of businesses in existence a few years later in 1994–99 (not very many years later, which does not allow for the programme to settle down and for the long-term effect to be observed). They selected all neighbourhoods from the city and then attached spending data to these units. They collected a range of controls to predict neighbourhood advancement in a statistical model. Their hypothesis, which they confirm, is that there needs to be a threshold above which expenditure starts to impact. This is a plausible idea: there is unlikely to be a policy impact at a low level of expenditure, but once it is concentrated, then it can start to raise standards, which may be self-sustaining. They examine the impact of spending (dividing it by the number of poor in the area and averaging the expenditures over three years) and allow for neighbourhood-level factors. There is a bit of data dredging going on with their analysis as they try out different specifications. In the end, they find expenditures above the average have an impact. Though their finding that including expenditures over a certain amount impacted on outcomes is plausible, it is not a pure test of the model as it does not test the spending hypothesis purely that there should be an average uptick in outcomes from expenditures. Perhaps they should have included total spending and below average spending in the statistical model? But this issue palls compared to the big problem. There is no account of why the neighbourhoods are selected to get the funds and whether they are in a good position to improve. The neighbourhood control variable only partly gets round this problem. A better solution would be to account for selection in the statistical model, but it would be hard to do this. The only way to test whether public expenditures work is to allocate randomly the neighbourhoods that get the money or at least allocate areas randomly in stages, in what is called a stepped wedge design, where all areas get the money in due course but it is possible to observe the impact of the programme for the time when some areas do not get the money. Observational studies find it very hard to get round the selection problem.

Oakley and Tsao (2007) seek to address the selection problem in their study of Empowerment Zones in Chicago. These are designated areas that get tax breaks so are tax expenditures. They also have regulatory freedoms, which make this study not a pure test of the expenditure model, but still a good test of a spatial targeting initiative. Rather than plug the data into a statistical model, they discuss the problems of evaluating the intervention. They identify the advantages of identifying a control group, ideally through a randomised design, though this is not often available in the urban regeneration field. What they do instead is to apply the fashionable matching design, where extra observations are matched to the treatment group. This gets round the selection issue in part as the control observations are created – there is a comparator group that is very similar to the ones that got the intervention. They carry this out in 92 matched census tracts in Chicago for the 1980, 1990 and 2000 time points. They compare the average effects, and carry out what is called spatial regression to capture the spillover effects of the programme. With all these procedures, they end up carrying out a much more robust test of the intervention. They show poverty reduced in the empowerment zones. There is also some evidence there are spillover effects. The problem is the statistical analysis and matching might not control for all the differences, which a randomisation design would avoid. But these authors have carried out the research carefully and are cautious about their findings.

One study directly tries to combat the selection problem. Bloom and Riccio (2005) report on an evaluation of Jobs-Plus, a programme that aimed to maintain and enhance employment of residents of public housing schemes in six United States cities from 2000 (preparations started in 1996). The programme was based on applying the ideas of William Julius Wilson (1996), who claims increasing employment will lead to dramatic increases in other policy outcomes, such as reductions in poverty, crime and substance abuse. There were three main elements to the programme, which showed the importance of the public finance instrument: support for job searching, a financial incentive in offsetting the rise in rents when holding a job, and then community support in terms of strengthening social networks (a softer tool the book discusses in later chapters). In terms of evaluating its effect, they acknowledge the superiority of random assignment for individuals in the programme but argue it is not possible to do this because all residents were eligible in the programme areas. Instead they matched up two or three participating developments in each city to the randomly assigned areas. Rather than just comparing the matched and non-matched groups, which would not be capable of statistical inference, they look at how both groups moved over time, what is called interrupted time series. This was done visually in this case, comparing employment rates. The study found no impact for the programme areas, partly because employment was growing over time in all places during the study period. It is hard to make a firm conclusion from the study, however, because the number of study units is small, which means difference could be due to chance rather than the absence of a programme effect.

Whereas non-experimental studies find weak or negative effects of these publicly funded training programmes, experimental work is more positive. Bloom *et al.* (1997; see Orr *et al.*, 1996) examined job-training programmes from the United States Job Training Partnership Act, which cost $1.6 bn and sought to benefit a million individuals. The study selected a sample in 16 areas. It randomly assigned the 20,000 people and then studied them over a two-year period, 1987–89. The researchers gathered data from surveys and administrative records, focusing on the earnings of those in the programme compared to those who were not. The study finds adult men, adult women and female youth benefited, but not male youth. As this was a randomised controlled trial, it is possible to be more confident about the results. There were no flaws in this study so there was not a differential selection into the experiment, at least none that it is possible to observe. The main problem is that the study areas selected into the experiment, so even though individuals were randomised, the results are not representative of what would have happened in the whole population had the intervention been rolled out more generally. This is a general problem of pilots, but randomised controlled trials suffer from it too.

Looking at specific outcomes in health is an experimental study of the New Deal for Communities regeneration, an important flagship policy of the Labour governments 1997–2010 (Cotterill *et al.*, 2008). Each New Deal for Communities area got a special package of resources to improve services. The researchers mapped six progamme areas in the West Midlands, England, and matched them to control areas. They then compared patient experiences, finding the rates are higher in the control areas, suggesting there was an impact of the programme on health outcomes in some areas. However, the numbers are small and often not statistically significant, so the differences may have been due to random fluctuation. The authors admit that five years is a short time period within which to observe changes in outcomes.

There are some studies of the effects of urban policy over the longer term. One was the research funded by the English Department of the Environment (1994) on how well the Urban Programme areas did over a long period. This tracked conditions in these areas over the 30-year period and found they had not improved very much over the period of the study, though it is hard to say whether they would have got worse in the absence of the programme. This is a theme of the literature – either mixed or negative results, but not the uplift as promised in policy programmes, but no counterfactual of what would have happened in the absence of the policy. However, a review of targeted urban initiatives highlights the long-term nature of the problems of the areas receiving funding, which are challenging to address (Smith, 1999). What is much harder to conclude is whether the urban initiatives have made it more difficult for these areas through reinforcing disadvantage. Another long-run study was carried out at the University of Sheffield (Dorling *et al.*, 2007), which showed relatively little change in the spatial distribution of poverty in Britain from 1968 until 2000, in spite of regeneration programmes. They do not have a direct measure of the impact of these programmes – they may have stopped things being as bad as they currently are. Ladd's (1994) review captures the conventional wisdom nicely. She looks at the evidence of enterprise zones in the United States, modelled on the United Kingdom ones also discussed above, but find the effects of tax incentives in localities is generally mixed. What happens is they help relocate firms from other localities nearby, so not leading to much benefit overall. On the other hand, there does appear to be some impact at the state level through multiplier effects.

The mixed findings of most studies appear in the many summaries of the literature, such as a systematic review of the impact of health targeting carried out by Thomson *et al.* (2006). This review selected 19 studies. Most found improvement, but not much different from national trends. One study found deterioration in health conditions and three showed a marked improvement. The modesty of what can be achieved is the key message. But even the studies included in the review had limitations. One problem is the quality of the data. This can be overcome in an experimental or quasi-experimental design, but there are few such studies.

Quantitative studies in less-developed countries

Many studies of the impact of spending are done on developed countries, which limits the ability to generalise. But a separate literature examines similar relationships in other parts of the world. One of the key studies is by Filmer and Pritchett (1999), who examine the impact of public spending on child mortality (under five years old) in 98 less-developed countries. Theirs is a simple test: they carry out statistical analysis of the impact of expenditures alongside socio-economic factors on outcomes. The control variables are income, female education (because of the effects of education on looking after young babies) and regional and religious variables, with the hypothesised variable being expenditure on public health as a share of GDP. They find the result is negative as expected, that is, spending reduced mortality. Overall, there is little effect and it is only statistically significant at the 10 per cent level. They test for endogeneity in a two-stage regression, but this generates the same results, with the main difference being a slightly larger coefficient. This study tends to confirm a wider literature that suggests the effect of health spending on outcomes is limited. The authors also argue there are limitations to the studies that show positive effects on health. They explain the low results from a series of implementation gaps that prevent the expenditure getting to the outcomes, such as whether health expenditures target child mortality as opposed to other services, the extent to which public health expenditures crowd out expenditure or activities that would have happened anyway and the efficiency of the public services in translating resources to policy outcomes.

Gupta *et al.* (2002) test for the impact of the effectiveness of spending on education and health care in less developed and transition economies. Their paper uses cross-sectional data for 50 countries to show increased expenditure on education and health care is associated with improvements in access and attainment in schools, and reduces the mortality rates for infants. The key twist to their result is to show a shift in spending may shift outcomes. As with the European studies, it is difficult to show a causal relationship, which the authors acknowledge. This is even though they sought to control for reverse causality through a two-stage regression model. A panel design would have helped in this context.

Such results of public spending may be contingent on other factors, however, in particular the institutional configuration. Rajkumar and Swaroop (2008) test the idea the quality of governance might mediate the relationship, partly because effective and fairer structures might give an incentive to implement the programmes. They use a sample of 228 observations over three years for both developed and less-developed countries. The outcome is health status – child mortality like in the earlier study. For the explanatory variables, they use measures of corruption and the quality of bureaucracy (for more detail on their findings for bureaucracy, see Chapter 4). These measures interact with public spending to show the joint effects. They control for the effects of time, distance from the equator and urbanisation. They find what they expect: spending when there is corruption significantly reduces outcomes, but the quality of the bureaucracy improves them. These things need to happen at the same time. They run a similar model of educational attainment, where it is harder to find a comparable variable over the countries, so this time they only have 101 observations over three years from 57 countries. They use the proportion of school-age children who enter and complete school. They apply similar control variables, but include numbers of school-age children and a variable to control for East Asian countries. The findings are very similar to health, with both interactions being negative and significant, but with public spending on its own being ineffective. Countries with low levels of governance get very little value for money out of their expenditure. Rajkumar and Swaroop test the robustness of their results with different specifications (for example, non-linear ones) and with measures of the quality of the bureaucrats. Like other studies, they seek to address the causal problem that public spending may increase if there is a more needy target population. Overall, these findings show the importance of governance arrangements to explain the effectiveness of public spending.

Sectoral studies

It is probably surprising to the reader to find so many studies that indicate a negative or weak impact of financial policies. But there is a wider literature that shows just this. For example, Finkelstein and McKnight (2008) find the first ten years of Medicare in the United States, a programme designed as a major pillar of social insurance, had no impact on health mortality. Though this went down overall in the United States, it was not an effect of the policy. They produce a graph that indicates a reduction in the mortality rate was not affected by the policy. The line goes downwards, with no interruption in 1965. Though the elderly got access to care, it seems they were getting it in any case before the reform. However, it did compensate for the out of pocket expenses of the elderly, but only in the upper end of the income range. These groups spent less on health, which made them better off. They test this with data from the United States from 1952–75. They cannot find any impact of the year 1965 when the policy was introduced. This does not rule out other medical benefits from Medicare, but it does illustrate a financial policy that would be expected to improve outcomes does not do so.

There is an experimental literature that shows increasing inputs into education does not improve education outcomes, like test scores. Glewwe *et al.* (2009) devised a randomised controlled trial to test the effect of allocating more textbooks to children in Kenya. It did not work, especially at low levels of academic achievement. The finding questions the results from the observational literature that shows these expenditure-led interventions work. They examined 25 schools that received the textbooks, randomly selected by the government from 100 schools. Except for one subject, they find no impact of having these textbooks. Different kinds of analysis yield the same results, though the high-achieving students got better scores. Glewwe *et al.* (2004) had already found that where textbooks are not available, flip charts assist learning. While retrospective analysis shows that the flip charts increase test scores by 20 per cent of a standard deviation, an experiment shows no impact. The researchers randomly selected 89 primary schools to receive the flip charts, compared to 89 others randomly allocated to the control group. They compared the averages for different subjects, which did not show much difference, and in different directions depending on subject, which is probably random variation. They then combined the individual and school level data and ran tests controlling for a range of factors. But the results again show no impact. What seems to have occurred is the charts are directed to high-performing students so they may perform better, as well as some selection into flip charts by potentially better performing schools. This is the classic selection problem that experiments can overcome, and which leads to different evaluations of the impact of the instrument according to the method chosen.

A case study: the United Kingdom 1997–2010

To finish this chapter, there is a case study to hand. This is the experiment the United Kingdom government undertook to increase the share of GDP taken up by public expenditure and to invest much of the increase in improved public services over a sustained period of ten years from 1997–2007. This is not an experiment in the true sense as it is not possible to show the connection between spending and outcomes as other things may have affected the latter. It is not possible to know beforehand what would have happened without the policy change, whether health outcomes would have improved anyway. But a dramatic change of policy after the election of a new government may be seen as an exogenous shock, taking a set of political decisions to change the proportion of GDP taken up by the public sector. Trends in the data over time should show the impact of the change in priorities. It has also become time-bounded at the end of the experiment because of the necessary reduction of public expenditure in 2010–11, reinforced by the policies of the Liberal–Conservative coalition elected in 2010.

It is worth setting out the magnitudes of the changes. There was an increase in public sector net investment from less than 0.75 per cent of GDP in 1997–98 to 2.25 per cent of GDP in 2005–06. The Labour governments increased the share of public spending as a proportion from 38.8 per cent in 1997–98 to 41.5 in 2006–07 (HM Treasury, 2008: 25). Total managed expenditure increased from £308 bn in 1997–98 to £523 bn in 2006–07 and in real terms in 2006–07 prices from £383 bn. Spending on health went up from £44.5 bn to £94.5 bn, a near doubling in money terms (26–27). In real terms, in 2006–07 prices, this was from £55.4 bn, a staggering increase. In education and training it went from £48 bn to £72.8 bn in 2006–07 prices.

With such large increases it would be expected there should be a good deal of improvement in the quality of services and service outcomes. Again much depends on interpretation about the extent to which this can be achieved over a short time period. If the bar is complete social transformation, then any result is bound to fall short of this ambition. If the indicator is any improvement, then such an expenditure increase would be bound to be successful because some improvement would have been observed. Much depends on whether the government gained sufficient outcomes for the amount of resources it put in, taking into account what else it could have done with the money and the benefits taxpayers could have got from spending it. In thinking in this way, the argument becomes a good test of the treasure theme even if one of the conclusions is about the importance of other levers. The difficulty is the changes have been quite recent so there is not a large academic literature to draw on.

One area that is indisputable is the high level of investment into certain aspects of health care, which have brought down hospital waiting times and allowed hospitals to meet core targets. The kinds of investment are increases in the numbers of front line staff, with the numbers of doctors rising by 22 per cent and nurses by 21 per cent. As a result, between 1998 and 2005, overall elective (planned) admissions to hospital rose by just over 605,000 – an increase of 11 per cent (Wanless *et al.*, 2007: 7). There has been a 20 per cent increase in the number of day cases. Attendances at Accident and Emergency have gone up by a third. The use of prescriptions increased by a fifth.

But with such a large increase in funds it would be unsurprising if this did not produce an effective outcome. The question to ask is whether the public have got enough outcomes for the money given the large amount that has been swallowed up in pay rises, reorganisation costs, a failed information technology experiment and extra administration costs. A further question to ask is whether the government was too impatient and moved from bust to boom too quickly and did not allow enough time for outcomes to feed through. Yet another question is whether the improved services actually improved other outcomes, such as heath inequality. But this did not alter in this period (Department of Health, 2008). Other outcomes are improving, such as mortality, which has caught up with France (Compendium of Health, 2003) – though there is a long-term trend going back to the 1960s. In 1997 the male mortality in England and Wales was higher than France at 878 deaths per 100,000. But male mortality in England and Wales reduced in the 1990s at a rate of 14 per cent, compared with 11 per cent in France. The Wanless *et al.* (2007) report summarises these changes, looking at the rise in input costs, the outputs and also the outcomes, such as the improvement in cancer recovery. This is not enough to counter the trends for poor health from obesity and other lifestyles changes that are threatening health. The report notes the failure to improve productivity during this period. There is a similar story from the report by the King's Fund (Thorlby and Maybin, 2010), which evaluated the changes over the whole period from 1997–2010 applying internationally recognised criteria for a high-performing health care system. It found patient waiting times were down and there was better safety for patients. It found there was a failure to deal with alcohol-related problems. This is a wider policy objective perhaps outside the purview of the National Health Service, which is concerned with treating, but arguably within it as the Department of Health has a major concern with health prevention and in joining up policy on health with other government interventions, such as with the more successful anti-smoking policy. Deaths from cancer and heart disease have fallen substantially since 1997 and suicides have also reduced. There has been rising satisfaction with the National Health Service. As with other studies, the King's Fund report notes declines in labour productivity. It also notes variations in performance as well as the lack of progress with preventable diseases and concerns about efficiency noted above.

If the story of extra spending in health is a good one, even with the lack of productivity, it is much harder to evaluate the gains in education, partly because the gains are long term and are harder to measure. Examination results may be artifacts of the measurement system, which may have got more lax over the years, making it hard to assess the rate of improvement. There is some indication that the basic level of skills, such as in mathematics, has not altered (Glennerster, 2002: 126). But given the doubling of spending per pupil, there are some positive statistics about the rate of progress of schools in poor areas, which have increased their performance more than the others (Glennerster, 2002: 127), though it is here there is the most potential to improve. An evaluation by McNally claims that there is evidence the 'increase in school expenditure between 2002 and 2007 led to a modest increase in educational attainment' (2010: 23). Rather than relying on examination results, where there has been grade inflation making it hard to know the actual change in performance over the period, the author uses the Progress in International Reading Literacy for 2001 and 2006 for pupils of about 10 years old; the Programme for the International Student Assessment for 2000, 2003 and 2006 for 15-year olds; and Trends in International Mathematics and Science Study, conducted in 1999, for 2003 and 2007 for pupils of about age 10 and 14. However, in spite of the rises being consistent with spending increases, 'Taken together the evidence suggests that any improvement in primary school achievement since 2000 has been modest, at best'. The authors claim it is cost effective because it brought Britain up to OECD average. But it is very hard to work out the opportunity costs of the expenditure: what else could the government have spent the money on and with what benefit?

In terms of overall objectives linking spending in health, education and poverty, one key finding is that some of the key indicators the government cares about have been very hard to shift. The Institute for Fiscal Studies report (Brewer *et al.*, 2008) shows how income inequality was at its highest since records began in 1960, which is backed up by Hills *et al.* (2010). The Institute for Fiscal Studies report points to some increases in poverty after 2005. However, this follows some reductions of poverty for much of the period up until 2005. This is not direct evidence whether the policies worked or not however, given the expansion of the economy during this period, which may have uplifted poverty whatever the government did. A claim that anti-poverty policies worked would warrant careful empirical consideration. But given the comparative evidence does support the idea that poverty-reduction policy does work, this may be one area where the public spending increases delivered value for money. For there are a number of respectable academic studies that deliver a favourable verdict on the government's policies (Hills and Stewart, 2005). The overall verdict is not surprising and is not particularly damning. The upswing in expenditure has delivered improvement in outputs and some outcomes; but the increase at the moment may not have been good value for money, partly because of the speed of implementation. Long-term outcomes such as levels of health, educational and other kinds of inequality remain at previous levels and in some cases are worse, except for the incomes of the poor. The Hills *et al.* report shows the incomes of these to be reducing in 2007–08 (2010: 38). Child poverty also increased at the end of Labour's period in power (2010: 46). The record of the 1997–2010 Labour governments shows both the possibilities and limits of extra funding. They may have been a luxury of when government finances were available in a period of economic growth and transition from a previous period of low levels of public spending. In a period from 2010 when public finances are much more constrained, any government is likely to look more critically as to whether government policies deliver enough given other commitments to spending and other outcomes that need protecting. The downturn in the economic indicators may also cause outcomes to worsen.

Conclusions

Only a cynic or sceptic would think altering public spending and taxation would not turn into outcomes of the desired kind; only an unrealistic optimist would believe the finance tool is a panacea to correct many social and economic ills. So the experience has been mixed. There is evidence of impacts in some areas, with very good results for poverty, much less on spatial economic programmes, and high impacts for taxation. But it is very hard to shift educational or health outcomes from spending-led policies alone. In part, spending money does not necessarily address the causes of long-term problems, even though it may alleviate them.

There may be obstacles to financial tools having the desired results. There may be poor implementation. Resources may be siphoned off to fulfil private objectives, either through corruption or through the influence of producer groups in the bureaucracy. Poor bureaucracies and the state of public management organisations may get in the way of effective delivery of new programmes so the clients of a programme do not get all the benefits. These factors may explain the varied impact of public spending. It may also matter what the money is spent on and what theory of human action it is based on. Financial incentives need to be consistent with the overall causal theory the policy-makers operate with. In the money sense, the account is in the realm of addressing incentives or providing additional inputs so actions can be achieved.

The other factor is that there may be costs associated with financial provision in terms of crowding out private or associational activity and creating unnecessary dependencies, though the dangers of this problem have probably been exaggerated. Moreover, the impact of finance may depend on the point in time. The impact of public finance as an available tool of government may depend on a particular phase of prosperity. Once the good times have gone and the public-sector funding becomes tighter, the positive kick back to effective outcomes may no longer be so available. Then it becomes more important to isolate the kinds of leverage it is possible to get from other aspects of political capacity. If the benefits of public finance are not universal and public finances are tight, what potential is there from more cost-effective instruments of government?

4 Bureaucracy and public management

Bureaucracy is the public organisation that implements decisions made by politicians and otherwise acts on behalf of the citizens living in a jurisdiction. It has been a feature of most societies, even in pre-modern times. As shown in Chapter 2, it is not enough for political systems to pass legislation, for laws need to be implementated effectively, which requires well-run bureaucracies. Even the levying of taxes requires organisations to collect the income and to chase up the non-compliers. Over time, bureaucracies have expanded in size and have extended their reach as states have become more powerful. As a result, the bureaucracies have come into contact with greater numbers of people who are influenced by what they do. Moreover, as politicians have sought to regulate more aspects of the economy and society, they have come to rely much more on bureaucracies to realise these ambitions.

Politicians often think they can improve the delivery of their policies by reforming the bureaucracy and introducing new systems of public management. They have good reason to direct their attention to these tasks. Surely bureaucrats and the organisations they inhabit are there to ensure decisions taken by politicians are followed? An efficient and responsive administration should ensure better implementation of political decisions. Getting the delivery chain in working order would seem to be an essential prerequisite for an effective policy. A well-run bureaucracy may have positive side effects given the extensive interaction between the state and the citizens. A high-quality bureaucracy could foster virtuous circles of rising trust in government and better cooperation between citizens and the state, which could then feed into improved policy outcomes.

The secret to the effective use of the bureaucracy tool is the management of organisational capacity, which is how bureaucracies are structured and co-ordinated so as to work effectively. Bureaucracies can, if properly organised, drive public action through the coordination of procedures and commands to a pre-identified end. This result does not always happen, which means governments lose out on one of the key levers of public action, often in ways that limit the application of the other tools of government.

In contrast with law/regulation and finance/taxation, bureaucracy is one step removed from the policy outcome. It relies on a chain of command within the state or public organisation and then the belief those commands influence the world outside the bureaucracy rather than the citizens and organisations obeying a law or being incentivised by a change in income. If there are many steps between the decisions of politicians in office and what happens on the ground, then achieving a desired change will be more difficult than more direct means of reaching citizens and organisations (though in practice all the tools rely on many steps being in place).

In spite of the potential abstraction of this method, policy-makers feel they have some control over it. It is within the domain of the state, which is what they are elected to steer. In general, politicians in office have extensive discretion about how the bureaucracy works and can carry out reform programmes and reorganisations without feeling they are treading on the toes of the organisations of civil society or intruding into the domains of private individuals, though this autonomy varies according to the country in question. Politicians often seek to change the terms and conditions of public employees, the structure of departments, the extent of hierarchy, the remuneration system, the extent of contracting out to the private sector and the external regulation of the bureaucracy, which may affect the extent to which it responds to commands, and the degree of innovation and creativity bureaucrats apply to their tasks. With this array of mechanisms and choices, it is hard to know what the exact levers within that work best even if the bureaucracy is energised and is given much greater capacity. Is it efficiency in the use of resources or the application of expert knowledge or the influence of the personal values and motivations of bureaucrats? Or is it the energy of entrepreneurial administrators or the bureaucracy acting in ways that connect well with citizens? In particular, does following hierarchy lead to better performance or is it about allowing the bureaucracy to innovate and to compete? As with many ideas for achieving better policy outcomes, once the causal connections come under more scrutiny, it is hard to know what it is about the bureaucracy that improves policy performance.

The key problem with the use and reform of the bureaucracy is that bureaucrats are largely in control. Politicians, in spite of their ownership of the bureaucracy, need to hand over many decisions to a group that has its own interests and values. Bureaucrats tend to prefer standard ways of doing business as an automatic reflex action. Bureaucratic organisations are very difficult to direct and steer because their cultures are strong. Bureaucrats tend to resist change. Moreover, they can limit the extent to which politicians are able to use and reform the bureaucracy by their control of information about how it works. This is a version of the principal-agent problem: the principal (the politician) in command cannot fully exercise their power over the agent (bureaucrat) because of the information asymmetry between the two (see Moe, 1984).

Partly because politicians fear lack of control and want more out of public services, public bureaucracies are often subject to continual reform. In recent years, these measures have been grouped under the term the new public management. This doctrine – and the associated set of practices – seeks to promote more efficiency and a leaner, fitter bureaucracy. It aims to reduce hierarchy, disaggregate bureaucracies and promote more competition in the public sector by contracting out services to the private companies, allowing units within the bureaucracy to compete with each other and giving more choice to the citizen-consumer. The new public management aims to create incentives based on appeals to private interest, such as with performance measurement and performance-related pay. These may operate either in competition or alongside the more traditional forms of control through the hierarchy and appeals to the public service motivation of the bureaucrats.

Public management reform is fraught with problems and it may not achieve its objectives. Failure can occur because the changes need to be implemented and accepted by bureaucrats themselves, which runs the risk the problems the reforms are designed to remedy will be perpetuated because the very people who are the cause of the problem are charged with finding the solution. Bureaucrats do not see the problem of policy implementation from the perspective of the outsider or the commissioner of policy, but from the viewpoint of the technocrat interested in how the machinery works and how it affects their conditions of work (Gains and John, 2010). The result is a self-reinforcing cycle of attempts at reform that result in failure or only partial success. Strong organisational cultures shape how reform is implemented and there is a tendency for the bureaucracies to retain past practices and ways of doing things. Assessing whether the ambitions of the reformers have been realised is a later task of this chapter, in a section on the new public management. But first the chapter discusses how classic or unreformed bureaucracies are supposed to get the job done.

The classic theory of bureaucracy

Bureaucracy is about the translation of means to ends, and the most effective and efficient way of getting there. In the public realm, it is necessary to have an organisation that turns collective decision-making by politicians and other decision-makers into reality in the form of implemented policies. The state cannot act like a committee overseeing contracts, for it needs people in place who have a stock of knowledge and capacity to do things, and are ready to act and work with the politicians. These people usually need to be located in a permanent organisation whose purpose is to follow commands from the elected politicians in office and otherwise implement the body of laws and rules on the statute book or implied by court decisions. Even the act of overseeing contracts in a market-led form of public administration may involve some specialisation, a division of labour between personnel, say in a department of contract compliance. It is very hard to imagine public life on a large scale without some kind of professional and dedicated organisation charged with carrying out political decisions and making sure private life is regulated and public needs are addressed.

At the beginning of the twentieth century Weber set out his influential thinking about bureaucracy, which offered an ideal-type, whose features may be compared with the practice of bureaucratic organisations (see Beetham, 1974 for a summary). It is important not to focus just on the various aspects of its organisation form, such as open competition for entry and the hierarchy. For these organisational characteristics are designed to apply rationality to solve public problems. The rationale and structure of the bureaucracy – its very existence – are solely directed to achieving goals imposed by legitimate external decision-makers. The bureaucracy, with its hierarchical command structure, becomes the way in which the political principals are able to achieve their ends. Bureaucracy is the means whereby society seeks to achieve its objectives through control, organisation and central direction.

It is worthwhile thinking whether this means–end rationale is the right way to understand the way policy-makers influence policy outcomes. As part of his cultural approach, Hood (1998) sets out the advantages of a Weberian or a hierarchical way of doing public management. For the hierarchicalists, bureaucracies can be effective means for dealing with control, for ensuring the employees do not contaminate the purposes of the organisation with their private interests and for preventing disasters created by employees who are out of the control of the line managers. Bureaucracies help to focus on the task at hand. For the critics, hierarchy can squeeze out the creativity within organisations. It can impede a flexible response to changing problems, whereby bureaucrats carry out commands in an unthinking way. Bureaucracy limits innovation because of focus on command and control. The resulting poor performance of an organisation means it is unable to deal with the commands in a sensible and practical manner. In some accounts, the bureaucratic organisation has low discretion and limits the ability to respond, which may be contrasted with the intelligence of high-discretion organisations. It is also possible to identify hierarchy as a cause of failure because of excessive rule following and lack of initiative. Hood gives the example of the Chernobyl experiment (1998: 36–38), the series of errors that led to an explosion at a nuclear power plant in the former Soviet Union in 1986, which was partly caused by excessive faith in the rules (though also the result of experimentation). Those in charge of the nuclear plant could not believe the rules had broken down, so they fell back on established procedures, which made the crisis worse.

The critique of hierarchy can go much deeper. In the public choice account, hierarchy allows the bureaucracy to be a monopoly provider to a population that does not have the choice over the supply of public goods. Whereas decision-makers in markets need to respond to signals from consumers, bureaucrats in hierarchies are positioned to follow their own interests, which limits the attainment of social objectives or outcomes societies could achieve if the state or public authority had less power. It focuses on the way in which the monopoly of information within the bureaucracy, the very thing that is supposed to help society achieve its objectives, may also lead to perverse outcomes. That insight Weber understood – what the public choice theorists do is to extend it to its logical extreme, where bureaucracy becomes a predator. As the state gets larger, its organisation becomes harder to coordinate and may be incapacitated by internal battles and the dominance of multiple interests. The bureaucracy becomes harder to control. The critique and reform of public administration belong to the next section, but before the chapter discusses the idea that outcomes may be improved by reform, it is worth dwelling on the long-term benefits of hierarchy as seen from within economic analysis.

The economic analysis of bureaucracy does not always predict inefficiency. In the literature on the economics of organisation (Williamson, 1975) bureaucracy reduces transactions costs because these are internalised within the organisation. The state does not have to enter into costly relationships with contractors and to monitor them. It can control affairs internally. This reflects the high costs of coordination outside an organisation and differences in organisational interest. It is balanced because those transaction costs occur within the bureaucracy as well. An internal department within the bureaucracy may have a strong sense of its own interests and seek not to reveal information to its principal, such as the leading politician and chief executive. But the implication of transactions costs analysis is that there is no necessary disadvantage of bureaucracy. A lot depends on how the incentives are set out and then compared between contracted in and contracted out scenarios.

A shorthand way of summarising these accounts of bureaucracy is to say the theory points both ways: an effective bureaucratic organisation is obviously a necessary condition of a successful policy. In the Weberian account it can give life to a rationalist conception of public policy, where the necessary procedures and systems can be put in place to ensure an effective and timely intervention. In transaction cost economics terms, the bureaucracy can help reduce the transactions of government by internalising them. But the very advantages of bureaucracy create problems, such as deadlock, inefficiency and irrationality, including high transactions costs. The tendency to inefficiency and the assertion of bureaucratic self-interest can limit the potential of this powerful tool of government.

Tests of bureaucratic effectiveness

Some tests of bureaucratic effectiveness would seem to bear out some of the critique of inefficiency. Several studies of education in the United States find bureaucracy worsens the performance of schools. For example, Bohte (2001) uses Chubb and Moe's (1990) argument that the bureaucracy tends to be top heavy, doing unproductive activities with a large number of personnel, who are detached from the day-to-day problems of students, which would be better addressed by the front-line staff, the teachers. He places this argument against the alternative view that bureaucracy can assist performance by providing support to teachers so they can focus on the core task of teaching (Smith and Meier, 1994). He uses data on 2,097 students from 350 Texas school districts, compiled from responses to a questionnaire filled out by school superintendents. Pooling the data between 1991 to 1996, he shows school bureaucracy is negatively associated with examination/grade performance, supporting the idea that resources directed to front-line staff, the teachers, could improve student performance. The measure of bureaucracy is the percentage of central administrators and campus administrators. This was used to explain student test scores along with the control variables of spending per pupil, low incomes and black students. There is a problem with this approach, as Bohte acknowledges. It is hard to separate out the impact of poor performance on bureaucracy, which is the argument of Meier *et al.* (2000). It may be the case that bureaucracy is put in place to deal with poor performance rather than bureaucracy causing poor performance. Boyte also does not analyse a panel dataset, which could help make inferences. Time, in the form of variables for each year of data, is only used as a control in the statistical model.

Wilensky (2002) tests for the effectiveness of bureaucracy using cross-national data. He argues that large bureaucracies may have either efficiencies through economies of scale or create problems through bureaucratic bloat. He creates a measure of public-sector employment adjusted for per head expenditure. He finds the United Kingdom, Australia, New Zealand, Ireland and Israel are high on bloat, whereas the Scandinavian countries, France and Belgium are efficient. Using regression analysis, controlling for corporatism, capital investment, strikes, Catholicism, leftism and social spending, bureaucratic bloat has a moderate downward effect on economic growth in the period 1951–74 (2002: 475). This is a useful finding, but it is important to distinguish arguments about the size of the bureaucracy from those about its organisation, which is key to understanding it as a tool of government. How the bureaucracy works internally is not considered in Lane's study.

Bureaucracy can promote positive outcomes by assisting social coordination and providing institutional incentives for pro-social behaviour. One direct effect is on corruption. Weberian organisational principles and the values that accompany them are ways to limit the pursuit of private interest among powerful regulators and their client groups, which can limit rent seeking (Rauch, 1995). A complementary mechanism is the way Weberian practices have an effect outside the bureaucracy by requiring those dealing with the state to be honest, and by implication straightforward with each other. There may be an effect of a hierarchy on values whereby the principles of accountability and transparency infuse societal and economic relationships more generally. Just as trust generates trust, a well-run, uncorrupt and formally organised bureaucracy might stimulate private organisations to behave in the same way. A final argument is that Weberian structures may promote infrastructure growth through the preference for pet projects. A hierarchically organised state may be able to promote economic development through planning and shaping the direction of economic activity (see Hood, 1998: 82–95). This idea influenced the ideas of English socialists in the late nineteenth century, who believed the rational organisation of the state and planning its activities could gradually transform society for the public good. There were similar ideas expressed by the Progressive movement in the United States, which aimed to wipe away the negative effects of corruption and introduce a fairer model of public administration.

A literature has grown up to test this hypothesis stimulated by Evans' (1992) work on the economic benefits of the developmental state. Rauch (1995) looks at the impact of the Progressive reforms in the United States, which sought to separate politics and administration as implied by the classic Weberian model, at least in its most straightforward formulation. He treats the existence of two kinds of administrative system as a natural experiment as some cities were reformed and others were not. He selected 144 cities with populations over 30,000 people and where data are available. He measured change in a panel dataset over 23 years from 1904, coding when the city became reformed and when it got an independent civil service. He is able to control for the effects of local taxation, showing the Progressive reforms in the form of an independent commission running the civil service, controlling for whether it is a city manager form of government, stimulates expenditure on public works and hence growth of employment in manufacturing in cities. Rauch believes his model is fully specified, but it may have been the case that the places that chose the reforms were more predisposed to spend money on infrastructure. In addition, spending is an output, not economic growth itself, though he estimates the effect of infrastructure expenditure in another paper (Rauch, 1994). His work relates to studies in urban politics that suggest the city manager form of local government produces different expenditure patterns and more efficient forms of administration (Kotter and Lawrence, 1974, see the discussion of mayoral institutional reforms in Chapter 5). His finding is consistent with the more recent literature that shows no difference in spending between the two systems of government (see Welch and Bledsoe, 1988 for a review), which supports his negative findings for the council manager as opposed to the positive findings for bureaucracy itself.

Evans and Rauch (1999) test this hypothesis cross-nationally. They non-randomly sample 35 countries to test whether those with more Weberian structures experience higher economic growth. The main problem is they have to gather data on the Weberian variable for they believe there is no reliable information about bureaucratisation. Instead Evans and Rauch survey 126 experts who score each country on the features of its bureaucracy, taking care to find out whether these structures antedated the period of growth being analysed, 1970–90. They claim this is a valid and reliable scale (though they do not seek to validate the survey responses or to do any scaling of them). Existing work (for example, Hall, 1963) indicates a Weberian scale is hard to locate in the features of organisations. So if the Weberian elements of the organisation do not co-vary with each other, how can the experts know how Weberian each country is? Nevertheless, Evans and Rauch find their

Weberian variable predicts the level of growth both bi-variately and in a regression model. The latter is particularly important because bureaucracy may be seen as the result of economic growth, or at least capturing countries that happen to be on high-growth trajectories, which may result from their high levels of human capital, which is then reflected in the bureaucracy. The authors control for the key factors that appear in economic growth equations: GDP per capita in 1965 and years of school age. They also introduce a series of regional dummy variables, such as the Tiger countries. The effect remains robust to all these specifications. Further regressions looking at change over time, and allowing for the number of revolutions, government expenditure and domestic investment do not eliminate this effect. So Evans and Rauch carry out an impressive study, but it hinges on the validity of the expert survey and no simultaneous cause of both bureaucratic structures and economic growth.

Overall, there is a group of studies that show the advantages of traditional bureaucratic organisation. The characterisation of bureaucracy as inherently inefficient may be something of a stereotype or a misrepresentation. However, the studies are not entirely convincing because they do not control for the factors that cause some places to have more Weberian bureaucracies, and there are some problems with their measures.

Better governance

A well-organised and hierarchical bureaucracy may be seen as part of high-quality governance, which may have positive outcomes for less-developed countries seeking to meet basic needs. The World Bank has collected a wide range of indicators for between 155 and 173 countries, depending on the measure (see Kaufmann *et al.*, 1999, which is regularly updated, for example, Kaufmann *et al.*, 2009). These measures are correlated with each other and then used to explain per capita income, infant mortality and adult literacy. The governance measures are clustered into groups, such as government effectiveness (which includes bureaucracy) and also corruption – as well as others, such as the regulatory burden. Along with other measures of govern-ance, government effectiveness is a significant predictor in its own right, which would indicate that bureaucratic quality is a positive driver of policy outcomes. However, there is an extensive debate as to whether these measures are correct (Kurtz and Schrank, 2007, and replies to that attack, Kaufman *et al.*, 2007). The main problem is the quality of the data, in particular relying on a survey of experts, which is not a direct measure of the phenomenon and, as the originators freely admit, is 'inherently subjective' (Kaufmann *et al.*, 1999: 2). In addition, there are problems in specifying a causal model. Indeed, Kaufman *et al.* acknowledge there may be feedback effects: countries with good economies get better ratings. But they carry out a wider range of speci-fications to try to get round these problems. Because governance is a function of economic growth, they specify a separate statistical model to test for this.

Possibly, there are better ways of using this cross-national data. As Chapter 3 shows, Rajkumar and Swaroop (2008) find better governance leads to an improved link between spending and public-policy outcomes. The key factor here is the quality of bureaucracy as an interaction term. This is negative, as predicted – lower quality administration leads to a lower impact of extra spending – though the interaction does not add much to the explanation in statistical terms. The result for the quality of bureaucracy on its own is not significant. They perform the same analysis for the education measure, the percentage of pupils that enter or complete full-time education. The advantage of these authors' specifications is they allow the reader to understand the causal mechanism, which in this case is about how bureaucratic efficiency allows governments to allocate resources more effectively and efficiently.

The implication of these studies is that reforms to introduce a more conventional bureaucratic form might have positive outcomes, especially for the economy. This is something to bear in mind when considering the reforms of the bureaucracy that have been carried out in the name of the new public management since the early 1980s. Most western policy-making systems, and many others, have often sought alternatives to traditional forms of administrative efficiency.

The new public management

In the 1970s and 1980s many commentators and politicians became disappointed at the quality of many policies states had produced in the preceding decades – even with large amounts of resources devoted to welfare and other services. In the context of poor economic conditions and new social problems, it was easy to criticise the group that had often been accused of stultifying policy performance: the permanent bureaucracy. Even a relatively establishment-orientated book, *Whitehall*, by Hennessy (1989), pointed the finger at the civil service as one of the institutions responsible for poor economic performance during the twentieth century, blaming it for lack of imagination and for holding back progressive change.

Advocates of the new public management claimed it would transform bureaucracy to deal with the problem of deadweight and inefficiency, offering more effective delivery of policy and better outcomes for the wider society (Osborne and Gaebler, 1992). Central is the use of market or market-like mechanisms in the public sector to encourage and incentivise bureaucracies to become more efficient and to improve their performance. These mechanisms include the contracting out of services to the private sector or to management buy-outs, the complete privatisation of services, procedures to allow consumers to exercise choice between different packages of services, decentralisation within bureaucracies to create more autonomy and flexibility and the introduction of quasi-markets, with shadow pricing, where disaggregated service units complete with each other to provide services. Competition and efficiency would be assisted by the publication of clear performance measures, backed up by sanctions and rewards. Moreover, by breaking down bureaucratic monopolies, officials would become more responsive, both to their political principals and to their client groups.

In addition, reformers wanted to take advantage of best practice in the private sector. Of particular influence was the argument for focusing on core competences. Such a reorientation may involve the break-up of an organisation by contracting out or transferring aspects of its structure that do not meet the central purpose, which leaves a central core of activity where there is genuine expertise (Dunleavy, 1994). The key idea is to find out what the organisation should focus on, which is what it is best at and where it has comparative advantage. The quest is to ensure the public-sector organisation emulates its private sector counterparts and creates, in Quinn's (1992) words, an intelligent enterprise. The doctrine makes great play of the benefits of leadership within bureaucracies and advocates giving power and autonomy to the entrepreneur/manager. It also means ending red tape, limiting hierarchy and creating mission statements. The bureaucracy would become more focused on results, interested in outcomes rather than process, and in putting its consumers first.

Policies based on the new public management were widely adopted by politicians in the United States, New Zealand and the United Kingdom. The new doctrine became a synonym for competitive government. It then spread round the world to be adopted in different forms in Europe and promoted by international organisations in the less-developed world. The reforms were designed to improve the capacity of governments to address policy problems. It became a means by which other interventions could be delivered, such as urban development and the finance of large public projects, for example though introducing competition for public funds in urban redevelopment and ensuring the direct role of the private sector in running capital projects.

One example is the creation of central government agencies in the United Kingdom from 1988 (see James, 2001). These detached certain aspects of government functions into discrete organisations, such as the Benefits Agency, charged with administering a range of income support schemes. Agencies show the different elements of new public management at work. The agencies had stronger leaders in the form of chief executives, some from the private sector, to take a more entrepreneurial role. Agencies show the disaggregation of the state and they are – to a certain extent – freed from operational control by central government, though government can always step in. Agencies are results-orientated as outputs, performance measurement and performance-related pay give incentives.

A second example was the Comprehensive Performance Assessment, which became Comprehensive Area Assessment, for English local authorities, which set up an annual assessment scheme for each local authority, which allowed citizens to make judgements about how well their local council was doing (see Boyne *et al.*, 2010). This also had strict lines of central control over bureaucracies in the form of officially measured performance information, but allowed the better-performing local authorities autonomy to manage their services and achieve better performance in a way they thought fit.

Both these examples show new public management incorporates the centralisation and regulation of some activities, such as performance measurement, but the decentralisation of others, such as the day-to-day running of the organisation. It is this mix between centralisation and devolution that helps create the improvement in performance as organisations have clearer objectives, but freedom to implement and to manage them. As a result, outcomes on the ground should improve because of the focus on targets that relate to service improvement, which are delivered by more effective organisations. Organisations should become more innovative as the entrepreneurial spirit takes hold.

Some care, however, is needed to ensure the new public management is not defined in a purely rhetorical way, making it vulnerable to what Hood (1991) calls a public management for all seasons so that everything – and therefore nothing – becomes the new public management. Hood (1995, 1998) questions the internal coherence of the programme for reform. He argues that there is no global convergence to one model of administration: management practice remains locally distinct; and some systems have not changed. Institutions and contexts count for more than global theory. The claim is the new public management is an incoherent amalgam of arguments that do not hold together; and culturally different variants of new public management can be identified. Some countries with large public sectors engage in cost cutting, but many new public management reforms are unstable and become unpicked, especially when negative consequences become more evident. This criticism is not entirely valid, however, as it is not inconsistent to argue a reform movement takes different forms according to the institutions and administrative traditions of the country in question, but still retains certain core features such as competitive government, performance management and incentivisation. The existence of book surveys examining the origins and diffusion of new public management is testament to its influence (Barzelay, 2001; Pollitt and Bouckaert, 2004).

Many of the criticisms of new public management fail to understand the grip that rethinking the conventional organisation form has had on reformers and politicians from the 1980s to the 2000s. It remains a powerful set of reforms, based on proposals designed to improve efficiency and to set out incentives for bureaucrats to improve their performance. It has an underlying theory of economic incentives that can be applied effectively to public organisations. It is different to other ways of using bureaucracy that depend more on internal organisation and hierarchy. The question to answer is whether it works by delivering more effective bureaucracies, better policies and improved societal outcomes. For the defenders of new public management, it means releasing the energy of reinvigorated bureaucracies. This is the path of constructive reform: learning from successful experiments in other contexts, allowing a greater focus on outcomes and on the needs and demands of clients, which is a line of argument in some of the academic commentary (for example, Aucoin, 1995; Kelman, 2005). For the critics, the new public management means rushed reforms that lose the acquired wisdom of bureaucracies, disrupting stable and effective systems of management and putting in place something untried and untested. It gives too much power to overambitious managers. Performance management and incentivisation create perverse incentives – and hence outcomes – across the public sector. New public management removes the mechanisms that ensure probity and the following of procedures, which at best leads to incoherence but at worst can encourage corruption.

In the light of the different approaches, the next section summaries the main studies of the new public management reforms to find out what account best captures their impact. And even these empirical studies diverge widely in their conclusions.

Evaluations of the impact of the new public management

Early evaluations are general surveys of the experiences of the most prominent countries that experienced these reforms, but do not constitute hard evidence new public management delivered better policy outcomes, more that it plausibly may have done so. For example, Aucoin (1995) reports on the effects of changes in Canada in relation to elsewhere, and Schick (1996) writes a critical account of New Zealand's reforms.

Later work presents more extensive evidence. Kelman (2005) reports on the reforms of the United States federal procurement bureaucracy – the United States Office of Federal Procurement Policy – in the 1990s as it went through a series of bureaucratic reforms. His book is partly based on his experience in the agency as it transformed after the National Performance Review of 1992. He provides considerable case study evidence of changed organisational practices. His survey of 1,593 frontline employees and face-to-face interviews with 272 bureaucrats shows a high level of entrepreneurial activity and the enthusiasm for organisational change, particularly among the change vanguard, bureaucrats who drove the reforms. But the book does not demonstrate the impacts of a changed bureaucracy. It is an account of a reinvigorated bureaucracy.

Many accounts and case studies make negative claims. Dunleavy *et al.* (2006a: 9–10) report high-profile information technology disasters caused by excessive faith in new public management principles, such as the United Kingdom Passports agency computerisation in 1999, whose breakdown came from a set of operational and strategic mistakes, though these were subsequently rectified (see discussion of overregulation in the previous chapter). Another conclusion is that new public management means a loss of control, such as through contracting services to the private sector. Many accounts of the impact of the new public management, however, remain impressionistic. For example, the Private Finance Initiative and the Public Private Partnerships, which try to hand over the risk of funding infrastructure projects to private sector organisations, have dominated infrastructure building in the UK since the 1990s. They have been associated with poor administration and failure of services. However, the research tends to be based on case studies or general reviews (for example, Hellowell and Pollock, 2009; Institute for Public Policy Research, 2001). There is not even a synthesis of the valuable National Audit Office reports that show a varied experience, with both poorly and well-performing schemes in evidence.

Overall, there is mixed evidence about contracting and service performance, with many studies indicating savings (for example, Walsh, 1995). Other studies take a wider perspective. Fernandez (2007) seeks to find out what factors influence successful contracting by analysing a mail survey of 982 US local governments in 2003–04 and seeing what is associated with high performance. The measure of contract includes cost, quality of work and customer satisfaction. Using a form of regression to identify high-performing cases, he finds a wide variety of factors within the contract, such as the degree of prior evaluation and trust between parties, influence performance rather than just to contract or not to contract.

There are some studies that try to measure the impact of the role of the private sector in providing public services. O'Toole and Meier (2004a) use data on over a thousand Texas school districts to examine the relationship between contracting and performance between 1997–99, some 3,122 observations. They carry out regression analysis on three years of data on student examination results, controlling for time with dummy variables and other factors affecting school performance (Black students, Latino students, poverty, gifted classes, teacher salaries, class size and non-certified teachers). But there is no significant negative relationship, except in one sub-sample of Latino students. The analysis does not deliver the knockout blow about the direction of causation with three years of data, no panel analysis and mainly non-significant results. It may be the case that contracting does not affect student performance, at least in the short run; but it might be associated with other aspects of running a school, such as the quality of the ancillary services, which may impact on school performance in the long run. Their analysis shows how contracting is associated with reduced spending on core functions such as money spent on teaching, so there could be a relationship, but it is not revealed in their data analysis. The study does not get round the problem of selection – why schools contract out in the first place, which may be linked to their performance.

Other aspects of new public management appear to deliver weak benefits, but again the evidence is mixed. For example, studies of the impact of performance-related pay seek to show that incentives do not operate because of the cooperative values of the bureaucrats, in particular loyalty to the work group (Makinson, 2000). An alternative view is the benefits are not high enough to motivate staff in spite of support for the scheme, as found in a study of the Inland Revenue (Marsden and Richardson, 1992). Subsequent research shows a stronger impact (for example, Atkinson *et al.*, 2009). Moreover, studies with better research designs show more positive results. Lavy (2009) investigates a new initiative in Israel to reward teachers in 49 schools with bonuses. These sums are $7,500, $5,750, $3,500, and $1,750, depending on performance, which are large compared to the average income of $30,000. Lavy deploys a quasi-experimental design to analyse the effects. He uses data from September 1999–June 2000, and the school year in which the experiment was conducted, September 2000–June 2001, recording the performance scores of the students. The experimental aspect comes from measurement error in the exam pass used to calculate entry into the programme – there was an element of random assignment, a natural experiment so the analysis can compare the scores across a sub-sample of 98 performance and treatment schools where these errors occurred. Subsequent regression analysis shows these performance regimes raised student performance in English and maths, which was due to teachers changing their methods of instruction (as found out by a separate survey). The effect of the treatment was a 10 per cent improvement for maths and 4 per cent for English. They show this was not due to gaming (manipulating) the scores. The only caveat is the study only observes change over one year.

Many accounts of public management reform stress its negative effects on organisational capacity, such as the break-up of the public sector, the loss of morale and the undermining of the public service ethos – the values that draw people into public service and motivate them to work much harder than one would expect for the rewards they get (Select Committee on Public Administration, 2002). The very incentives that are supposed to motivate people may have the opposite effect. But one study shows a commitment to wider social values, as reported in surveys, increased during the main years of public management reform in British government from 1997 to 2005 (John and Johnson, 2008). They use the British Social Attitudes survey as part of the International Social Survey Programme, with data for both 1997 and 2005, examining the survey question 'Important attributes of a job' and comparing the responses between private and public-sector employees. They find the number of people working in the public sector who said their job was socially useful increased from 22 to 32 per cent over that time, which was when a large number of public management reforms were introduced. That the opposite happened to what might be expected during this period, especially among young people joining public services, would appear to question one of the alleged negative impacts of public management reform.

While these kinds of studies can show costs and benefits for particular aspects of management reform, the question remains whether the reform of the public sector, targeted against traditional hierarchical structures, has benefits for the wider society. Answering this is not an easy task. Pollitt (2003a: 39) argues that it would require complicated before-and-after studies, with all the costs identified as well as the benefits. Governments rarely set out the objectives of the reform, making an evaluation very difficult; there were also many reforms taking place at the same time; and there were no official esti- mates of the costs. Pollitt suggests even good evaluations of the reforms, as happened in Australia and New Zealand, found it very hard to come to firm conclusions. Nevertheless, Pollitt and Bouckaert's *Public Management Reform* (2004) seeks to find comparative evidence for the effectiveness of the reforms. They review extensive surveys of public management reform and data on policy outcomes for the OECD countries. There appears to be some evidence of cost savings, process improvements (better and fairer procedures), gains in efficiency, cultural changes and improvements in management capacity, even if it is hard to make these inferences with a high degree of certainty. The bigger question is whether countries that embarked on public management reforms improved their economies and other outcomes, such as public finan- ces, in contrast to countries that did not. The reform argument is plausible because the key English-speaking countries improved, admittedly from a lag- gard position, as these economies previously had worse performance inde- pendent of other factors (see Castles and Merrill, 1989). Though Pollitt and Bouckaert qualify the results of their enterprise quite considerably, they pro- vide some evidence that supports this claim, even though other factors can explain the improvement. The analysis is based on associations within a small number of cases, which makes the review more of an interpretive exercise than a scientific analysis. Overall, it is very hard to say from the comparative evidence whether new public management has had a positive effect – it depends on the context, as Pollitt (2003a: 50) argues. They claim it is very hard to say whether something as amorphous and ever changing as public management reform as a general phenomenon can even be measured and assessed as to its impact. In that sense, it is hard to disagree with the pessi- mistic outlook of Pollitt and Bouckaert's review. It is better to build up the evidence base by studies of particular aspects of new public management, as the discussion below on performance measurement illustrates.

Another survey is United Kingdom bound. Boyne *et al.* (2003) carry out a review of the evidence of the impacts of public management reforms from the sectors of health, housing and education. They review the secondary evidence, summarising the existing studies in a series of sector-specific chapters to find out if the objectives of efficiency and responsiveness had been realised. There is less evidence than in the Pollitt and Bouckaert volume, but they summarise many studies in these sectors for this time period. They conclude there were efficiency gains and more responsiveness in housing and education, but less in health. This does not inform about the outcomes, such as whether levels of housing quality, the health of the citizens and their education levels have improved as a result of these reforms. But it does indicate that service quality improved.

Performance management

One area of public management change that has received considerable academic attention is the impact of performance measurement in the public sector. This is the idea a clear measure of performance acts as a means to regulate public-sector organisations and gives them an incentive to improve public services. Performance management, however, is not short of critics. There are five main sorts of attack. The first is that performance is hard to measure or at least hard to quantify though grading and ranking schemes. This means the targeting of performance is not efficient at addressing matters that might not be close to the optimal outcome. Second, in relation to the first point, the performance regime distracts the organisation from its core aims and makes it concentrate only on those that are in the performance regime. Prendergast (2001) provides an example of this through performance measures and the police, whereby more scrutiny of the police causes them to reduce the number of criminals they arrest because they fear external review. Third, organisations have an incentive to game the results so as to achieve the desired performance score rather than actually improving services. This is the idea organisations would seek to hit the target by manipulating information. An example is the creation of temporary hospital rooms on corridors by means of curtains in British hospitals in order to fulfil a national target (Hood, 2006: 517). Fourth, meeting performance targets may undermine important values, such as the public-service ethos amongst its staff, which may sustain organisations in the long run (which the John and Johnson, 2008 results question). Fifth, performance management becomes a political tool for governments seeking to be seen to be improving services, which means there is added pressure from the centre to force organisations to improve and meet the targets, which may accentuate distorted goals. This typically leads to too high expectations, and often ends up with the target being abandoned. Finally, performance management regimes suffer from regulatory capture: the people doing the regulating are likely to be composed of expert members of a regulated group which may be adept at lobbying. This means performance management may be a game played from the top down, with the regulator pretending to be policing the regulated parties. It should also be added that performance management regimes are often resisted by the groups who are being regulated, typically organisations in the public sector, who are much more concerned with administration than other publics, like consumers, and have effective professional representatives to put forward their points of view.

However, performance management regimes should not be seen necessarily to fail. Analysts should not succumb to the negative images of such regimes, for probably the critics of performance management outnumber the defenders (see the review in Boyne *et al.*, 2010). Within performance management is a clear articulation of incentives in the form of rewards and punishment, which should allow senior managers within organisations to put in measures to improve performance. It may be the case that economic incentives can work if correctly applied. Much depends on the intelligence of the performance regime itself and how its instigators can adjust it to respond to changes and to gaming by bureaucrats, often by poaching people from the regulated organisations as regulators and inspectors – one of the oldest tactics regulators use to get compliance.

Much work on performance measurement tends to be case studies or is based on anecdotes and stories, which may suffer from selective reporting. The better evidence base is from the quantitative studies. For example, Propper *et al.* (2010) test the familiar idea that organisations may hit a target, so improving outcomes in one area but worsening outcomes in another. In the United Kingdom, there has been a considerable effort to reduce waiting times in hospitals. These authors use a natural experiment design, comparing Scotland, which did not have targets (but still encouraged reduced waiting times), with England's target-driven system. They examine the period from 1 April 1997 to 31 March 2004, with quarterly data, using the difference-of-difference method to remove aspects of the data specific to England and Scotland. This means the study has data from before the intervention of targets. Using regression on the panel dataset, they test for the impact of performance on two outcomes: waiting times and mortality. The study design is able to show whether the introduction of the policy affects these outcomes, when controlling for any differences between the countries that have not been accounted for by the differencing method. They include the countries as controls in the statistical model so the policy for England is a dummy variable for the country cases from 1999 (there are 48 cases). What is relevant is the interaction between the policy and the English variable, which shows performance management has an effect. The differenced estimates on 56 cases show mortality decreased. The study also looks at the effects within hospitals by examining the impact of the pressure of the target. This did have an impact on admissions, so showing some gaming in the system, but nevertheless it had no effect on patient outcomes. Overall, this study gets round some of the problems of evaluating interventions without experimental data. The main issue to raise is whether it is easier to rely on performance measures in affluent times when resources are increasing, for there may not be such capacity to improve when the public sector is more financially constrained, as the authors admit. The second is whether study design really is a natural experiment, for there may still be non-observed differences between Scotland and Wales. The authors are not able to rule out the counterfactual that if the regime were introduced in Scotland it would have had the same effects as in England, which is what the research design is asking readers to believe. For the authors write, 'The assumptions required for the difference-in-difference analysis to identify the impact of the policy are that the two countries were subject to the same policies pre-devolution and that the policy change must be exogenous to waiting times' (Propper et al., 2010: 322). Both assumptions can be questioned.

Some United States studies show similar results. The introduction of student tests in the No Child Left Behind legislation, which introduced performance evaluation in schools, has prompted an assessment of whether it worked (Jacob, 2005). Using a panel dataset of students and administrative data from Chicago schools in 1996–97 (370,210 older students who got a high stakes test and 397,057 others who got a low stakes test), the author finds scores increased by about 0.20–0.30 standard deviations due to the legislation, much larger than could be explained by pre-achievement trends. There was a much stronger effect among the high stakes students. By differencing the data and carrying out an interrupted time series analysis, it is a robust evaluation of the reforms, while not being able to rule out other explanations completely, as an experiment would, even though he has a panel of achievement data from large, mid-western cities outside of Illinois from which to compare.

Performance management can be a part of a wider project to improve performance, which involves setting clear measures of performance, voters assessing the competence of politicians charged with running performance regimes, changes of administration as a result, replacement in the top management team charged with improving performance and then improvement in outcomes as a result. Researchers have tested these ideas on a panel dataset on the Comprehensive Performance Assessment system in English local government from 2002–08 (Boyne *et al.*, 2008, 2009a, b, c, 2010a, b, c) using data from its 148 principal local councils. The results show citizens vote according to the level of performance of their council, punishing the poor performers, and new administrations are elected as a result (Boyne, 2009a; also see Revelli, 2008). There was a virtuous circle of improved management and better performance because managers were replaced when there were poor performers (Boyne *et al.*, 2008, 2009c, 2010b) and a change in political control (Boyne *et al.*, 2009b). The turnover led to improved performance (Boyne *et al.*, 2010c), which then fed back to electoral support (Boyne *et al.*, 2009c). All these changes have been analysed with a statistical model using fixed effects, so the results provide good estimates of the direction of changes in the absence of an experiment.

So it seems the performance management – if implemented correctly – can work, which shows aspects of the new public management are useful for improving policy outcomes. While there is evidence for the disruptive effects of decentralisation and fragmentation of the reforms, other aspects of the regime can be effective. Often positive impacts occur because of careful and selective forms of intervention rather than from the broad brush of the new public management. Reformers need to be sensitive to which aspects of the bureaucracy/management tool work, and should fine-tune their interventions accordingly.

Digital era governance

The new public management is not the only way to create better outcomes through the bureaucracy. The argument of Dunleavy *et al.* (2005, 2006) is that the digital or e-revolution has undermined the arguments for contracting and disaggregating the structure of the state. Instead, it points the way to re-integration. New technology and its applications, such as web-based software, can closely link government information systems to the reactions of citizens, who are using new technology increasingly in their private lives. With citizens providing feedback to government, there is an opportunity to provide better services, particularly if government is equipped to respond quickly and appropriately. In addition, citizens may co-produce services alongside the state or public authority, for example by filling in the tax returns online, which is both more efficient for government and more convenient for the citizen. There is no longer a need for central bureaucracies to be divided up according to function because a large amount of government activity is carried out automatically through zero touch technology and citizen interaction with a website, which need not have departmental ownership. So, after a long period of fragmentation, the state can reap the benefits of a more integrated administration focused on advanced, interactive websites and by meeting the needs of citizens in the round. As government becomes more efficient and responsive to the needs of citizens and citizens do more and more online, virtuous circles of increasing trust and confidence could take hold.

So the arguments for digital era governance are powerful, and could mean a reinvention of the bureaucracy/public management tool, moving it to the centre stage as the preferred resource of government. If the new public management was only a partially successful attempt to carry out this project, digital era governance might actually be the silver bullet that policy-makers are looking for. The transformation argument may, however, be limited by the extent to which states are able to overturn conventional bureaucratic processes by digital means and by the way new mechanisms sit within existing bureaucratic processes and procedures, even if a lot of routine activities are automated. The institutionalist account of digitalisation charts the evolution of new technologies within this wider institutional framework, and investigates how they fit in and adapt to the prevailing rules and standard operating procedures of bureaucracies. In this view, existing routines of bureaucracies dominate the implementation of digital government, possibly limiting its scope and impact (Chadwick and May, 2003).

In the United Kingdom, Dunleavy *et al.* (2006) argue that 25 years of the new public management have fragmented the state and contracted out its core functions. The loss of capacity may mean the potential for digital era governance is hard to realise. In addition, the contracting out of information technology functions to outside organisations, such as private companies, is a loss of a core competence of the state and results in difficulties of co-ordination. Greater policy errors may come from the lack of control and the failure to monitor effectively the companies charged with introducing new technology. In other parts of the world, such as Finland and Singapore, the move to digital era governance is much easier because of the integration of the state and a focus on bringing in change. The impact of digitalisation thus varies according to national context, which can limit the ability of politicians to deploy this tool of government. Not only do they introduce digitalisation, they have to overcome the limitations of their bureaucracies at the same time.

One problem of evaluating digital era governance is that it is still too new to generate much evidence about its impact, and many of the likely changes are in the future. Much emphasis is placed on examples, such as the introduction of a transport card, the Oyster card, which has reduced queuing for tickets (Dunleavy *et al.* 2006a: 487), or case studies such as the experience of online tax returns and the experience of countries that have moved closer to digital era governance. Some studies do suggest a transformation, but the evidence is partial. West (2004), for example, tests out the claim in federal and state administration in the United States. The research is based on a survey of state public managers, a content analysis of 1,680 federal and state government websites, a survey of 1,003 people to examine the impact of the web on public trust and confidence, and an experiment, which involved sending an e-mail and a letter to four offices in each state asking a series of questions. This is not a full test of digitalisation, but at least it is a step. The results overall show modest impacts. As with other studies of government websites, the results reveal their lack of development and weak potential for interaction with the citizen. The survey shows no impact of the use of the federal websites on trust in government, confidence in government, belief in government effectiveness, except for an association with political activity. Naturally, the cross-sectional survey cannot point to any causal relationships. The responses to contact show the offices were efficient at getting back to respondents and at providing information, but the study provides no comparison with other forms of contact, for example telephoning. Even with its limitations, this study shows the current weak development of this tool of government, but its findings can be contrasted with other studies, such as Tolbert and Mossberger's (2006). They analyse a survey of 815 people to test the impact of the use of e-governance on political trust. They find a positive relationship. It appears the improvement in the process of government has the following effect: 'E-government at the local level was also perceived by citizens as making government accessible and responsive, but only responsiveness was directly linked to increased trust of local government in the two-stage model' (2006: 366). This suggests increased government trust is produced by improved interactions through e-government at the local level. Again, it is cross-sectional data so it is hard to know whether people who trust more select into using websites, but the authors seek to control for this in a two-stage estimation.

So the internet and digital governance have the potential to transform the delivery of policy. But it is hard to test these claims at such an early stage of the development of the technology and its introduction into bureaucracies. There are illustrative case studies and some evidence for the impact on citizens. But there are no randomised interventions that evaluate its effectiveness, which may be hard to do given the innate holism of the project. It is probably the case that public services will change fundamentally as a result of digitalisation. Hood and Margetts (2007) argue that information technology is transforming all the tools of government, digitally sharpening them for greater efficiency. Future work will need to test out this claim.

Management matters

The efforts of governments at wholesale reform – whether it is new public management or digital era governance – are hard to evaluate or are at best patchy in their impact. But there are other aspects of public management, not completely linked to new public management, which do vary over time, and may be influenced by government reforms and the decisions of politicians. These are the management structures and forms of leadership, which may have long-term impacts on performance and policy outcomes. This is partly because Weber was wrong to think there is one kind of bureaucratic organisation, from which there is deviation. In fact, there are several kinds, as scholars working in the field of organisational theory have long argued (for example, Perrow, 1986). With these alternative forms of organisation available to them, public managers may seek to use their discretion to shift the focus of their organisations to process information more effectively and produce better results.

The claim of a group of studies looking at the different dimensions of organisational structures and behaviour is that management matters. This idea can be expressed in different ways. At its most sophisticated it argues that governance has a logic, which may have traceable impacts on societal outcomes, and where managers may use what discretion they have to improve the leverage of governance (Lynn *et al.*, 2000, 2001). Lynn *et al.* write 'governance generally refers to the means for achieving direction, control, and coordination of wholly or partially autonomous individuals or organisations on behalf of interests to which they jointly contribute' (2000: 235) – which brings public management closer to the network governance theme of Chapter 7. The idea is more creative management can achieve better leverage on societal outcomes by thinking through the linkages. Forbes and Lynn (2005) use this framework to carry out a meta-review of studies, which concludes the direction of findings gives support for the management matters set of hypotheses, though the main purpose of the article is to set out the different methodologies of current public administration studies. In spite of the virtues of this overview, it may be too general and over-complex to make causal claims. It tends to describe good administrative practice rather than offer a model of the relationships at work.

It may be better – if more prosaic – to examine the strategies organisations can take to improve their performance. There are many varied claims in this literature, which range from the need to integrate policy and provide focus (Ingraham *et al.*, 2003: 24–26, and see discussion below) to the dimensions of organisational impact (see Boyne *et al.*, 2003: 371). An important theme is the impact of leadership styles, such as a transformational form of leadership, which may be revealed when a new chief executive takes over. Then there is the content of the strategy itself, which may reflect the freedom of the managers to dictate priorities and the stability of the environment (O'Toole and Meier, 1999). Meier and O'Toole (2006: 155–57) set out these leadership effects in a model of performance which involves environmental constraints, management and then the ability of management to exploit opportunities and to buffer external shocks. In their view managers are not passive, but are able to resist unwanted change and to shape their environment.

Out of the many claims, one that appears again and again is that stronger and more focused forms of leadership will improve policy performance. The idea is some kind of top-down direction, depending on force of character and the skills of persuasion, can energise the bureaucracy and encourage it to produce desired outcomes. Without good leadership, the organisation falls apart and becomes subject to internal dissent, so reducing its performance. Such ideas link to the new public management, and are about releasing managers to get on with the job of leadership. Indeed, there is an industry of policy advice and comment about the potential of better or more facilitative leadership. Governments also introduce measures to promote leadership, largely based on the idea that changing leaders will improve organisational performance and hence outcomes, such as better health care from new leadership teams in charge of hospitals or better outcomes from new heads of schools.

There is less robust evidence to indicate whether leadership does matter. Wolf (1993) finds evidence that leadership affects organisational effectiveness in his analysis of leadership, but it is based on a subjective assessment of leadership books written by scholars on the particular agencies. Brewer and Selden (2000) report a survey of 18,183 federal employees in 23 United States agencies. Leadership is measured by general questions about the ability of supervisors, with questions of 'My immediate supervisor has good management skills', 'My immediate supervisor has organized our work group effectively to get the work done', and 'Overall, I am satisfied with my supervisor', which is about the diffused leadership qualities in the organisation rather than the impact of high-level leadership. This study finds the leadership variables predict organisational performance. In a similar kind of study, Moynihan and Pandey (2005) survey 274 state government health and human services officials in the United States. It uses regression analysis on self-reported performance scores – asking managers to rate the performance of their agencies. This is a problem because they may have an interest in over-reporting performance and linking it to their own efforts: it is a very subjective approach to measuring the impact of leadership. The study finds that, over and above environmental factors, the ability to create a developmental organisational culture and to establish a focus on results improves the effectiveness of the organisation; these are not the classic leadership factors, but are more to do with strategy. The measures of centralised control associated with strong leadership do not have an impact – rather the sign on this variable is negative: it is decentralised decision-making that influences performance, which in the authors' view supports a more new public management type of argument. In a finding that refers back to the discussion about bureaucracy earlier, they find hierarchical culture is not a factor – neither negatively nor positively. Given the limitations of the study, it is not possible to use these results to come to any positive conclusion, even though they are suggestive. In general, scepticism is the appropriate reaction to these survey-based studies that measure both the dependent and the independent terms from the same instrument.

Much of the management matters literature is concerned with examining the impact of managerial capacity on policy outputs, such as the Government Performance Project examining state performance in the United States (Ingraham *et al.*, 2003). One exception is the paper by Coggburn and Schneider (2003) which explores the relationship between the state performance scores and the quality of life. The argument is that good managers could promote a better quality of life through better management of social relationships, improving public services and by increasing economic investment. The quality of life is measured by aggregate scores, which combine different factors, such as crime, infant mortality, hazardous waste sites, political participation (which might be an independent variable) and local government debt. The model seeks to predict quality of life as a function of managerial quality, which is measured by the performance grades for 1999 (aggregating grades for financial management, human resource management, information technology, capital management and managing for results). The other variables are external policy choices made by the states and economic conditions (which is state per capita income which might be part of the dependent variable). The statistical analysis finds states that have targeted resources to particular groups (the policy variable) perform worse on the quality of life, which echoes back to the ambiguous results for the finance tool elaborated in Chapter 3. For one measure, management capacity affects the quality of life; but for another, it does not make much difference, even though the other variables show the same results (the authors do not seem to notice the non-significant coefficient in their regression as the t-value of 1.2 is much less than the 1.96 needed to meet the 95 per cent test). Given the problems in separating out the independent and dependent variables, the absence of any relationship across time, the mixed results across the two measures, and an inability to test for the relationship between quality of life and government performance, that is, that causality works in the opposite direction, it is hard to conclude much from this study. This is a shame, because it is a relevant piece of research, and few studies of public management explore the long-term relationships between performance and policy outcomes.

One exception is Meier and O'Toole (2002). Using the Texas school data set, they assume performance is the difference between the actual and predicted salary of school superintendents in a statistical model of 5,127 cases over five years (1995–99). The dependent variables are test scores and the models controlling for instruction spending, black students, Latino students, low-income students and class size, teacher experience, non-certified teachers, parental support, community support and student attendance (the results are repeated for an additional ten performance indicators). The performance measure has a positive impact on pupil test scores. But it depends on the bold assumption that salary difference is a measure of quality. This would have to be determined by a perfect market in head teacher hires, which is unlikely given the lack of information in the sector and the weak level of competition between schools. It also assumes schools with high results are not seeking to recruit good teachers in the possibly mistaken belief they keep scores high – which is the problem of attributing the direction of causation once again.

Andrews *et al.* (2006, 2008) and Meier *et al.* (2010) use a framework elaborated by the organisational theorists Miles and Snow (1978). Miles and Snow hypothesise strategy content influences performance. They set out a four-category typology of the different kinds of strategies managers use: prospecting, defending, analysing and reacting. The argument is prospecting kind of organisations should be able to obtain a performance pay-off from running services because they are more likely to be pioneers and innovators. Defenders have the opposite characteristics, and will be very late to adopt innovations. Andrews *et al.* (2006) test this idea out on data from English local authorities. They use a survey of 119 authorities, which has several participants in each authority as respondents. The responses to a series of questions then generate the categories. For example, the question 'The service or authority is at the forefront of innovative approaches' is used as the prospector measure. Then it is possible to correlate whether an authority has this characteristic with its performance. They elaborate a statistical model of performance as measured by the Comprehensive Performance Assessment score, controlling for other attitude measures in the survey and deprivation. They find prospecting predicts performance, and defending is negatively associated (though this is outside the normal range of statistical significance). The problem is identifying a causal relationship in cross-sectional data even though the attitudes were measured in the years before. The authors need to test whether a change in attitudes creates a change in performance, which they cannot do because they only measure attitudes once.

They continue this line of work on Welsh local authorities (Andrews *et al.*, 2008) – a survey of respondents in 51 service departments carried out in 2002. They obtained the Miles and Snow categories from the survey questions. They seek to predict a performance measure calculated from individual service measures divided by the mean score, using predictors (which are rather different to the Andrews *et al.*, 2006 measures) of expenditure (which might be a consequence of the management strategies) and past performance. There is a result for prospecting, but nothing for defending, which the authors regard as surprising and which does not confirm the model on English data.

The difficulty of this line of work is it depends on making some strong assumptions about the differences in management styles from agreements with statements in survey responses. It is also hard to show this kind of causal relationship without panel data. Moreover, a recent attempt to examine these categories on United States data on school districts, using just three of the Miles and Snow categories because of a limited number of questions, fails to generate positive results when seeking to predict test scores (Meier *et al.*, 2010). Meier *et al.* use the Texas school district survey 2000–05 to generate 3,041 cases (though some of the measures are from one year: managerial strategies from 2002 and the networking measure from 2000, and they impute the missing values for the intervening years). The measures of Miles and Snow come from the surveys, such as the prospector measure from the question 'A superintendent should advocate major changes in school policies'. The other variables are environmental turbulence and decentralisation as measures of managerial strategies, then the control variables of teacher's salaries, class size, teacher experience, non-certified teachers, instructional funds, and black, Latino and low-income students. The statistical model for students with high scores shows defenders get better scores when compared to the other categories, including prospectors, which is not predicted by the theoretical model. The authors' analysis and discussion of marginal effects do not get round this problem, so they admit the Miles and Snow categories do not hold in this case.

One line of work looks at the impact of the replacement of the top managers on performance. In one point of view, changes amongst the top management team might help an organisation adapt to changing circumstances and consequently lead to higher performance. Stability would ossify organisations, whereas change allows bureaucracies to respond to new pressures. In the new public management literature, newly appointed bureaucrats may be associated with reform, bringing with them fresh ideas for achieving change. The alternative idea is that attempts at top-down change are destabilising and doomed to failure, especially if the system as a whole is considered. At the top end, the loss of good managers in high-performing organisations may be one of the perils of excellence. In this case, the shuffling of successful senior managers between local authorities may not help the low performers but may damage the high performers. Paradoxically, then, the turnover and transfer of managerial elites could weaken the performance of public management as a whole. In the organisation itself, replacing the top managers may not make much difference to the organisation if sources of poor performance are deeply embedded, such as in the values of the senior managers and in standard operating procedures. As a result it can be hard to change organisational practices. If the new manager is resisted by the existing personnel it will be very hard to overthrow this culture by force of personality and drive – the top manager needs to use a variety of strategies, which may involve strong direction, but at bottom there needs to be some degree of consent, and also an enthusiastic coalition within the organisation whose members believe in the new changes and see a benefit for their careers. So the disruption induced by the departure of experienced specialists among the top management could lead to a drop in organisational performance. It is even possible that such changes are largely ritual, largely for scapegoating, to demonstrate the organisation's agility to stakeholders, but without much of a performance effect. The causal mechanism is the way in which existing bureaucrats use their experience and knowledge of where the bodies are buried to ensure the organisation moves on from existing levels of performance. New bureaucrats need to find out what works and also to recruit as followers other officials down the chain who can follow their commands. This is an account of bureaucracy that stresses the importance of informal networks within organisations and the limits to top-down command and control strategies. It is possible personnel stability is the cause of good performance. O'Toole and Meier (2003a) test this idea with five years of Texas school district data – they use personnel stability to explain educational outcomes, controlling for a wide range of factors as before. However, they cannot fully verify their hypotheses, and it is better education performance that creates stability over a long time period – teachers want to stay in schools with good pupils.

The project on turnover of managers in a panel dataset of English local councils – described above – finds turnover of chief executives positively influences measured performance (Boyne *et al.*, 2008), but this only occurs when performance is low. There is no general impact of turnover on performance, but new managers can raise performance from the floor, which does seem to show that managers can turn organisations around given the right circumstances. However, it is very difficult to control for the factors that cause a local authority to recruit a new manager, which may be to do with a realisation within the organisation that it needs to change, making the arrival of a new chief executive the result of a willingness to change performance rather than the effect of managerial qualities. The conclusion to draw is leadership strategy does appear to have some effect, but there are limitations to many of these studies.

Conclusions

There is ample evidence that politicians regard the bureaucracy as a means of affecting outcomes they care about and they will use the powers of office to get the most out of this tool of government. They are right to think in this way. In theory, getting a policy effectively implemented – and thereby achieving desired policy outcomes – should rely on a series of organisational characteristics, such as the ability of bureaucracies to coordinate, to lead and to receive correct signals from the wider society and its citizens. The problem is knowing how best to organise a bureaucracy. Though it is possible to combine elements of the two models on offer, there is a choice between a traditional hierarchical organisation that carries out commands or a more decentralised set of arrangements whereby incentives get to the desired result.

Only a few studies support the more conservative view of bureaucracy, one that is wedded to formal procedures, has a separation between formal politics and administration, where the roles are clear and there is hierarchy. This organisational framework appears to support the performance of economies and contributes to other desired outcomes by the clear application of objectives and the effects on the wider society of good bureaucratic behaviour. Unfortunately, these studies do not present decisive evidence, partly from using faulty measures.

The alternative perspective is to believe the bureaucracy suffers from dead-weight, and it needs strong reforms to create better incentives to improve performance. Once the organisation has been reconfigured, there are gains to be had. Indeed, there is evidence that taking control of the bureaucracy and reforming it will have the desired effect of changing outcomes on the ground, such as education scores and patients who live longer. Some aspects of public management reforms appear to work, in particular performance management. The best studies, done by economists using sophisticated designs, show this (Jacob, 2005; Propper *et al.*, 2009; Lavy, 2009). They reveal that there is leverage from precise interventions that understand how incentives work. It is possible reformers need to develop a more sensitive use of the bureaucracy/management tool, keeping some formal procedures where they can, rejecting the excesses of the new public management, making uses of digital solutions, but not forgetting the particular mechanisms that can improve the delivery of public services, such as in performance management and recruiting better leaders.

5 Institutions

Institutions are the rules of the game in a political system, which are often formal in the sense they are binding upon participants, though they do not have to be. Typical examples of well-recognised institutions are the constitutional rules in force in a nation state, like an electoral system, or institutions charged with decision-making, such as a supreme court that adjudicates on fundamental political disputes or a central bank that decides interest rates. But there may be other rules that are in effect binding because they are accepted by most people and because they have powerful social sanctions attached to them if they are breached. Examples of these embedded practices are the standard operating procedures of bureaucracies and informal constitutional conventions, which politicians and bureaucrats do not want to break or fear sanctions from doing so. Whether formal or informal, institutions have the characteristic of being sticky, that is, they are hard to change (Riker, 1982). This semi-permanence means political actors and citizens have to live with them, in the short term at least, or face high costs when changing them. As a tool of government, then, they are hard to use. But even though institutions are embedded within political systems, politicians do seek to change them, and increasingly so in recent years, such as introducing power-sharing agreements, decentralising power to devolved governments, legislating for directly elected mayors and reforming electoral systems. The question is whether, over and above the arguments from justice and fairness, these changes are likely to lead to positive policy outcomes.

The chapter concentrates primarily on the formal rules of the political system, such as the impact of the electoral system or the creation of new institutions like independent central banks. In many senses, institutions share a stable with law and regulation (discussed in Chapter 3). But the focus here is less on legal instruments to change behaviour, and more on the rules of the game in the political system. It is less about the resources politicians can use than the resources that control the politicians and help them make better and more legitimate decisions. There is some overlap with bureaucracies too, although the focus is not on the internal operation of institutions as in public management, but on their impact on how society makes collective choices. In terms of the tools of government, institutions are a higher-level resource, which can govern how politicians and other decision-makers use the other tools of government.

As such, institutions may be seen as internal to political systems; they are the ways in which political participants solve problems, and are not intended to have a direct impact on policy outcomes as such. They may not be seen as a conventional instrument of government by policy-makers. If they work and are seen as fair that surely is enough. But it is also the case institutions are supposed to have desirable qualities that produce good outcomes, such as stable governments, economic prosperity, well-informed policies and more social cooperation. How does this work?

Institutional rules usually are authoritative; that is, they are respected and obeyed within the jurisdictions in which they operate. They are so because they have become accepted as the way in which difficult decisions are made. These rules are particularly useful and appropriate when the main political actors are gridlocked and need to appeal to a higher level of authority. There is a close link between the effective practice of politics and the workings of political institutions: if politics is about arguments about collective choices, then institutions provide one way in which these disputes can be adjudicated, resolved or attenuated, often because they are at one step removed from the fray of the political debate. Thus the rules of parliament help get votes through; constitutional courts resolve constitutional disputes between the levels or branches of government; and bureaucratic rules adjudicate on the claims of various interest groups advocating policies within a ministry. Rules can assist the production of local public goods by helping to get agreement; knowing whose turn it is to do a civic act can enable local public goods to be provided, such as in a citizen-run crime prevention scheme. By encouraging different ways of doing business, it is possible to imagine knock-on effects, say from more efficient decisions, which lead to better public policies that have an effect on policy outcomes on the ground.

One of the most powerful arguments, one that aims to unpack the causes underlying institutional impacts, has come from transactions cost economics (North, 1990). The argument is that if people were left to their own devices, human beings would not cooperate, so there is a need for cooperation to be routinised and incentivised. Pre-set rules affect the pay-offs people get from cooperating or not cooperating. In addition, institutions can help actors give signals so they can adjust their strategies. Institutions affect the nature of the political game and the gains actors get from being a part of the political system. The key argument is that there is a positive effect of cooperation, which comes from the stability of policy-making and incentives for people to work together.

A strand in this debate, much favoured by North (1990) and also Weingast (2002), is that institutions provide information which can help coordination and reduce the transaction costs of doing business. An example is information flows between companies, when they decide with whom to do business. If institutions free up and increase the quality of information, these transactions costs will not transfer into the cost of a product, that is, the cost of checking whether the other partner is seeking advantage. The state can reduce these information asymmetries, so common in many economic relationships. Some rules mean opportunistic behaviour is observed and possibly punished. For North, the example of the early development of capitalism is evidence for the impact of institutions whereby rules concerning the recording of business transactions, central standards in product quality and the enforcement of contracts are the key factors that permit economic growth to take place. North stresses the informal rules of the game as well as the formal rules.

However, institutions do not necessarily have these desirable qualities. Indeed, there is a long line of thinking that complains the existing sets of institutions are inefficient. For example, there has been an argument – reaching back to the beginning of the twentieth century – that suggests the United Kingdom Parliament is too weak to be able to carry out effective scrutiny of administrative and executive action (Crick, 1964). What the political system needs is more powers for legislators and more independence from the executive. But in *Constitutional Democracy*, Mueller (2000) argues that the failure of western democracies to address key problems lies in the excessive separation of powers, which is the opposite of this view. The existence of contrary views about the same institution is a common problem: what is the bane for one set of commentators becomes the longed-for institutional reform of another. This reveals the familiar envy principle when studying political institutions: people in one country end up overrating other countries' designs and thinking there is something wrong with their own. Often views are a mirror image of each other, such as with critics of electoral systems wanting proportional systems in first-past-the-post electoral systems whereas those from countries with proportional representation systems sometimes propose to have majoritarian ones.

So what kinds of institutions affect outcomes? In one line of argument, the preference is for institutions that make decisions in a speedy and timely manner, without excess delays and prevarication, which then have positive effects for good policies and constructive relationships between citizens and the state. What is desirable is an effective system for aggregating public knowledge, which can assess a problem without too much day-to-day political inference and excessive cross-checking by self-interested and factional interest groups. The more opportunities for veto players there are, the more stable the government is, and by implication the worse it is for policies (Tsebelis, 1995, 2002). Tsebelis sets this out in formal terms, but the logic is very simple. The more opportunities there are to block decisions, the harder it is for governments to depart from the consensus to make hard, but necessary decisions. These ideas have been used by Immergut (1992) to study the effectiveness of health policy-making in comparative context, finding a larger number of veto points, especially when used by doctors, limits the ability of the executive to pursue reforms, which is to the detriment of health policy.

This relates to the familiar defence of simple forms of executive government, which relies on setting up lines of command and accountability to one institution or office-holder, visible to the public and to stakeholders, who can be judged on this basis and who in return has a degree of freedom over the legislature and control over the bureaucracy. This is the argument for greater clarity of responsibility of decision-making, whereby office holders enter into a credible commitment to implement difficult policies. If other decision-makers do not hold much power, it is impossible to shift blame onto them. They have to be held to account, which can lead to more responsible decision-making. It is also a justification for stronger and more visible forms of individual leadership, such as vesting authority and decision-making in one office held by an individual, such as a president at the national level or a mayor in the locality, who may preside over a fragmented legislature and plethora of interests and voices. Typically such a direct line of accountability is not vested directly by a party or a legislature, but by a mandate from the people in the form of direct election, so the person can appeal over the heads of other politicians, such as legislators. This is a non-parliamentary form of government, where there is more of a need for one individual to counter the fragmentation of political institutions outside the formal executive.

Thus the design of institutions affects political accountability. Different rules may hold politicians to account for their actions; they may also promote a culture of responsibility, based on mutual cooperation extending the ideas above. This may be desirable on its own terms as political systems are expected to have these qualities and they may be better able to uphold the rights of the citizens, for example, but they may affect other kinds of behaviour that in turn affect policy outcomes. In particular, if accountability is low, then corruption may be high, which will affect economic growth, because it becomes more costly to do business and more risky to carry out transactions. In this sense there is a crossover between the impact of institutions and of organisations, the topic of the previous chapter.

Parliamentary systems do not usually have formally and directly elected political leaders, but they do seek to give prominence to the executive in the form of the cabinet and the strong role of the prime minister. By virtue of the ruling political party's majority in the legislature, the strong powers given to the executive and the attention of the media on political leadership, the system can produce powerful and visible independent leaders, sometimes giving them more power than to a president in a system of division of powers.

There is an opposed line of thinking that suggests centralised institutions may be worse for decision-making, partly based on a suspicion that strong executives in a parliamentary system of government, such as Britain's, are unresponsive and do not listen to a wide range of evidence. The claim is an unaccountable executive prefers to use its power in more naked fashion. It tends to make short-term or radical decisions that in the end lead to poor policies. In short, a government that tends to make radical ill-thought-out decisions will not be able to sustain a long-term improvement in policy out-comes, partly because it will be focused on disaster management and because policy errors will soak up badly needed public expenditure and may even have negative consequences as well.

The veto player argument can be stood on its head, for if there are more veto players it is likely there will be an equilibrium, which may give the necessary stability to produce well-thought-out policies that have time to succeed. But the problem is veto players can have different effects on out-comes depending on what the problem is: if the task is to create a stable institutional framework to attract, for example, a reliable flow of inward eco-nomic investment, then veto players are a good thing to have; but if the need is to respond with a dramatic policy choice, say to combat global warm-ing in the face of entrenched economic interests, then veto players could be detrimental.

The strong institutional form of executive-dominant systems limits the number of access points for interest groups and reduces the capabilities for constructive and well-evidenced policies through debate and the consideration of different arguments and sorts of evidence, which may be more likely to occur in a separation of powers system where power is shared between pre-sident, leglisature and constitutional court. This is an extension of the approach of Braybrooke and Lindblom (1963), who stress the learning potential of complex decision-making systems, and is associated with the pluralist critique of rationally ordered procedures and institutional rules. In the British case, the idea is the centralised political system is not able to deliver the intelligence and responsiveness needed for effective policies. At the core of the debate is whether countries with more pluralist and divided institutions have achieved better outcomes because of greater responsiveness and legitimacy or whether pluralism prevents political leaders from guiding those outcomes. It is a question that goes to the heart of what is the purpose of government and how the way of making decisions at the top can affect the quality of policy-making.

Some public choice models also support the diffusion of power. The links between electors and politicians at the national level may act as a source of inefficiency because of the need to win elections, which may be manipulated. In this scenario more centralised institutions may be inefficient. Central authorities may seek to manage the economy in the short-run interests of voters, such as stimulating the economy just before the election so as to get more of a chance of being re-elected, but which has the effect of mismanaging the economy because inflation is higher than it should be. The other factor is the misallocation of public funds to marginal or swing voters, which means resources are not going to those who need them but to those places that are more electorally attractive to the central office holder.

An example of this line of thinking is Weingast's essay on the impact of federalism (1995). He argues that economies need an institutional structure that promotes growth. In part this comes from the authority of the state in upholding property rights. But the fear is this very authority may be used to take wealth and property away – the state needs a self-limiting ordinance to carry out its market-protecting role, a kind of credible commitment, hence the constitutional role of federalism, which limits the power of the federal state to intervene. The result of federalism is the protection of markets. He backs up these arguments by looking at the development of limited government in the United States and more controversially in the unitary state, England. Weingast defends his English account by describing as federal the limitations the constitution placed on the central state and the way regulation of enterprises sustained economic growth. But this account suffers from relying too greatly on the decentralist tendencies within federalism, when federal governments have persuaded constitutional courts to intervene in the economic welfare of the nation's inhabitants, and where these states can be just as authoritarian and careless with the economic rights of the citizens as other governments. The other impact of decentralised forms of political accountability is through political competition, whereby less monopoly control, such as by one political party, can assist economic outcomes, partly by raising the quality of the politicians, and reduces the incentives to govern just through vested interests (Besley *et al.*, 2010). The implication is that if political institutions through voting rules, such as proportional representation, increase political competition, higher economic growth will follow.

Thus there are two main views about how institutional designs deliver efficiency. The choice is between a conception of beneficial decentralised arrangements protecting self-organising processes from interference from a mighty state or the coordination potential of strong lines of accountability to one institution and office holder. It is this point of ambiguity this chapter seeks to confront.

The chapter first reviews some of the core arguments for institutional effects, before addressing some classic studies and whether institutional reform can have positive consequences. The next part of the chapter considers the growing literature seeking to test the proposition that institutions matter, using data largely from comparative politics.

The impact of types of democratic system

This section takes one of the key debates of recent years to examine the impact of political institutions on outcomes, that of types of democracy, in particular the operation of different kinds of rules to decide the vote for electoral representatives. The electoral system has been described as the 'most fundamental constitutional rules in democracy' (Persson and Tabellini, 2003: 11), so it is worthy of particular attention as an example of the impact of political institutions on policy outcomes. Reformers can make a clear choice to change their electoral system, such as the UK faces in 2011 with its referendum on whether to keep first-past-the-post or to introduce the alternative vote system.

One proposition is proportional representation systems lead to a much better management of the economy than first-past-the-post ones. If true, it would mean a switch of electoral systems would yield benefits or costs depending on the direction of change. The argument is that first-past-the-post systems tend to have majority governments, a smaller number of parties from which to choose and alternating parties in government, which leads to the claim these systems institutionalise conflict. In contrast, proportional representation systems are more consensus-based, with many parties in coalition governments. The tendency to include interests produces more responsive and considered governments, which are more pluralistic and make more informed policies as a result. Majoritarian systems do not deliver such generally welfare-improving policies as they are based on narrower sectional interests.

The claim that majoritarian systems perform worse than other kinds of democracy system has been a major theme in the work of Lijphart (1984, 1999; also see Lijphart and Crepaz, 1991). Lijphart's argument is not just about the electoral system, but is about the whole pattern of government linked to the electoral system. He sets out various dimensions of policy-making according to linked institutional features of government and the party system. On the executive-parties dimension, there are differences according to whether there is concentration of executive power in a single-party majority cabinet or executive power sharing in broad, but not minimum winning multiparty coalitions. This boils down to whether the executive (president or cabinet/prime minister) is dominant over the legislature as opposed to where there is a legislative–executive balance of power; whether it is a two-party or a multiparty system, which may be a function of electoral rules; the electoral rules themselves; and whether there is a pluralist form of interest group representation as opposed to more state-structured corporatist system aimed at compromise and concertation. Lijphart moves beyond the more formal rule-based definitions of institutions to a more informal and societal aspect as in his inclusion of the interest group system. Consensus-based systems tend to produce oversized cabinets that include political interests. In addition, it should be noted that Lijphart also finds differences according to the dimension of unitary versus federal systems.

In his earlier work, Lijphart (1984) finds these two different types of system do not differ with respect to inflation rates and economic growth. Only unemployment is lower in majoritarian democracies. But the later analysis, carried out with a wider selection of countries and enhanced definitions, finds that unemployment and inflation are higher in non-consensus democracies. Lijphart develops the notion of kinder, gentler democracies that produce more desirable policy outputs, such as lower incarceration rates, less use of capital punishment, better environmental policies, more foreign aid and more spending on welfare services. Also they elect more women into public positions, reduce economic disparities, have higher voter turnout, produce citizens that express higher satisfaction with their political system; they select leaders with opinions that are more congruent with those of the citizens; they enhance accountability and lessen corruption; and they ensure that the government is always backed by a majority, not just a plurality.

Political scientists have carried out further analysis with the Lijphart conceptualisation. Crepaz finds strong evidence to support Lijphart using data from eighteen countries and nine elections per country (162 cases). He finds consensus democracy, when linked with inclusive and consensual forms of decision-making, can cause lower unemployment, higher growth and inflation. He measures the level of popular cabinet support, which is the number of popular votes for the governing cabinet, to operationalise this term.

The Lijphart–Crepaz claims have been contested. Anderson (2001) finds the economic benefits of consensus democracy depend on two features of government: having an independent bank and a corporatist structure of government–interest group relationships. He runs regression models of inflation and employment for 1970–90 and finds central bank independence and corporatism reduce inflation, but that consensus democracy increases it. Central bank independence reduces unemployment and there is no impact of the type of democracy (see the discussion below on central banks). If a dummy variable of Switzerland is included in the statistical model, consensus democracy increases unemployment. He argues that both of these institutions do not follow or are consequences of consensual argument – central bank independence is not part of the Lijphart model – nor is it theoretically part of consensus democracy. The key issue is that there is a well-known relationship (Soskice, 1990), if a complex one (Calmfors and Driffill, 1988), between corporatist bargaining institutions and economic performance. Accepting this argument does not mean the effect of institutions is diminished, but it does mean that there is a difference between political institutions and patterns of interest group relationship. The later Lijphart and Crepaz (1991) argument is based on the association but not complete identity of consensus democracy and corporatism.

Anderson rejects Crepaz's arguments about the benefits of encompassing institutions that incorporate social groups, claiming consensual democracies fragment political interests whereas majoritarian ones solidify them into parties. Moreover, in consensual democracies there is often dissent which leads to the termination of coalitions. Even if this is a strong, somewhat under-founded counter claim, Anderson's is a valuable piece overall; but the data are limited to change over the period rather than a panel, which is a better technique to estimate change over time. There is a limited number of countries, but only with two time periods. It is odd he does not test his ideas using Crepaz's dataset, which is larger and would be a replication and an extension, a more robust way of challenging the results.

So it is necessary to adjudicate between these different versions of the impact of institutions. A lot depends on how much – for some of the post-war years at least – the corporatist variable matters for the analysis. Perhaps right is on the side of Anderson and other critics (for example, Roller, 2005) who argue consensual democracy is about political institutions, such as the electoral system, rather than interest group arrangements and traditions of state accommodation. The other problem is that regression analysis on so few cases, with little switching across different systems, makes it hard to be firm about the direction or even the existence of the causal arrow. It could be the case that by virtue of location, say in the central, more prosperous part of Europe, the countries that happen to have better economies also have proportional representation electoral systems and these have happened to co-exist together without a necessary causal relationship between the two. The problem may be the determinants of both economic growth and the functioning of certain kinds of institutions (for example, corporatism) may largely come from societal rather than institutional factors.

There may be a particular temporal relationship between a certain kind of democracy and economic growth – the success of the managed and corporatist systems in the post-war period, but where the relationship, if it exists, vanishes in an age of the breakdown of state structures and privatisation in the period since the early 1990s, which is not covered in most datasets. In part, majoritarian systems were able to impose radical policies to reform the labour market and inefficient state sectors, options that were not so available to more consensual democracies where the veto players occupied key roles in the government coalitions. Partly as a result, these countries were able to use the power of the state in their majoritarian systems to incur short-run pain, but achieved better economic growth rates in the 1990s and the early 2000s, in the United Kingdom at least, but also in New Zealand and Australia. A lot of these years of growth do not appear in the datasets, when the United States and the United Kingdom were powering away whilst classic consensual democracies, such as Germany, were becoming more sluggish. As the German economy grew again, it is less clear whether its revival is due to the resilience of its political-economic structures, or whether it has imitated the market practices of majoritarian countries, or whether its industry has done this task on its own, independent of state structures altogether. Or it may be the experience of the 2010s shows the continued vulnerability of competitive systems after the economic crash of 2008.

The economists Persson and Tabellini (2003) have carried out the most comprehensive analysis of the impact of constitutions. They are highly critical of political science studies they regard as 'Largely based on simple correlations in relatively small datasets of developed democracies' (2003: 4). Their findings are generated with a much larger sample of countries and more sophisticated data analysis. To allow for selection they use matching methods and regression with instrumental variables. They utilise the idea of limits to political rents – where political institutions may be able to limit the influence of private interests. Presidential regimes may be able to restrain corruption in politics. The main causal mechanism is through the public visibility of the leader, which then limits corruption. Lack of corruption improves policy-making, which then benefits the economy.

Presidential regimes usually have a separation of powers where the direct accountability of the executives to the legislative can limit leaders' behaviour. There is no dilution of responsibility that characterises some coalition governments. They argue electoral systems are likely to have an impact. Contrary to Lijphart, they believe majoritarian systems are more sensitive to public opinion as they encourage citizens to control the incumbent. As a result, political rents are lower. This argument is open to challenge largely through the perverse effects of majoritarian systems, which means that the electoral connection is likely to be muddied by extensive regional voting and the existence of third parties. In addition, Persson and Tabellini (2003) have identified the ballot structure and the number of legislators elected per district as key factors. Electing politicians by party lists weakens their incentive for good behaviour because it breaks the accountability chain as how can an individual be punished (though there could be a selection problem whereby politicians who wish to be corrupt select a voting system that is least likely to punish them). There is the same argument against multi-member districts as the exact chain of accountability is weakened.

The authors say less about how limiting rents and reducing corruption encourage economic growth. The effect is largely because rents reduce competition and create the wrong incentives. There is the same effect with corruption. But they qualify their argument by admitting any constitutional feature is likely to have an impact on corruption, which means the theoretical model is not fully worked out. In the end they advocate a conditional model whereby under certain conditions presidentialism will have a positive or negative impact.

Overall, they find lowering the barriers to entry for new parties and candidates as measured by the number of legislators elected to each district and more direct accountability of candidates leads to corruption, high productivity and the greater effectiveness of public services, whereas the effect of the electoral system is not so efficacious. Some effects are double-sided: presidential democracies have the ability to limit corruption among the best democracies but encourage it in the worst democracies. Large electoral districts of proportional representation systems have more corruption. Majoritarian and presidential systems harm worker productivity, though the results are sensitive to the inclusion of certain cases. They extend this discussion of work examining the impact on government policy (also see Persson and Tabellini, 2004), which shows the governments in majoritarian democracies spend more and proportional systems have higher levels of debt, and tend to exhibit less fiscal control over the business cycle, which points to poorer economic management as a key consequence of a proportional representation system. Later extensions and replications confirm Persson and Tabellini's results (Blume *et al.*, 2009).

Overall, this line of work is a significant advance on Lijphart and his associates' studies, and one that questions the underlying assumptions of the virtues of proportional over majoritarian systems. In that sense, it is not possible for institutional designers to read Lijphart's work as a justification for moving to a proportional representation electoral system, at least not for policy outcomes or even better policy-making.

An extension of this vein of work comes with the work of Aghion *et al.* (1994), who take a larger sample than the Lijphart studies. They look at the impact on economic growth of ethnic fragmentation as moderated by the extent to which the regime is insulated from the pressures on fragmentation. This is a subtle and not necessarily democratic argument, and works in the opposite way to Lijphart and Crepaz's – do blocks to decisions act against economic growth? However, the argument is that political institutions are dependent on economic growth and ethnic polarisation rather than the other way round. Thus high-growth countries tend not to need such insulating institutions to promote economic growth, making the supposed link between more open democracies and economic growth a spurious finding. Proportional representation systems tend to be less insulated, producing the Lijphart–Crepaz findings, but with a different theoretical import.

Some of the problems come from differences about what the institutional differences are between different sorts of democracy; another is that the impacts are solely seen as affecting one outcome, economic welfare, which does not reflect the balance of trade-offs a democracy faces in the light of preferences from its stakeholders. An attempt to reformulate the definitions and to expand the range of outcomes of democracies has been attempted by Roller (2005). She sees limitations to the veto player approach because of the way in which it does not gradate the type and power of the veto. Critical of the typology offered in Lijphart's *Democracies*, in particular the executive-parties and federal-unitary dimensions, she argues 'These designations are based on different logics. While the first dimension encompasses two separate sets of facts (executive and parties) the second focuses on a dichotomized aspect of the degree of centralisation ... both are misleading and imprecise' (2005: 98).

She starts with a description of the content of the rules, which goes beyond counting the number of veto players, to indicate the power of the players. Then Roller seeks to incorporate informal rules in the definition of institutions, which reflects the preoccupations of the new institutionalism. She adds factors of the stability of the government. In the analysis she uses a partisan veto player index, the veto players in the lower house and the number of governing parties as well as variations on Lijphart's consensual democracy measure. She examines five dimension of effectiveness: international security, domestic security, wealth, socio-economic security and socio-economic equality. Controlling for economic globalisation, the level of wealth and ideology, she finds the governmental system as measured by the constitutional veto player index has varying impacts in specific policy areas. The relationship between governing and opposition parties, as measured by the partisan veto player indices, has a positive influence on the outcomes in most areas, which indicates more consensual political patterns appear to influence performance. But the only statistically significant effects appear for poverty, social policy and on municipal waste production: overall the effects are limited. The argument supports the idea informal institutions are important. There is weak support for Lijphart's argument that more consensual institutions produce better outcomes.

A more applied test of the impact of consensus democracy, but outside the example of economic analysis, is offered by Scruggs (1999, 2003). Scruggs is mainly interested in extending the well-known effects of corporatism on economic growth into environmental policy, where critics have been more critical of the environmental impacts as opposed to more traditional producer-friendly outcomes. He tests this by looking at the environmental performance of 17 of the OECD countries. But he is also interested in testing out the impact of consensus democracies on environmental policy. He argues that consensus democracies will be more interested in following environmentally friendly policies because of the larger constituencies for multi-member electoral jurisdictions, which means they follow more diffuse interests rather than the sometimes intense preferences associated with smaller ones. On the other hand, the separation of executive and legislative accountability means governments find it hard to follow environmental policy because of the difficulty of producing consensual environmental policies when there is divided government. Then the operation of federal governments may find it more challenging to coordinate to provide environmental policies. Scruggs examines pollution emissions to make his case. He finds corporatist institutions seem to help environmental performance, but consensus democracy does not. There are some limitations with the study, which has only 17 cases measured at the same time point. However, even with the limitation of a small number of cases, the controls do not wipe out this impact. The factor to bear in mind is that it does not control for some unobserved factors, such as a cultural predisposition to favour environmental policies, which may just happen to be associated with corporatism.

As Hicken *et al.* (2005) discuss, there are only a few adjudications between these two models. Their research on 44 countries in 1997–98 facing forced exchange rate reduction seems to point in the direction of the benefits of accountability-enhancing institutions, but from the way the leaders build coalitions. Controlling for particular regions, lagged growth, per capita GDP in 1997, ethnic fragmentation and income inequality, they find the breadth of the accountability of the chief executive creates a stronger recovery. Those countries where the executive has a larger coalition and with a larger group that select the leader get better growth. And even in this piece of research, there are selection concerns as the factors that lead countries to have accountability relationships may be the same ones that raise growth. The piece does seek to control for this, however. The research appears to support the importance of larger electoral coalitions and there are no disadvantages of cross-checking, but many of the results are inconclusive.

Overall, the debate about consensus democracy reveals the difficulties of specifying and testing the causal mechanisms. One problem is the lack of clear theory about what kinds of democratic institutions promote good policy outcomes. There is a debate between those who think consensus and pluralism are the correct route to more effective policy solutions and those who think clear lines of accountability to the top provide a more effective route, preventing the drift in decision-making and its stultification by sectional interests. Even though the evidence is muddy, the direction of findings seems to point in the direction of the accountability-enhancing reforms, mainly because the tests are better; in particular, Persson and Tabellini address the selection issue. The implication is that reformers could introduce accountability-enhancing institutions, such as directly elected presidents or mayors. They should avoid accountability-diluting institutions, such as some forms of proportional representation, at least from the perspective of policy outcomes.

The new institutional economics

The next strand in the debate is whether differences in informal institutions make a difference to policy outcomes, which implies reforms of informal patterns of decision-making could offer a more constructive route than – or in addition to – changing an electoral system or introducing a central bank. The argument is that reformers need to get over their obsession with formal mechanisms, and understand how institutions operate in practice. The path dependence argument is the key, which is the idea that institutions create an equilibrium that persists even when conditions change. This idea suggests that institutions may not necessarily mean efficient outcomes, but they may ensure that very bad outcomes are also avoided. The key point is if there are variations in political systems to the extent they protect against the amplifications of moves away from equilibrium. In this light, the Hall and Jones (1999) analysis looks at productivity growth with capital formation as a key variable, but where institutional legacy in the form of distance from Europe and differences in government policies and institutions – what they call social infrastructure – influence worker productivity.

More broadly, economists and political scientists working in the varieties of capitalism stream of research (for example, Hall and Soskice, 2001) argue complex institutional forms, including labour market regulation regimes and systems for regulating the governance of corporations, have an effect on economic and other outcomes. They represent a developing set of thinking by economists and those who study political economy about how institutions affect economic choices, whether over investment, labour productivity or company performance.

The varieties of capitalism approach classifies economies into different types. But the project is not just descriptive as there is a causal model to account for the different outcomes. The mechanism draws on a view of the firm that depends on a variety of institutional mechanisms to stay in business. In coordinated market economies, firms reside in networks that self-monitor and seek to overcome coordination problems. These writers go beyond using the formal institutions, and believe informal institutions are important in this process, which are also political because they create binding decisions. In addition, political institutions also variably provide arenas for deliberation so political actors can make strategic intervention to support. The result is a complex pattern of interdependence between the state and the economy that supports capital accumulation, but in different ways. Liberal market economies, like the United States, are different to the coordinated market ones. In the former, the regulation of company governance and a different pattern of share ownership are geared to short-run profits, whereas the latter can sustain longer-term investment decisions. The implication is coordinated market economies, in spite of greater regulation of business, which might appear antithetical to the private sector, actually help business invest for the future and yield benefits for the supply of labour, whereas market economies are vulnerable to short-term pressures for growth and are more susceptible to the forces of globalisation. The account suggests these institutions will persist even in the face of intense international economic competition. In addition, coordinated market economies are better able to deliver a range of other outcomes that are desirable in the form of social policy benefits, worker protection, fairer distribution of income and better environmental outcomes that do not interfere but even sustain economic growth.

Many outputs from this research programme are descriptive – outlining the institutions and establishing the distinctions between the different systems. The main problem with the argument is it is hard to test it out with so few country cases and it is hard to know whether it is the type of capitalist regulation that is responsible for the successful paths of growth or some other factor. Some accounts even dispute whether the systems are as different as is suggested (Hiscox and Rickard, 2002). Other papers seek to test out its central propositions, such as Hall and Gingerich's (2009) quantitative comparison of the similarities in economic structure, which then shows how the coordinated economies have an impact on economic growth.

It is hard, however, when considering the argument about embedded institutions, to imagine policy-makers being able to embark on a programme of institutional reform to reap the benefits of some of these institutions. It might involve re-regulating the relationship between the public and private sectors, restricting Anglo forms of capitalism, and increasing consensus-building institutions. It might involve new forms of regulation (see Chapter 2) of the economy so as to alter the operation of institutions, such as capital markets. These effects would take a long time to work through and would be dogged by the path dependence of institutions themselves, which tend to reinforce old ways of working.

City regions and political leadership

One area where there are clear choices for policy-makers about institutional design is about the economic fate of cities and other urban policy outcomes, partly because of the considerable social and economic changes happening within these areas that both constrain and give opportunities for governing institutions to shape policy outcomes. In the nineteenth century, cities were at the heart of industrialisation; by the twentieth century many experienced decline because economic growth moved outwards to small urban centres on transport links or to developments near suburbs. By the late twentieth century there were pressures for localities to become more flexible in response to international economic pressures. It is clear a range of social, economic and demographic factors influence city economic growth, but what is the role of institutions? Institutions can create the conditions for effective decision-making, in particular by affecting the quality of leadership in cities, which can be directed to linking different organisations across the city and to making effective decisions about investment. There are two aspects of this argument that are of interest: one is in the number of local government units; the second is the powers of the leaders, each of which can be tested.

Within cities, the number of jurisdictions will alter depending on where the boundaries were drawn and national rules about their size, so there is extensive variation both within and across nation states. A small number of units may reduce the costs of coordination, make coalitions easier to sustain and allow stronger leaders to emerge within large urban areas by reducing transactions costs. This leads to the hypothesis that a smaller number of jurisdictions leads to better performance (Carr and Feiock, 1999). Cheshire and Magrini (2009) find evidence to support this hypothesis in a European setting, arguing there would be more energetic growth promotion policies as a result of this strategy (Chesire and Magrini, 2006). They test this hypothesis with data on functional urban areas across Europe, especially the number of jurisdictions in each city. They find a positive effect when controlling for a large range of the possible determinants of city regional growth. The problem is the data tend not to measure the type of institution at work, just the jurisdictions in the area. Greasley *et al.* (2010) also test this idea on urban areas in England, taking larger sizes than the local government units, the 56 primary urban areas, using data between 1995–2005. Controlling for a wide range of factors, they do not find consolidated government predicts jobs and population growth.

The second leg of the argument is more powers given to the institutions of leadership can help that person mobilise resources and organisations, both within and across cities. The idea is that leaders will be able to forge coalitions, creating what some call urban regimes (Stone, 1989), which develop a constructive relationship between the public and private sectors. One person may be able to drive through the changes needed, as Chapter 4 discussed with respect to urban management. Leaders may also be able to lobby for the area, engage in strategic planning and focus on the quality of urban services. This argument draws on a long United States literature on the impact of the reforms on urban leadership (Kotter and Lawrence, 1974, and see the debate on bureaucracy discussed in the previous chapter), which has influenced a series of reforms in West European countries that have introduced local political leaders with stronger powers and direct election by the public (John, 2001). There is a considerable body of case study research that examines the very particular conditions whereby creative leadership can emerge, such as through links to businesses (for example, John and Cole, 1998), but less quantitative evidence (but see Cusack, 1999).

In the United Kingdom there is a debate about the extent to which local government was held back by an institutional structure that diffused decision-making in committees, which in the past hid the party machines that guided decision-making in local councils (Stoker, 2003). The problem is that local councils had little connection to the public, low visibility and weak accountability. A reform movement gathered pace to reform the executive and legislation in 2000 introduced directly elected mayors or cabinets into the English local government system. Early evidence shows that councils were better run and provided services more effectively where they had more developed leadership structures (Gains *et al.*, 2007). These authors use a survey of local authorities in 2002 and 2007 to find out the extent to which the local authority took advantage of constitutional provisions for leadership powers and then correlated these powers with the quality of public services. The problem is that potentially better performing local authorities may have selected more constitutional powers, so it is not a full test of the phenomenon. However, Greasley and John (2010) perform a better test using the same data, but use regressions based on the measurement of leadership and performance at different time points, using a variety of measures and specifications. While falling short of a randomised controlled trial or natural experiment, the study provides some evidence that reforms designed to strengthen political leadership lead to better policy performance.

Decentralising government

The urban example – and also the discussion of federalism earlier – points to the effects of decentralisation on policy outcomes. The argument links to a theme of this chapter – that there might be benefits (or costs) of making decision-making more plural and open with many access points. It is a counter to the argument about the advantages of clarity of responsibility and one line of accountability to one key decision-maker (reviewed above) in the urban leadership and types of democracy debates. In this formulation, the autonomy given to a decentralised unit is supposed to generate efficiency because – as indicated in the Tiebout (1956) model – local units are closer to the preferences of citizens and more responsive to them, providing preferred bundles of services and taxes. In addition, the competition between service units is supposed to enhance this responsiveness and to yield efficiency benefits of its own. Decentralisation yields – in the terminology of Besley and Case (1995) – yardstick competition whereby citizens compare the decisions of decentralised units. This encourages greater efficiency because of the enhanced responsiveness of politicians and bureaucrats. The decentralisation of power might also constrain the ability of the central state or Leviathan to introduce welfare-harming policies (Brennan and Buchanan, 1980: 197–217). More generally, it is assumed that more pluralism leads to more intelligence and innovation in decision-making overall. Finally, a decentralised administration might permit the emergence of local solutions to collective-action problems whereby citizens and groups decide to provide local public goods through agreement. In short, there are likely to be welfare-enhancing advances from institutions giving more powers to decide matters locally and for the responsibilities of the central state to be limited.

Decentralisation is also likely to be a preferred constitutional choice of government, because of the many examples of reforms that have been made to local government, and decentralising power to regions in, for example, the United Kingdom, Spain and France. It is probably easier to decentralise than to change some of the core institutions of government. In addition, decentralisation of financial budgets has been a frequent policy reform associated with the new public management (see Chapter 4). Many international institutions prefer direct contact with decentralised organisations in less developed countries.

The argument against thinking there is a link between efficiency and decentralisation is that decentralisation may be associated with inefficiency and lack of professionalism, which might be due to the invisibility of decision-making and its domination by local elites (Smith, 1985; De Vries, 2000). It may mean vesting power in politicians and bureaucrats of lower calibre than their national equivalents. As a result, decentralisation may also promote corruption (see Fan *et al.*, 2009). There may be wasteful competition between levels of government.

A line of work suggests a lack of clear relationship between decentralisation and economic performance (Treisman, 2007: 258–62 for a review), in particular economic stability and growth. As Treisman writes, 'The results for economic growth are as difficult to read as those for macro-economic stability' (2007: 262). Studies show complex interactions in the data, suggesting there is no simple relationship. The argument is about the benefits of policy stability: decentralisation may act as a break on more reckless macro-economic management by making policy change harder to carry out. Central policy-makers have to keep the commitments because of the presence of veto players. Treisman (2000) examines the relationship between decentralisation and inflation in a panel dataset of 87 countries from 1975 to 1989. He uses the shares of sub-national spending and taxation as measures of federalism, which are used to predict inflation, controlling for previous inflation, the turnover of the central bank executive, central bank legal independence, GDP, the exchange rate, imports, civil war, the number of revolutions or coups, bank lending to private sector and years of democracy during the period. The results give contingent support for the hypothesis: decentralisation is not effective overall, but it appears to lock in either good or bad economic management, which produces either low or high inflation. He makes this claim by examining the interaction between the measure of decentralisation and inflation in the previous period. It is the degree of central bank independence that influences the results. Regional governments help police the centre and keep the central government from interfering with the central bank. The reduced effect of decentralisation on inflation in less developed countries is due to the weakness of central banks. In this sense, the paper is less about decentralisation, more about central banks (see below).

There are studies of the impact of decentralisation on non-economic policy outcomes. The first study in this vein is by Khaleghian (2004), who tests the relationship between decentralisation and public services with the case of immunisation coverage in 140 low and middle-income countries from 1980 to 1997. He measures decentralisation by the presence of taxing, spending and regulatory authority in municipalities and other decentralised bodies, coded as a binary variable. He deploys control variables to predict immunisation, such as national income per capita, the durability of democracy and each year of data. The statistical analysis finds decentralisation positively predicts immunisation. There are different effects for the kind of country: decentralised low-income countries have higher coverage whereas the effect is reversed for high-income ones.

Treisman (2002) provides a more sophisticated example of this kind of work. He calculates the level of decentralisation in 130 countries in the mid-1990s using constitutional documents, which he admits is not reliable but better than any other method, and where the measurement error can be controlled for in a regression. He also sought to control for local accountability by noting the number of elected tiers of sub-national government. He measured competition with the size of the local government units. He examined a number of measures of the quality of government in various sectors, healthcare, education and infrastructure, such as number of immunisations rather than infant mortality, the share of the population for which a minimum of twenty of the most essential drugs are continuously available and affordable at public or private health facilities or drug outlets within one hour's walk, rate of youth illiteracy, a measure of the number of kilometres of paved road per resident of the country, two indicators of sanitation services: the proportion of the population with access to an improved water source and the percentage with access to improved sanitation facilities. After controlling for the economy, the stability of the democracy, the size of the country, ethnic diversity, religion and type of legal system, he regressed the outcome variable on these factors. The measure of sub-national autonomy was never a significant predictor, showing no impact of decentralisation on policy outcomes. Nor did federalism make an impact. There is even evidence of negative impacts, with the average size of area negatively related to corruption, so working against the Tiebout-efficiency hypothesis. Regional vetoes over legislation seemed to pull down outcomes, and the number of tiers seems to increase corruption. This finding is consistent with the work of Fan *et al.* (2009) that shows that decentralisation is directly associated with corruption. More tiers of government seem to reduce inoculations. The limitation of the piece, which the author discusses, is whether the decision to decentralise affects the results because there may be factors that affect both decentralisation and performance, but the author believes there is no effective instrument of control to carry this out. He also checks for the measures by running analysis on subsets of the data and with a different measure of decentralisation. The author is rightly cautious about the results because of the measurement error associated with the choice of variables.

Barankay and Lockwood (2007) try to get over the problems of using cross-national data by looking at education in the Swiss cantons over the period 1982–2000. This also has the advantage of looking at changes in the institutions over time, which can capture the policy choices of this tool of government, as well as using fixed effects in the panel to control for the factors affecting performance. The paper uses fiscal decentralisation to measure the impact and adds in a range of controls. This finds a relationship between decentralisation and productive efficiency in education. If decentralisation increases by 10 per cent, it leads to a 3.5 per cent increase in the share of students getting the Maturité examination. The paper argues that the changes to decentralisation were exogenous.

Finally, in this run of studies, Dreher (2006) examines a smaller number of countries than Treisman but obtains data for 129 over the period 1991–2001, then 70 over the period 1984–2001. The study uses several measures of decentralisation: the number of sub-national employees relative to central government, financial measures of decentralisation, a dummy variable for federal or not and finally a measure for the number of sub-national units. The dependent variables include law and order, costs of opening a new business, judicial independence index and a measure of the rule of law. Then there are the controls of GDP per capita and population. Most of the regressions are cross-sectional except for the measure of law and order. The regressions seek to control for endogeneity by running two-stage equations. The results show the impact of decentralisation on law and order, on starting a business, judicial independence and rule of law. The two-stage regressions strengthen these results. The number of sub-national tiers reduces law and order.

Overall the link between decentralisation and policy outputs is a positive one, and it is reasonable to assume these translate into policy outcomes. The main negative study is Treisman's, but it is hard to work out the reasons for this, perhaps because it uses a greater number of covariates or he has a different measure of decentralisation.

Institutional design and the local commons

There is a line of work that takes some of the insights of the advantages of theoretical benefits of decentralisation in public choice, arguing that decentralised forms of institutional design, in particular locally owned rules for decision-making, can facilitate the production of collective goods. Ostrom (1990) examines the problem of the global commons, the way in which common pool resources, such as fish from the sea or water supplies, generate a collective-action problem because there is an incentive to carry on consuming them until they deplete or degrade. The lack of private ownership means there is no incentive to protect them. In the classic collective-action problem, even if there is an individual benefit from cooperating to protect these supplies, the choices may be structured in such as way so as to create an incentive not to cooperate. Thus the seas carry on being overfished even though the people in the fishing enterprises know in the long run there will be no fish left.

Ostrom suggests actors can cooperate to solve public problems by designing institutions that create the conditions for collective problem solving. Ostrom noticed examples across the world of long-running and legitimate systems for managing these resources, which are part communally owned and managed. The idea is to have an institutional framework that allows the actors to control the institutional design. This does not mean decisions are privatised or handed over to enterprises – the state remains important. Once in place these kinds of institutional solutions can survive over many centuries, such as schemes of mountain grazing in Switzerland based on the communal ownership of property rights, and irrigation systems in Spain, which are highly effective in resolving conflict over scarce water supplies. Ostrom (1990) and her colleagues (for example, Keohane and Ostrom, 1995; see http://www.indiana.edu/~workshop/) have investigated the operation of these kinds of institutions and their reform, such as fisheries and irrigation, which they believe could address key environmental and other policy problems. Often solutions come about by thinking carefully about the property rights involved, such as removing rights to consume, then letting the participants design a system for conserving common resources. As such, the institutional solution to common pool resources provides a powerful theoretical account of key failures of public policy, and provides evidence for the merit of decentralised solutions, offering institutional remedies to collective-action problems, particularly for the environment. The lesson for policy-makers is they need to get the incentive structures right, and a process of careful institutional design is the best way to ensure the incentives produce cooperation to manage common pool resources. There are a number of institutional design principles these regimes have which allow them to survive successfully over time, such as clearly defined boundaries, effective monitoring by a group of people who are part of or accountable to the appropriators, graduated sanctions for appropriators who do not respect community rules and an arena for the resolution of conflict, which is cheap and easy to access. Thus the institutions for managing common pool resources are not guaranteed to be successful, but they depend on a careful institutional design that prevents loss of confidence of the participants and monitors and sanctions those who decide not to conform to the rules.

There are a large number of studies using Ostrom's framework, which cannot be reported here (but see Ostrom, 2010 for a review). This chapter reports one experiment and one study. Castillo and Saysel (2005) carried out a field experiment on coastal communities in Providence Island (Colombian Caribbean Sea), which had been suffering from overfishing. The experiment recruited 80 fisherman and crab hunters, and randomised them into the three treatments of communication, tax and subsidy. The researchers then asked the participants to play a public goods game structured by these treatments. The researchers found the decision-rules, the ability to communicate, affected the extent to which they contributed. This is one of many experiments that show how the rules affect cooperation and provide a justification for creating institutions that promote cooperation. Because the experiment is simulation it is difficult to know what would happen if such an institution were introduced in the real world. This is a problem of a large number of these kinds of experiments – they are more useful for developing theory.

Most of the work testing out on common pool resources on the ground has been based on observational data. Ostrom and Gardner (1993) studied irrigation systems in Nepal, where the authors created a database of 127 systems with different kinds of management system, sometimes run by the farmers, or by an external agency. The researchers wanted to find out why some irrigation systems distributed water more effectively. This effectiveness could be measured and then used in data analysis to see if the governance system was more effective, which it was. Farmers controlling their own water had a better distribution system. But the case studies show there were considerable asymmetries of power in a system where farmers needed to bargain very hard. But out of these bargains came some effective examples of agreements about rules that led to more effective distribution of water. The main problem of the research is how the governance systems were selected and whether this may have made it easier to have a more effective system of distribution. They have updated their work and have obtained similar findings (Joshi *et al.*, 2000).

The analysis of common pool resources is a powerful argument in favour of institutional reform, and becomes ever more salient when considering the current state of the environment, especially the warming of the planet. The limitation of the framework is that not all public policy problems, even those for the environment, boil down to common pool resources, though most involve some externalities. The other problem is this form of institutional design works well when the problems are local, but there are few examples of successful mechanisms to solve larger problems. It may be the case that the solutions to common pool resource problems are a limited case based on less-developed societies rather than complex industrialised economies or the environment at the international level. Nevertheless, if some of the learning potential of designing institutions can be transferred, it may be one arm of a strategy to improve the creation of institutions at the international level to solve some of the current policy problems. The question is how to use this institutional tool, when it is predicated on local solutions. Central interventions may undermine the conditions for its success. The secret is the correct design for institutions: 'a core goal of public policy should be to facilitate the development of institutions that bring out the best in humans. We need to ask how diverse polycentric institutions help or hinder the innovativeness, learning, adapting, trustworthiness, levels of cooperation of participants, and the achievement of more effective, equitable, and sustainable outcomes at multiple scales' (2010: 665).

Constitutional engineering

In spite of the difficulty of reforming institutions, governments make institutional choices and seek to reform institutions from time to time, either in response to external pressures or from the movements of ideas, such as giving power to regions, enhancing the power of constitutional courts and making changes to the voting system. These reforms depend on the knowledge about the impact of institutional reforms discussed earlier. If the claims of many of the studies cited above are true, it follows a change in institutions should lead to the desired outcomes. However, the act of choosing may reflect special conditions that need to be evaluated alongside the reform. For one, reforms take place in times of crisis, which may mean it is difficult to create the conditions for a successful transplant – better to reform when things are going well and there is a good chance a reform may bed down. The second factor is the successful introduction of a reform may depend on a number of minor implementation decisions, kinds of calibrations administrators need to make, which affect the introduction of a constitutional reform. The third factor is it is possible to implement an institutional reform formally in the sense of introducing new rules, but the more informal rules and values that underpin such institutions remain unchanged. This factor is stressed by the new institutionalism, so elites and publics carry on behaving as before and undermine the effective operation of new institutions. The fourth factor is transplanting institutions fails to understand the organic and adaptive characteristics of the institutions themselves, which resist a mechanistic implantation. The conclusion is institutional reform is bound to fail unless it is suitable for the context. Thus attempts to introduce institutions from above could end in failure. It may be the case that institutions are appropriate for certain contexts so the same institution may work in one place but not elsewhere. Fifth, it is likely the introduction of institutions is not independent. It is not possible to separate out the choice of institutional design from the conditions that create a perception of the need for institutional reform. Thus it is likely institutional reform will be influenced by a critique of the existing system, so in some sense will be contaminated by it, either reproducing aspects of the old system or overreacting against it – both sets of considerations may mean the detail of the institutional transplant will contain the seeds of failure. Finally, one of the conclusions of the institutional economics is that it takes a long time for these effects to yield an impact, perhaps 50 years of more, which is usually beyond the time-span of a reforming government and where some countries may quickly reverse institutional reforms before they show their effects.

There is a literature on constitutional engineering (Sartori, 1994), which shows the problems as well as the opportunities of reform. The best known example is Lijphart's recommendation that constitutional engineering can help cure divided societies, based on his inference that particular institutional rules, such as large cabinets, the provision for a mutual veto and that civil service recruitment should be proportional to the composition of groups in the society, can help elites cooperate and trust each other. This seemed to be a good explanation for political stability and thence economic growth and policy stability in divided societies, like the Netherlands, the first study of consociational democracy (Lijphart, 1968), and was replicated in comparative contexts (Lijphart 1969, 1977). Lijphart concluded it must be the institutional rules that matter. The grand coalition, the mutual veto, proportionality and the partly institutional factor of segmental autonomy had a role in causing stability. The problem was that those societies that seemed to be stable, like Cyprus and Lebanon, blew up in civil war in the 1970s, so undermining the claim of the efficacy of consociational institutions, at least at first base. The problem is that consociationalism is both a consequence and a cause of those factors that cause instability. It just is not possible to look at history of both stability and instability to say institutions were the factor. There may be something else at work, like political culture (Barry, 1975).

The big test is whether the introduction of consociational institutions can reduce stability, which can then assist economic growth by making a country more attractive for inward investment. On the surface this reform appears to work. Northern Ireland, for example, experienced over 30 years of violent conflict between entrenched communities, but this came to an end in 1998 when outside decision-makers, including the British government, proposed consociational institutions with moves to more proportionality of appointments, veto points and a grand coalition – just as Lijphart recommended (but note Lijphart's (1975) pessimism about Northern Ireland in the 1970s). But it is much harder to know whether the introduction of these arrangements reflected a wider commitment to reform or a change in strategy on the part of the elites of the divided groups, which saw it as in their interests to cooperate and so agree to the imposition of consociational institutions. And then there is the problem of applying these ideas outside the relatively stable culture of Western Europe to societies where the divisions are even greater.

The crucial problem for constitutional engineering is that examples of success, such as constitutions bedding down, say, in West Germany in the years since the Second World War, are hard to separate from long-term conditions that drive stability, economic performance and the support for those institutions themselves. This is because the impact of institutions is long term – there is no quick push for institutions to work; they need to affect incentives and choices in the long term and the ideas behind institutional arrangements need to influence wider social and behaviours and norms.

Is it the case that no simple change in institutions in one location is going to show us the smoking gun of evidence of a causal effect? One piece of research that does show a change in institutional practice matters is by Acemoglu *et al.* (2009). They have a design that attempts to get at the long-term impact of institutional reform – over a hundred years – and try to model an exogenous shock whereby some countries get one set of institutions and others not, a kind of treatment effect. The example is the export of the French Revolution after 1789, mainly by conquest, which tore down restrictions to trade and introduced a clearer legal framework. The argument is that even when the French troops had gone, the occupied countries were left with the legacy of elites that had been challenged and the legal institutions themselves, which stayed in place. This helped economic growth by reducing the constraints on trade and creating a fairer system of legal regulation.

The design takes economic growth of European countries as the dependent variable, using the growth of railways and employment as the measure. They examine the growth in cities with more than 5,000 inhabitants, calculating the growth rates of 41 political units (21 present-day states, eight German and 12 Italian pre-unitary states). They also look at city growth in Germany as a case study of the reforms. They control for economic growth in 1750 to try to get over the problem the French may have invaded places with higher chances of growth. They apply a dummy variable to code for French occupation (excluding pure military occupation), and also analyse the length of occupation. They use as controls the population who are Protestant and the latitude of the capital city. They use ordinary least squares regression in a panel dataset for seven periods up to 1900 for the GDP data, and five periods to 1900 for the urban data. The results for urbanisation show no negative impact of the revolution, but a positive impact that rises over time. They try out these results in a variety of specifications, such as different measures of French occupation (for example, number of years), different kinds of regression model and with interaction terms. The results are robust. There are similar results for GDP per capita and for urban growth in Germany. The latter allow for instrumental variables estimation (two-stage least squares) to predict the impact of the occupation on the reforms themselves in the first stage equation. Even though there were areas that reformed without invasion, the statistical model shows occupation had an effect. The final model shows the reforms helped improve economic growth through their forcible introduction by the French. There are also powerful results for railway construction as the dependent variable. Overall, the study produces some powerful findings about the impact of institutions, with a variety of statistical tests, different forms of data and checks for robustness. As with any study there are some criticisms. One is the data are not very good, being of weak quality because of the long time period. Another is they have not fully specified their model, for the places the French chose to invade might have had better economic chances. Maybe France, as a prosperous economy, had trade routes with other potentially prosperous places the armies naturally followed, which means the regressions pick up what would have happened in any case? But many of the tests in the paper, such as the control at 1750 and the instrumental variables regression, go a long way to allaying these criticisms. The implication of the paper is not a defence of military intervention as a tool of government! But it does suggest countries may wish to change institutions in a more liberal manner and so reap economic growth from more efficient transactions.

Independent central banks

One of the clearest examples of an institutional impact, and one where there is a clear choice for policy-makers, is the experience of independent central banks. Central banks regulate the money supply largely by setting the interest rate and taking control of financial institutions. These banks vary in the extent to which they are independent from politics in the form of day-to-day control over their activities by the national government. The argument is independence causes the bank to regulate the economy in a more beneficent way than the politicians, who may succumb to short-run influences to win over voters with low interest rates and a stimulated economy, as the model of the political-business cycle would predict. The result of political interference would be higher inflation, which would lead to worse economic outcomes than would occur with independence. Central bank independence thus saves politicians from themselves and allows them to produce outcomes they would ideally like. It is a form of delegation that creates a credible commitment.

One of the clearest examples of governments wanting to capture the benefits of central bank independence was the Labour government's decision in 1997 to give independence to the Bank of England, with the direct responsibility for hitting the inflation target. Such a decision led commentators to praise Labour and has been seen as part of the credibility of those governments as an effective manager of the economy, and perhaps associated with inflation control and economic prosperity from 1997–2007, though it is hard to prove bank independence had this effect in this case.

The literature finds central bank independence is indeed associated with lower inflation (for example, Cukierman *et al.*, 1992; Alesina and Summers, 1993). Alesina (1988) also generates strong evidence to suggest central bank independence produces the same inflation impact with both left and right wing governments. However, there are many other studies that question these effects, especially for less-developed countries, using sophisticated panel designs to address the problem (see Acemoglu *et al.*, 2008: 9–11 for a review). Many studies find independence is not related to economic growth.

This might follow from the view of some economists that low inflation is not necessarily bad for economic outcomes, including growth, though there is some evidence for an effect on growth in less-developed countries.

As Eiffinger and de Hann (1996) note, these studies do not seek to define independence precisely. The other problem is the direction of causation – just because central bank independence is associated with lower inflation does not mean the former causes the latter – it may be the case that countries with a low-inflation tradition, which helps them achieve low interest rates, are more willing to set up central banks, something Eiffinger and de Hann (1996) show in their review of the causes of central bank independence. Countries choose central bank independence for a reason, and low-inflation countries may be able to influence the policies of the bank to have low inflation. It should not be forgotten that as well as determining the wider policy framework within which banks operate, central governments do not lose control over other economic policy instruments that have an impact on inflation, such as taxation, public spending and, crucially, the level of public debt. Put crudely, if government wanted to reduce interest rates it could buy government bonds (within limits). But it chooses not to just for the same reasons it wants to have independent central banks. It may be the case that high inflation causes low independence as politicians need to find ways to control inflation. This is another example of the common problem with institutionalist studies. It also demonstrates the close link between the impact of tools and the politics that constrains their selection.

So it is important to place the argument about central banks in the wider political context, which may determine the success or otherwise of the reform. This is the argument of Acemoglu *et al.* (2008), who use bank independence as a case study for understanding the relative failure of institutional and policy reforms in less-developed economies. They develop a model of the interaction between reforms and contexts where they are introduced. The beneficial aspects of the reform may be more limited where there has been distortion. They reason that 'effective reform may sometimes lead to the deterioration of other (unreformed) policies: a phenomenon called the seesaw' (2008: 4). The seesaw is the greater use of fiscal policy after the reforms. Using data from 1972–2005, they match the effectiveness of central banks on inflation, controlling for the institutional design in the form of constraints on the executive in the form of an interaction between independence and institutional design. They find high-constraints countries only have a weak impact of central banks, as predicted, while there is no effect for the low-impact countries. Middle-impact countries have the seesaw. They discuss case studies, such as Columbia, which introduced reforms and reduced inflation, but where the government increased expenditure. This example contrasts with neighbouring Argentina, which introduced central bank independence in 1991, but its better set of political institutions helped it avoid the seesaw. The important point for this chapter is the authors are not pessimistic about the impact of institutional reforms. This is because reform can work in some circumstances for predictable reasons, not that the institutional design was flawed: 'The general message from our paper is that the analysis of policy reform should start with an understanding of the political economy constraints leading to distortionary policies in the first place' (2008: 34).

Central bank independence is a discrete example of an institutional impact on performance. But even here the impacts are not clear. As ever it is hard to identify the direction of causation, and identifying the causes of the problem may also be part of the response. But at least governments can introduce this institutional change in the knowledge it can produce a benefit in the right circumstances.

Conclusions

There is robust evidence from the range of studies across different fields that show there is a connection between institutional design and favourable policy outcomes, especially economic performance. It would be surprising to find institutions do not matter given their centrality in the way in which decisions are made and how they are likely to affect collective action, which has benefits for the health of the economy, the state of the environment and other desirable outcomes. An analyst would have to have a very weak faith in politics not to think the way authoritative decisions are made would have an impact on decisions, and then to be very cynical indeed that those decisions have no effect on policy outcomes.

Nevertheless, endogeneity and selection are big problems of studying institutions: the very factors that create institutions often create the outcomes of interest. But only an extreme believer in the epiphenomenal character of politics would explain away all the variation from common processes; for that is to be a kind of sociological determinist, of the sort that may have stalked certain university corridors in the 1960s, and even that person was a phantom. In any case, the advantage of studying institutions is they tend to be in existence for long periods of time, and change either very slowly or occasionally in a burst of reforms. So it is likely that outcomes will be mediated by institutions because institutions will tend to precede the other factors researchers are interested in. The literature shows a lack of clarity in understanding the causal mechanisms, in particular on the exact character of the institutional form that is most efficacious. There is the division of the institutionalists into two schools, each of which claims a separate route to outcomes: one believes policy outcomes are affected by the limits to decisions, with advantages coming from decentralised and plural forms of decision-making; the other identifies benefits from the accountability-enhancing aspects of institutions, which are a spur to performance, as captured by the winning-coalition idea and the role of the leader in pushing policy forward and being held to account for it. Given the diversity of studies and their findings, it is still uncertain which way they point. Nevertheless, the strongest claims come from the effects of institutions that consolidate decision-making and have clear lines of accountability rather than those that diffuse power and promote excessive pluralism.

Given the impact of institutions, can policy-makers use them to promote outcomes? The answer is yes, they can, as institutions can be changed by constitutional and rule-making procedures, which are within the control of political actors, even though they are harder to enact than day-to-day decisions. Some decisions are relatively easy to carry out, like when the United Kingdom made its central bank independent in 1997. But some countries require a long process of constitutional ratification. Institutions are hard to change because they are embedded in existing social practices, which often explain why institutional transplanting does not always work in the manner intended. Institutions tend to bed down in existing political and social relationships, which may be the environment that caused the problem in the first place. However, institutions will affect the incentive structure of politicians, so once they are enacted, even if the existing political actors want to continue with the old way of carrying out business, there are incentives that give power to others and promote new ways of achieving public action. Overall institutions have some claim to be a magic bullet, making institutional reform part of the armoury of outcome-enhancing reformers. How far they compare with and complement other ways of enhancing outcomes is the concern of other chapters in this book.

6   Information, persuasion and deliberation

The earlier chapter on law and regulation discusses how the state and other public authorities use the instruments at their command to try to achieve behaviour and other changes they believe to be desirable. The conclusion is there are high costs of this kind of action: citizens and other actors often resist commands, no matter how reasonably conceived and well set out they may be. Top-down regulation often encourages strategic behaviour on the part of those who are regulated and the result need not necessarily promote the objectives of the law or rule, but instead advance private aims. But there is another, gentler way, which can communicate the reasons and motivations behind a desirable course of action that the state or other public actor wishes to promote. It does not have the consequences of having to do something, but instead aims to encourage people to carry out certain actions willingly and without compulsion. There may be kinds of activity that it is way beyond the reach of the state to compel people to do, either because it would be unenforceable or illegitimate to do so or just because it would be impossible to reach people or organisations.

In fact, acts of persuasion might not be so different from other requests coming from the state and other public actors. One way to look at law and regulation is to consider them as a certain kind of information that is presented to the citizens or organisations, which usually has the same qualities of reasoning and persuasion, but sanctioned by authority and with sanctions if not followed (though these may be hard to enforce). The argument this chapter considers is that the provision of information helps the tools, such as law and regulation, work effectively. So there is every reason for the state to present the same kinds of information without sanction, simply as a message that can be received by the citizens or associations as a piece of advice, if backed up by expertise, evidence and the implied authority of public authorities. If citizens freely discuss these messages – and own them – then so much the better. Thus information and persuasion are part of a family of soft tools that states and public authorities have always used, which have grown in use with the rise of professionalisation and expertise within the bureaucracy. State officials are keen to spread their advice more generally as they increasingly rely on expert forms of information collected by themselves and their agents.

The kinds of activities that are purely information or persuasion-based are public information campaigns, which may contain key messages backed up by evidence. There may be – in addition to or in place of – efforts at persuasion using symbols to try to influence behaviour, where the means are exhortation, encouragement and even negative warnings. The means of information and persuasion might be a leaflet, a magazine, a media campaign on the radio or on television, a door-to-door canvassing exercise, putting up posters and an attempt to get someone to pledge to do something. Alternatively, it might be more indirect, through carrying out interviews with the media, the dissemination of research findings, the briefing of journalists and the sponsoring of events. These campaigns are sometimes targeted at the general population, such as health or car-driving campaigns, or toward specific groups, such as the elderly, those in ill health or young car drivers. Hood and Margetts (2007: 31–33) discuss the way in which governments provide bespoke messages, which are directed to certain kinds of citizens, say in the form of a customised letter, or which citizens can access, say electronically, if they search for it. Alternatively some interventions can be information rich. There may be an incentive, but the key to the intervention is providing information to change behaviour.

Information provision is not costless. It needs to be collected, designed and commissioned; but it is not at the high end of expenditure choices of governments. It is an attractive policy tool because it appeals to the higher human motivations, both to government as it uses evidence and considered actions, and to the citizens because it appeals to their goodwill, their willingness to listen and to decide themselves what is the best thing to do. There are also situations where providing information is a no-brainer option. As Balch (1980: 36) writes, 'Often people fail to use a new product, service or behaviour because they are unaware of it or uncertain about its consequences ... In such case, where information is the main gap between the potential and the new behaviour, information is what must be provided' (emphasis in the original). 'There are numerous examples of this kind of information provision, which we do not appreciate much normally, such as notices saying that the cliff edge is near or the water is deep. And people even ignore these pieces of information.'

It is more likely information and persuasion are directed at people who might not necessarily act on it immediately or see it as in their interests to act. So the information needs to persuade as well. An effective message depends on its presentation and ensuring the message is adapted to who is likely to respond. There is a marketing industry, which governments have employed, to try to do this. Why should many activities of government, such as actions to promote the take-up of welfare benefits, be any different to the private sector? Effectively the state is persuading individuals to do something and to see the action as beneficial to themselves, with the difference – and advantage – that the state can appeal to wider motivations, such as the desire to do good.

The main weakness of information and persuasion is there is no compulsion involved, so these messages can be avoided without immediate cost. By conveying information, the public authority might be suggesting that the public need not obey. It is in effect saying, 'We can't force you not to eat high fats, and we will treat your heart disease that may result, but we would like you to stop because there is this evidence that shows it would be bad'. It is possible to imagine several kinds of response to public information of this kind. One may be immediate cessation of a diet of chips, burgers, sweets, cakes and soft drinks, and their replacement with muesli, steamed fish, vegetables and spring water based on the power of this new information. But it is not likely that one act of providing information will have this effect. It is more likely that people will ignore the message because they enjoy their foods of habit, which are provided cheaply and are easily available locally, and which it does not require much effort and knowledge to cook and eat. People cannot observe the immediate consequences of their habits, so they may choose to ignore the message or to think that it is really not so bad. They may even decide they enjoy their lifestyle so much they do not care what happens later or prefer to have a shorter, unhealthy life, positively valuing current pleasure and negatively valuing future costs. This is a well-known phenomenon, called hyperbolic discounting, and explains a range of apparently non-rational behaviours, such as why people do not save for retirement even though they know they should if they are to be comfortable in old age. The problem for information and persuasion is that the need to persuade arises from the future costs that people do not take into account, but changing the way people look at the world is hard because it is so engrained. Information can make people aware of the costs and benefits, and might induce a short-term change in behaviour, such as toward healthy eating; but it is likely that people will return to their long-term pattern of behaviour once the short-term stimulus has been removed. The diet is kept to for a few weeks, and then the attraction of the old foods reappears and encouragement by family and friends takes its course. This is described by the term preference reversal, where a commitment to a new lifestyle can be reversed by even a weak counter stimulus – so the dieter sees a box of chocolates in the office and then consumes them voraciously. Once the diet is broken, there is a downward slide and the person returns to what they did before.

An example was the attempt by the chef Jamie Oliver to change the diets of communities in towns in the north of England, a project called the 'ministry of food'. In spite of the extra incentive (or maybe the disincentive) of a media campaign, many of the participants made half-hearted attempts to change their behaviour and to pass the message on. It is hard to say whether the campaign was a failure, but it does illustrate the limits to persuasion. The other aspect of persuasion the Oliver campaign illustrates is the tendency for people to resist the message, as a kind of reaction, which is equivalent to taking the opposite point of view in an argument even if you agree with the position of the opponent. Halpern *et al.* (2004: 25) refer to the psychological concept of reactance, where people see an act of persuasion as a threat to their freedom. Finally, too much information makes the information itself routine as it loses its effect – the recipient becomes bored with it. This is easily done in the information-rich western societies with many sources of information. Government announcements will be easily lost amid the many messages the general public receives.

The claim that information is important depends on how malleable people are in the face of official messages. There is a long line of research that goes back to the 1920s and 1930s that claims mass media messages are very important, and have become increasingly so in a mass society of more disconnected individuals, which some see as atomised and so responsive to official messages (Kornhauser, 1959). Modern states with their access to the mass media would seem to be able to use this influence to advance wider objectives or just to stay in power, something that came to its apogee with totalitarian regimes of the 1930s. The early academic accounts of propaganda would seem to bear out the power of simplified messages (see McQuail, 1979 for a review).

With such a strong set of claims it is no surprise to find a line of sceptical thinking about the power of information and persuasion, partly in reaction. So Hyman and Sheatsley's (1947) paper 'Some reasons why information campaigns fail' argues that 'the very nature and degree of public exposure to the material is determined to a large extent by certain psychological characteristics of the people themselves of knowledge' (1947: 413). The consensus of the communications literature of the 1950s was people's cognitions and social networks limited the impact of persuasion (for example, Klapper, 1960). If messages are going to be mediated by the social context in which they are heard and seen, they will be limited – unless the purveyor of the message knows how to use the social context to good effect.

The power of human beings to resist new information and to trust information from peers, family and friends is a powerful obstacle to the impact of new, potentially beneficial information. It can also be seen as a useful corrective against over-zealous central authorities keen to peddle the last advances in knowledge. This does not mean messages are bound to fail. There have been significant changes in behaviour as a result of information. Thus research on the harmful affects of smoking has diffused over time, helped by government information campaigns and by other instruments, such as taxation. The chapter will look at the short-term effects of those campaigns later, but it is not possible to argue human behaviour does not change from information and persuasion. The question is how much and over what time period. In addition the academic consensus has switched around again. In a riposte to the earlier article about why information campaigns fail, in 1973 an article appeared in the same journal called 'Some reasons why information campaigns can succeed' (Mendelsohn, 1973). Mendelsohn draws attention to the design of studies, and where more targeted campaigns can have an effect, particularly if they give some thought to the context and viewpoints of the individuals being targeted as well as use evidence about what exactly is it that works. This links to more recent work on agenda-setting, deriving from McCombs and Shaw's (1972) classic paper that suggests the media are important influences through their role in setting the agenda. Later work talks about the framing effects of the media.

This line of thinking about media influence highlights the many practical things governments and other public actors can do to improve the quality of the information, such as improving the clarity of the message. Part of the reason for the variation in these responses to public information campaigns comes from the varied objectives of these campaigns and how they relate to different kinds of factors linked to the commissioning of the campaigns themselves. Weiss and Tschirhart (1994: 85) identify different tasks of campaigns: '(1) to capture the attention of the right audience; (2) to deliver an understandable and credible message; (3) to deliver a message that influences the beliefs or understanding of the audience; and (4) to create social contexts that lead toward desired outcomes.' It is possible that commissioners may need some element of all these activities, or in combination, but the exact formulation will vary according to the type of task and the nature of the group being targeted. The other factor that may vary is the degree of intelligence that is applied to conveying the message. They summarise the rules and research findings, which show ensuring a credible source of information, the clarity of the message, fitting in with the respondent's existing knowledge and the duration of exposure have an impact. It is possible to use some well-known techniques of persuasion that involve implying reciprocation, the giving of a commitment, the appearance of more people doing this, the respect for authority (important in public policy) and liking the persuader (Cialdini, 2001).

As with the chapters that came before, this one reviews the different kinds of intervention governments can carry out by using information as the primary tool. It then considers more direct forms of persuasion and the use of personal contacts from state representatives to change personal behaviour. Finally, it assesses citizens' direct involvement in public decision-making. Part of the aim of the chapter is to show there is more behind this tool than might be thought, particularly as information campaigns often appear to be worthy but ineffective. It is plausible to think of information/persuasion (along with the potential for deliberation) as a more powerful lever than it first seems.

Public information campaigns

The simplest example of a persuasive tool is the public information campaign. Here information is presented in an attractive, noticeable way to seek to change behaviour. This kind of campaign has been subject to many studies and reviews, but, as Weiss and Tschirhart (1994) note, it is very hard to evaluate the impact of these initiatives because of methodological problems of examining cause and effect. They give the hypothetical example of a public campaign on cocaine in the United States use happening at the same time as extensive media coverage about it (1994: 85), making it impossible to separate out the general and campaign effects. In addition, public campaigns tend to happen when there is a particular problem, which means people will be behaving rather differently than at other times, so limiting the generalisability of studies of information campaigns. More generally, it is hard to identify a comparison or a control group or even to know who has been exposed to a campaign as people do not remember exposure in a survey and it is hard to make inferences from aggregate data.

An example of a study is Henry and Gordon (2003), about a 1998 campaign to reduce driving in Atlanta that the city had enacted following the 1990 Clean Air Act. The area had been classified as not meeting the standards in the act and it was required to put into place a plan to put things right. The authorities commissioned a campaign to reduce emissions when ozone was above a certain level. This created conditions for the effective evaluation of the programme because there were some days without a campaign and some days with one, creating what the authors call a natural experiment. The study could not use actual data because of reliability problems, so it used a rolling survey instead. The paper uses Weiss and Tschirhart's (1994: 84–91) summary of the four desirable objectives for the campaign's design and administration, discussed above. They constructed a visible campaign, such as using electronic signs on the main roads the day before the action day. They used different proven instruments in the campaign as it provided information intended to create new knowledge, linking the pollutant with identified health and social problems. The messages were intended to alert people to the problem of air pollution and to change underlying values and preferences by increasing the preferences for alternatives.

The statistical part of the study sought to measure the campaign and non-campaign influences on awareness, then to predict behaviour, by carrying out a two-stage ordinary least squares model with predictors for awareness but not for behaviour. It would have been better they had used aggregate data, but the authors conclude this would have been too variable and hard to isolate the causal effects. It would have also been better with panel data so as to observe the effects over time, but this was not available either.

The study was particularly interested in the differences between government and non-government employees as it was a government policy to reduce commuting by car. The rolling survey interviewed 4,860 respondents over the 153-day period, using 2,935 responses from people who worked outside the home and had a car. The researchers did not find awareness predicted behaviour. Instead, they find driving – in terms of hours on the road and number of trips – does reduce on campaign days. The authors still think that awareness may predict behaviour. They found there was a difference between the sector of employees: non-governmental workers did not show a statistically different reduction of their mileage but the government employees reduced their mileage by 11.8 miles. Overall, the authors conclude that working with a mediating institution, such as a supportive workplace, helps public information campaigns, which is one of the Weiss recommendations. But it does mean it is hard for the authors to disentangle the effects of campaigns from the effects of the employers. The fact the effect on non-governmental employees was non-significant suggests the employers were important rather than just having an additive effect, though the authors argue the employees could not have known what days not to drive without the campaign. What the study needs are some government employees who did not receive the campaign to isolate this effect. Overall, this is a valuable study that shows this kind of campaign does have an effect. There are limits to what government can do with these kinds of campaigns, however.

Another example, which is similar to the car-driving campaign, is about crime reduction (O'Keefe, 1985). This study looked at the United States Advertising Council's Take a Bite Out of Crime public service campaign, which ran in many locales across the United States from 1979. Adverts were placed in newspapers and on the radio. The content aimed to get greater involvement of citizens in combating crime though neighbourhood co-operation and burglary protection schemes. The campaign deployed an animated dog called McGruff to get the message across by taking various common situations which helped 'take the bite out of crime'. Using a panel survey of 1,200 adults to see if attitudes and behaviour changed between 1979 and 1981, the study had a particular focus to evaluate whether citizen competence had changed as a result. The results from the analysis of the panel showed that campaign exposure appeared to have increased what people knew about crime prevention, and gave them more positive attitudes about working with other people to reduce crime – findings which held when controlling for other variables in a regression model (the paper does not say which kind of regression). But the campaign appeared not to have had an effect on people's sense of responsibility for doing something to prevent crime and on personal concern for having to prevent crime. It is hard to work out the size of the effects as the paper does not show the estimator or the variables, but they appear to be small, ranging from 0.08 to 0.1 (about 10 per cent). The paper moved on to look at behaviours. To measure this campaign's effects, respondents were asked at both time points to nominate items from a list of 25 activities aiming to protect themselves and others from victimisation. The aspect of the survey that is most noteworthy is that it mentioned activities in the campaign and outside of it. Respondents were more likely to mention activities mentioned in the campaign, which is an effective test of the intervention. The only activity respondents cited was getting a dog for security – but the author thinks the dog triggered a subliminal response. The paper also explores differences between the areas and the campaigns to see if there is an effect. Finally, the paper seeks to get a handle on the causal mechanisms: those in need of more confidence felt reassured, those with more knowledge tended to behave in the intended direction.

The programme gave people the information they needed, which may explain its impact. In terms of design, and in dealing with the problem of survey-based responses, it is an effective study.

There are a large number of tests of information campaigns and the chapter cannot do justice to them all. Fortunately, there are meta-analyses and systematic reviews that allow some general inferences to be made about the impact of these campaigns. One area where research is common is health promotion so it is not surprising to read a meta-analysis (Snyder *et al.*, 2004). As discussed in earlier chapters, what meta-analysis does is to calculate the average effect size from a range of studies so a conclusion is not based on one study. This meta-review is interested in testing some particular hypotheses, such as whether a new adoption is easier to market than an older one, whether addictive behaviours are harder to move, and whether the laggard component of a group finds it hard to change, as well as testing whether the timelines of the effects of these campaigns are as predicted from diffusion theory. These authors used search and selection criteria to scrutinise 300 studies, many of which were rejected because they were reviews or studied just the workplace. So the total reduces to 48. The average effect size is 0.09, which is similar to the 10 per cent discussed earlier. As predicted, they find the studies show addictive behaviours are harder to change. Media campaigns are much less effective than interventions in a clinical setting – which is no surprise. They were not able to confirm or reject the diffusion hypotheses. But there does seem to be an effect in relationship to the baseline level of effectiveness, with those people already not inclined to participate being hard to move. Snyder, in a later piece, carries out a review of meta-studies, what could be called a meta-meta-analysis (Snyder, 2007). This sums up the findings of nine meta-reviews, from the United States, Western Europe and less-developed countries, which is about as good a summary of the effectiveness of these campaigns as it is possible to have. In the United States, the effectiveness of health media campaigns is about 5 per cent, a finding that seems to apply in Europe too. This does vary as to the type of campaign, with high effects for seat belt campaigns. The population affected will determine its effectiveness, and the degree of tailoring is important too, which is increasingly possible through new technology. There is a lot that can be learnt from the content of messages to increase their effectiveness, for example including information that is new. The paper notes most of the literature does not look to see if the effects are sustained in time, whether people get a habit from the changed behaviours as a result. The literature does not get very far setting out and testing for the causal mechanisms – about what it is about the information that causes people to behave differently. Overall the studies and meta-reviews do not establish a strong or certain effect from this type of intervention. Consider the quotation: 'Evaluation researchers of the 70s and 80s have ... found it difficult to produce unambiguous evidence of impact. The absence of strong evaluation results can be attributed in part to the methodological difficulty of isolating the contributions of information campaigns to complex behavior that is bombarded by many competing influences. … One major problem is finding appropriate samples to permit comparison between those exposed to a particular campaign (either directly or indirectly) and comparable people who are entirely innocent of the campaign's message.' (Weiss and Tschirhart, 1994: 85). So here again is the central methodological concern of this book: the difficulty of showing the impact of a tool of government. Experiments can overcome this, but they have not been used greatly in the evaluation of these kinds of public policies (though it would be easy to do so). These have been contained within political science, which has evaluated the effects of campaigns on political behaviour.

The main examples of experiments in this field are on voting behaviour, such as Gerber, Karlan and Bergan's (2009) experiment that randomly allocates different newspapers to groups of voting to see what the impact was. Those allocated to the *Washington Post* were more likely to vote Democrat. Another example is the work of Moehler and Luyimbazi (2008), which examined the impact of radio campaigns in Uganda, where random groups of radio stations broadcast information about the past performance and current projects of some local governments. The experiment seeks to encourage a feedback loop where the interventions act as a form of accountability to governments.

There are experimental studies of the impact of advertising on outcomes. One by Borzekowski and Robinson (2001) is a randomised controlled trial which exposed 46 children in Northern California from the United States Head Start programme to a videotape that contained an embedded advertisement in the middle of a cartoon, which showed pre-school children in this group were more likely to choose certain kinds of foods – whether healthy or not – mentioned in the advert. This draws on a line of work that shows advertising affects children's choices. The conclusion from this experiment is that advertising is likely to affect food choices in the short term. There was a strong effect for juice, but not for cereal. This study, however, is based on very small numbers in an unusual setting and does not evaluate what these campaigns do in practice, even though it is suggestive that limiting exposure to adverts would help prevent children choosing unhealthy foods.

Persuading the citizens directly

Using the media to effect change is only one way to communicate messages, and it may be one where the impact of the message diffuses through the large number of pieces of information the citizen gets from different sources. It may be better to persuade the citizen directly, by a face-to-face communication on the doorstep or by telephone. Here the government tries to resemble the private sector through foot-in-the-door techniques, but with the advantage that the state or other public actor should be expected to get more respect than salesmen trying to offload their products. So the foot in the door is an effective technique in overcoming citizen barriers. In political science, there has been much interest in evaluating Get Out the Vote campaigns with experimental research designs to see if voters will turn out more if mobilised by a dedicated field-force (see Green and Gerber, 2008 for a review). These studies use field experiments which get round the problem that those canvassed may be more likely to vote anyway, which dogs a lot of studies of this kind. Rather than the treatment – canvassing – being automatically correlated with the outcome, the study varies the treatment to identical sets of voters to understand the impact. The experimenters randomly allocate one part of the sample to a treatment group, and the other to a control group: the former receives the campaign, the latter is left alone. After the election, it is possible to compare the electoral records – which are public documents – of voter turnout in the two groups to see if the intervention has an effect. There have been a large number of these studies, most of them carried out in the United States. Door-to-door campaigns get a treatment effect of about 7–8 per cent, which is remarkable given the light-touch nature of the intervention; phone banks do much less at about 3 per cent. Posters and mailshots have less impact still, but they may be cost effective. E-mails can even be negative in effect. It seems the factor here is the personalisation of the message – people respond to the personal and face-to-face touch. But not all studies show this. John and Brannan (2008) show for the United Kingdom that it is possible to get the same effects of about 7 per cent from both canvassing and telephoning when comparing responses from the same group, randomised into two treatment and two controls. What seems certain is that mass e-mail does not seem to work, nor do automatic calls (robo calls), but that some forms of impersonal contact do have an effect, such as direct mail and radio broadcasts, but this is quite modest. This conclusion is similar to the evaluation of those public information campaigns – there is a crossover here, but it may be the case the more modest effects from experimental studies are closer to the true estimate.

Can these canvassing studies be extended to be a more general tool for use by governments? State-sponsored organisations may sponsor bands of citizens or professionals to canvass the general population more directly. One example may be effort to assist the recycling of household waste, which is important to achieve environmental objectives, such as reducing landfill and carbon dioxide emissions. Households are encouraged by recycling facilities and exhortations by government advertisements and local council leaflets; but it may take a door-to-door campaign to encourage them to carry out the activity, with the emphasis on the face-to-face contact and on providing pieces of information provision about recycling as well as an attempt at persuasion. There have been a number of studies to test this idea. Schultz (1998) conducted a randomised controlled trial examining the impact on recycling behaviour of providing written feedback on individual and neighbourhood recycling behaviour. Cotterill *et al.* (2009) tested for the long-term effect of an intervention to increase the level of recycling in 194 streets and 6,580 households in Trafford, in the North West of England, United Kingdom. The streets were randomised into a treatment and a control group. When comparing the first follow-up to measures at the start, the level of recycling in the canvassed group rose by 4.3 per cent, whilst the control group fell by 1.1 per cent. When comparing second follow-up to baseline, recycling participation in the canvassed group rose by 4.9 per cent and the control group rose by 3.2 per cent, showing a decline in the impact of the intervention over time. The intervention showed the impact of face-to-face groups, especially those with low baseline recycling rates.

The positive results for door-to-door interventions do not mean that leafleting is ineffective, and it may be more efficient in terms of amount of resources used for the amount of recycling it raises. But the results are less encouraging. Lyas *et al.* (2004) undertook a randomised controlled trial to examine the impact of different types of motivational leaflets, but did not find a statistically significant effect. Another alternative is asking people to make a verbal pledge or commitment to recycle, which Bryce *et al.* (1997) find works. A study of student housing found pledges secured through personal contact led to higher recycling rates than pledges through indirect contact or providing information, but it may be the personal contact that makes the difference rather than the act of making a commitment (Reams and Ray, 1993), reinforcing the usefulness of a door-to-door campaign.

Schultz has shown giving feedback to recyclers increases their participation in the scheme. Feedback cards left by collection crews to highlight boxes that contain contaminated material can be effective in reducing the amount of contamination and it also is a cheap approach (Timlett and Williams, 2008, and see discussion below). Nomura *et al.* (2010) show in a randomised controlled trial that giving feedback to streets about their use of food waste can raise the amount of recycling. The study randomised 318 streets into a treatment and a control group. The researchers and study team sent the treatment households two postcards providing feedback on how their street performed in the form of a smiley or a frown face depending on how well the street did compared to the average for the neighbourhood. The results, using regression analysis, showed giving feedback had raised participation by 2.8 per cent.

The conclusion to draw from these mobilisation exercises is they offer potential for state-sponsored groups to engage with the citizens and to encourage them to change their behaviour, not just on the environment, but with regard to political participation and other desirable outcomes, such as low crime and health. But it is likely such attempts will not have a large impact, and will affect those individuals who are more likely to and who have the capacity to change. Recall the Cotterill *et al.* (2009) results that recycling works more with those with low baseline rates of recycling and appears to target those who have recently moved into an area. They also find the impact of the campaign tails off when measured three months later. Canvassing is an important aspect of communicating information and persuading, but because of the limited time to do it and the complexity of organising it, it is never going to be a major tool of government. The effects are modest and tend to be short-lived.

Smart information provision – nudges

The preceding text has drawn attention to the weakness of attempts by government to persuade citizens and other actors to behave differently. Such attempts to encourage citizens to act can get better leverage by paying attention to the techniques of persuasion. Cialdini (2001) has highlighted some of the means sponsors use to persuade consumers and other participants. The idea is that respondents often comply with requests. The secret is in the framing of the question, such as if it implies reciprocity. Getting commitment, as with pledges, might be an effective way of getting a request accepted. Cialdini's assertion of the importance of authority may be a technique that public-sector actors might wish to use. For example, with an airborne disease alert, the public will listen and take notice of public information advertisements. The association of a campaign with the actions of peers will also enhance its impact.

Telling an informant his or her peers have been or will be informed about their behaviour is a powerful form of social pressure. Going back to voter turnout, Gerber *et al.* (2008) carried out an experiment to find out if telling the voter that neighbours will be informed about their voter turnout would make them more likely to vote, which had a strong impact. This idea can be applied to use social pressure to improve public outcomes, such citizens contributing their resources for the good of the community. Cotterill *et al.* (2010) test the idea that the numbers of books citizens donate to charity will depend on the manner in which they were asked. The research team randomly allocated 11,812 households in two electoral wards to a control group that were just asked to donate books to Africa, a pledge group which were asked to pledge and a pledge-plus-publicity group, which got the pledge but were told that if they donated their names would be put up in a public place as a token of appreciation for their contribution. The findings show that making a request into a public act encourages compliance, raising the number of donations from 7 per cent to 9 per cent of the population, a 22 per cent increase in people pledging, whereas there was no difference between the control and pledge groups. It is the form of the request that matters because people want to be recognised for their public acts.

In addition to making people feel good, making them feel anxious when getting the feedback also increases compliance. Experimental work shows that if an authority becomes threatening, then removes the threat, compliance is more likely (Dolinski and Nawrat, 1998). They tested this idea with three groups of 56 people, one group walking legally, another group jaywalking, and another group jaywalking who had whistles blown at them when they crossed the street, showing people tended to comply and be more anxious (when measured by a questionnaire). The second experiment was about illegal parking, where the researchers placed a document resembling a parking ticket on illegally parked cars. In fact, the ticket was either a request to give blood or a hair enhancement product. The idea is the person returning to the car would feel anxiety about getting a ticket and then relief at not getting one, so being more ready to comply. There were two other treatment groups where the leaflet was not left in the manner of a parking ticket and a pure control group. The group that thought they had a parking ticket felt relief, especially when informed they should contact the police. These and other experiments show the power of relief and link it to contributions. It is possible for policy-makers to use information in such a strategic manner.

In recent years, the idea that information may be used in a clever or smart way to encourage citizens to behave in ways that are in their own or society's interest has been referred to by the term 'nudge', popularised by Thaler and Sunstein (2008) in their book of that name. This draws on work in behavioural economics. Behavioural economists regard individuals as cognitively bounded, where they prefer to economise on information and use their instincts instead where they can. This kind of behaviour may lead to sub-optimal outcomes, both for the individual and for society at large.

The best example is savings for retirement. In classical economic theory, the individual generates a savings rate that yields a desired level of income after full-time employment ends. But this does not happen, because people don't bother with the calculation and they tend to prefer current benefits. This is not done in a one-off decision, but without much thought and planning over a long period of time. If individuals really thought about it they would prob-ably want to save enough, but they just do not do it, or if they do they revert back to their old ways pretty quickly. Rather than this being a private act, it is possible to see it as a policy problem. The state may have to pick up the costs if people do not have enough pension or a group in society is very much worse off from poor planning. In addition, individuals might like a helping hand from those in public authority so they can use their current income more wisely. To cope with the inability of individuals to save for retirement, governments have set in place expensive pensions schemes they fund to com-pensate (the financial solution, as in Chapter 3). The nudge approach is different in that it uses an element of information provision to get the indivi-dual to where he or she wants to go. The state or public authority gives a signal that does not compel the person to do something, but alerts them by affecting the way they carry out choices, say by altering the choice architecture, such as the default options on a website, for example. This is what Thaler and Sunstein call liberal paternalism, not directly controlling what people do, but influencing them through reminders and cues. Important is a default option, or ensuring if someone has to make a choice, the default or lazy option is the more beneficial one. The state is in an apparently weak position of seeking to alter the information flow as it reaches the citizen, rather than command-ing and controlling. Thaler and Sunstein give some examples of the types of changes needed. One is a red light that goes off when air conditioning filters need to be changed, so reminding consumers (2008: 234), or an automatic civility e-mail reminder that sends a message to someone sending an angrily worded e-mail to encourage them to think again about sending it. This is not a rule in a hard sense, but the state or other public bodies arranging things for consumers so they have a chance to think about their choices. Thaler and Sunstein are not above advocating a mild form of bribery, such as paying a dollar a day to teenage girls with a baby for each extra day they are not pregnant, so avoiding the perils of many pregnancies among young girls (though this might be a bit too late – it is the first baby that makes the difference).

The approach is best illustrated by an example. Thaler and Benartzi (2004) test a plan to increase employee saving. The assumption is that employees have the desire to save but lack the willpower to carry out a good plan. The idea is they can commit to saving in advance. The study tested whether a programme called Save More Tomorrow, SmarT, would encourage employees to save a portion of their income. This plan starts a long time before the saving programme, where employees are contacted about increasing their contributions. If employees join, they start contributing after a pay rise, so they will not notice the contribution. Then the contribution increases each time there is a pay rise on the same expectation. As they write, 'In this way, inertia and status quo bias work toward keeping people in the plan' (2004: 170–71). Finally, freedom is maintained by allowing the employee to opt out at any time, but the expectation is they will not do so for the same reasons of inertia and status quo bias. The article reports the first implementation at a mid-sized manufacturing company in 1998. Of the 315 eligible participants all bar 21 got to meet the consultant. The advice was tailored to the employees' responses and willingness to save. The paper reports 71 who agreed to take the advice; the rest got a version of the plan. Overall, 162 (78 per cent) agreed to join. Only 25 participants dropped out. Even those who dropped out maintained their rate of saving. The results for savings show those who joined the plan saved at 6.3 per cent, whereas those who joined SmarT saved at 13.6 per cent. The authors admit this is not an experiment with random assignment, so they are observing those who selected in rather than the effect of the treatment. To push this limitation further, the research should see the whole group, both those who select in and out, as the treated group, with another company as a comparison – it may be the case there would have been an increase in savings rates without the intervention, though this is probably unlikely. They reject the idea it was advice alone that caused the effect as it was the incentives in the scheme that changed behaviour, showing this sort of nudging is more than information. There was a second implementation at another mid-sized company, also in 1998. Employees just got a letter and did not have the visit from a consultant. The only other action was a few posters, which removes the personal touch of the intervention and so tries to separate out information about the scheme with persuasion plus information. The increase was a 2 per cent increase in saving every time there was a pay rise. Even this modest intervention was popular. Of those already in the existing savings plan, 615 (18 per cent) joined. In addition, 165 (8.2 per cent eligible) joined who were not in a savings plan. The first group achieved a savings rate of 9.4 per cent compared to 7.6, the second group achieved 2.3 compared to zero. All eligible employees saved 5.8 compared to 5.5 from before. There seems to be an effect, but much weaker because of the lower level of intervention. The third example was in two factories, with different ways of delivering the programme, one with just option seminars not one-to-one meetings, the other having strong encouragement to attend the seminars and the offer of a one-to-one meeting with an advisor. The rest of the firms were the control group. The results show similar saving rates for both firms of 3.1 per cent and 3.7 per cent, compared to 2.9 per cent, so it seems the nature of the intervention does not have an effect, though the authors offer some qualifications to this finding from differences between the firms.

As a result of these separate studies, the authors conclude the programme is moderately successful. Care is needed when seeking to generalise from this study because there are no experimental or even statistical results. Even the final study with a control group does not present a statistical test, which it would have failed. But it does reveal the secrets of its programme – the idea of creating a scheme that appeals to employees and then locks them in by default, not by compulsion. The role of government is to provide a light-touch intervention that affects the information upon which citizens make decisions. It works with the human grain rather than up against it. The limitation is the nudge does not yield large effects, such as increases in saving of a few percentage points in this case.

Social support

As with the door-to-door approach of mobilising people to do things of collective benefit, the interest of one person in another can lead to behaviour change. Targeted support, involving one-to-one relationships, may be generalised to where voluntary sector sponsored by government or public agencies themselves employ people to offer support to a person to change their lifestyle. As Chapter 2 reports, legal and punitive methods of control often do not work. In the drugs field, governments tend to have a top-down and highly legalistic approach to getting people off drugs, which involves enforcement, and then compulsory treatment, combined with prescription of drug substitutes. This makes them look strong in the gaze of public opinion about drugs and makes them appear to be keeping control of the problem. In the United Kingdom this was the essence of the government's ten-year drug strategy 'Tackling Drugs Together to Build a Better Britain' (1998–2008) (Home Office, 1998). So the arm of the law is applied, there is a lot of regulation, and in terms of policy output, it is possible to state there are a number of people receiving treatment. But is there an effect on outcomes? People carry on taking drugs. They use the officially prescribed substitute methadone in addition to illegal drugs. There is not much change in lifestyle; and there remains welfare dependence.

Approaches that emphasise a more personal intervention based on interest in the person and dealing with a wider set of motivations can have a positive effect (McLellan *et al.*, 1998; Wanigaratne *et al.*, 2005). The McLennan study looked at two groups of treatment programme, where the non-randomly allocated treatment group had counselling, managers to coordinate and speed up medical screenings, housing assistance, parenting classes and employment services. The study carried out surveys in three waves, the last one being enacted 26 months after the first. Those in the treatment group reduced drug use, and had fewer physical and mental health problems. The regression analysis confirmed the result. Though it is not as robust as a randomised controlled trial, the results look robust and plausible. Another small-scale study looked at a range of interventions based on the needs of the client, giving them opportunities to do something different with their lives, to try to reinvent themselves with the opportunities to train, do sport and other activities (Askew *et al.*, 2010). The study of drug users showed these diversionary activities did not work – the people in the programme used one-to-one support from the workers on the project to confront their problems and this reduced their consumption of illegal drugs.

These forms of social support may be extended to a range of people and behaviours, such as support for older people, and those who need to improve their diet. Such kinds of action may help substitute for the kinds of supportive networks that generally assist positive outcomes (Halpern, 2004), but the problem is knowing whether these kinds of interventions have the desired effect as it may be the case that those who have the most potential to improve get selected to have them, either because they are easier to locate or more willing to do so, which means observational studies will overstate the benefits of this tool. A review carried out in 1985 complained it was hard to make observations about these kinds of intervention because of the lack of experimental evidence (Cohen and Syme, 1985). Since that time much experimental work has been carried out. For example, May *et al.* (2006) tested out a buddy system for trying to get people to stop smoking. They randomised 563 smokers who attended a smoke cessation clinic into 237 who were paired with someone to buddy them and the rest to a control group who got the same treatment without the buddy. Even though the results were encouraging, there was no difference between the groups, once the statistical model had accounted for any differences between them. The problem might be that both groups had high social support anyway, as the authors discuss.

Another intervention examined the impact of social support for the time before women give birth to see if it affected the outcomes of the gestational ages at completion of pregnancy (Bryce *et al.*, 1991). The trial randomised 1,970 pregnant women with poor obstetric histories into 983 who got the social support and 987 who did not. The intervention was home visits and telephone calls to the women who agreed to take part. The people calling round aimed to be empathetic and sympathetic. There was no difference in the number of births that occurred before the normal pregnancy time period. However, some studies show the longer-term impact of social support. For example, Oakley *et al.*'s (1996) follow-up on health outcomes of a randomised controlled trial of support during pregnancy carried out seven years prior showed improved health outcomes. They sent a 28-page questionnaire to the original participants, managing a 67 per cent response rate of 241 respondents. They found improved health outcomes of mothers and children. Interventions for elderly people generally show the influence of visits (see Hendrikson *et al.*, 1984, and the meta-review in Elkan *et al.*, 2001). Even though some studies show negative results for hard-to-change behaviours, this frequently used intervention in the medical and social policy fields has much support from the evidence of randomised controlled trials.

Thinking, not just nudging

The penultimate informational act the state can sponsor is allowing the citizens to reflect upon the policy choices, and by supporting and providing information to citizen forums. It is possible that nudge messages are rather cynical and might not allow citizens enough input into decision-making. Nudge relies on the notion that the state knows best, has expert information on the policy choices themselves, and then uses techniques to get citizens to comply, whether through regulating behaviour, persuading or nudging. Better to be a more democratic state and assume the best way to solve problems is to decentralise, and give ownership of the issues to the citizens themselves, and to rely on their problem-solving capabilities. This may be seen as an aspect of ensuring collective action, whereby there are obstacles to achieving collective ends, but where cooperation between citizens built on growing trust may allow solutions to emerge. Ostrom has set out this problem and explores various kinds of solutions to this problem, in the form of building institutions in local contexts to create the conditions for collective action (see Chapter 5). This topic crosses over with the discussion of institutions in the last chapter because it is not just information that is the key part of the tool but also an institutional innovation that makes discussion by the citizens possible. It blurs into the account of decentralised networks too, which is in the following chapter. But deliberation may be seen primarily as an information tool as it is a means of communicating with the citizens more directly, conveying messages and influencing decisions, but in a way individuals and communities own and so shape the proceedings. The result should be more citizen energy and commitment to public problems, thus more willingness to cooperate. It can develop into what is called co-production, where the citizen produces public goods, instead of or in partnership with public authorities. There is a limit to complete decentralisation and democratisation, which might even challenge the state, but the public authority can facilitate this kind of institution, ready to provide the necessary support and follow-up.

One example is the initiatives to generate participatory budgeting which have been influenced by an experiment in Porto Alegre, Brazil, which started in 1989 and turned into a world-wide movement (see Smith, 2009: 32–39). In this initiative, the citizens make the decisions on large budgets in a series of neighourhood assemblies and meetings to distribute the money, which in spite of the natural implementation issues and a lot of power remaining with the bureaucrats, has generally been regarded as a successful exercise in popular participation. Much of the writing about the innovation suggests this also led to an improvement in policy outcomes (Santos, 1998: 485; World Bank, 2003: 3), such as the public amenities relevant to the quality of public welfare in the municipalities that adopted it, for example improved housing and the number of water connections for households. The initiative also appeared to lead to a rise in participation (Nylen, 2002), with a spillover between participatory budgeting and wider civic and civil participation, but usually affecting those already involved. Note there is selection at work – about 40 per cent of the municipalities in Brazil adopted participatory budgeting, which might be one reason why there are improved outcomes as a result. In part, these outcomes are also a result of ensuring poorer groups are represented in decision-making, which means resources are distributed more equitably. Participatory budgeting stresses accountability, responsiveness and transparency, which is also associated with better policy outcomes. There is a view that participatory budgeting can lead to better planning for more socially useful resources and for resisting short-run gains such as inward investment decisions, which show little long-term benefit. It also can limit corruption and put in place good governance that in turn improves outcomes.

Such an account of policy outcome improvements – as well as the increases in political participation – needs to be very carefully assessed. These are selective exercises, so are not a random or representative sample of local authorities or people getting involved in them. Assessments of participatory budgeting suggest the particular context matters, and a combination of factors needs to be in place that are not transferable or often only transfer weakly (Smith, 2009: 65–67). The other factor is that it is not clear whether the improvements in policy outcomes come from better policy-making or were the result of redistribution. After all, a centrally imposed form of redistribution could have had the same effect if it was redistribution rather than participation that was driving the improvements. The other factor is the demonstration effects of such schemes themselves – whether the improvement of outcomes is the result of the interest and energy offered by the new scheme rather than the intervention itself, which is a common problem with pilot projects (though participatory budgeting in Porto Alegre has lasted a long time). So the report and study cited above can only make claims that policy outcomes improved; they do not show it was participatory budgeting that caused those changes, which could have occurred anyway, or because of the interest created by the innovation, or because of the factors that led to the introduction of participatory budgeting. It would seem likely the outcome change would be more modest because these special factors are not in place.

Fung (2004) presents an analysis of participatory mechanisms in Chicago. This research describes the monthly meetings that let residents decide local matters over policing and schooling in a series of local initiatives, which replaced a top-down, hierarchical kind of decision-making. What the theory suggests is that giving citizens the space to deliberate allows them to own their decisions, which improves the quality of the policies. Outcomes, such as the quality of policing or education in this context, improve as a result. The approach of the research is to find out about the nature and impact of these initiatives in six cases in three neighbourhoods (2004: 115–72), looking at the initial conditions and following through the evidence. The cases vary to the degree they have poverty and have a similarity of dispersion of interests, though, as the author admits, they are a small number of cases from which to evaluate the intervention. It is very hard in any case to examine the impact of deliberative mechanisms in a way that has high external validity. Each case may be unique. Moreover, it is very hard to work out the causal mechanisms between information exchange and decision-making – empowerment – and the improvement in outcomes. Take the case of 'Southtown Elementary Becomes Harambee' (2004: 142–51), a Chicago elementary school in a poor area, which underwent a transformation under a new head teacher, involving a new name and focus. It then improved its internal governance and increased its test scores. But Fung is careful to say 'test scores do not offer evidence of particularly effective governance' (2004: 150). Moreover, the school experienced conflicts and problems in implementing deliberative mechanisms. The policing example works much better: citizens used the deliberative forums to improve policy-making and the level of crime, which was partly based on encouraging intelligence-led policing. Overall, the book lacks a robust test of deliberative mechanisms, which could have been achieved by more counterfactual analysis or an experimental or quasi-experimental design.

The information tool in its extreme form – deliberation – has possibilities in theory, but there are few robust tests, such as randomised controlled trials, in spite of useful case studies, such as Porto Allegre and Chicago. Researchers just do not know the impact of deliberation on wider outcomes, even though there is a lot of evidence about its impact on decision-making and public opinion (see Fishkin, 2009). This is probably because the focus of deliberative democrats has – understandably – been on whether these innovations deepened political participation rather than on outcomes on the ground.

Education

The final aspect to the provision of information-based tools is one of the broadest and wide-ranging. But it is also the hardest to influence when governments think about change. Education is about how societies and families seek to transfer knowledge and understanding though instruction, usually carried out by professionally trained personnel in specialised institutions for this purpose. Education, both at primary, secondary and higher levels, transmits essential skills without which the economy and society could not function, in particular by providing human capital. Providing more education in relation to the GDP improves outcomes, as Chapter 2 shows (see Riddell, 2006 for a review of the evidence). But it is a different proposition to say whether government can use education to provide messages or to transmit norms that have beneficial consequences. In theory it may be possible to change the content of the curriculum to transmit new messages or to change behaviour indirectly in beneficial ways, or to encourage a change in values, say toward responsibility or toward more wealth creation, for example. This argument assumes those values, even if achieved, will achieve the outcomes policy-makers desire. But it is difficult even to get those changes, for three reasons. One is the familiar charge Chapter 4 discussed: bureaucracies often resist these kinds of directions, in particular education bureaucracies, which often have their own ideas about the purpose and content of education programmes. The other reason is that human beings tend to fend off new ideas even when exposed to them in contexts outside their peer group, such as from schools. Finally, the principle of a liberal education usually prevents governments from using education to seek to influence behaviour directly because it offends against the idea that education should be neutral as to ends. The idea is to give citizens the ability to make up their own minds, though this is not necessarily inconsistent with shaping messages as the nudge advocates claim.

One illustration of this difficulty is the effect of citizen education programmes across the world, which is when governments prescribe the content of school programmes, including classes on political institutions and desired forms of citizen behaviour. But the impact of such programmes tends to be modest, usually limited to small increases in student knowledge (Niemi and Junn, 1998). The reason has to do with the limited ability of governments to change the core part of the curriculum, the level of priority schools give to education and the sheer difficulty of influencing students, who are influenced by their families, peers and communities rather than one or two lessons a week. The main effects of such programmes are to raise student knowledge. For example, John and Morris (2004) report a study of the impact of citizenship education on 15 and 16-year-olds in 27 schools in 2000 shortly before the introduction of compulsory citizenship education. Using multi-level models on the 1,249 respondents to control for the clustering of students in schools, they find that citizenship education predicts social capital, in this case the amount of volunteering a student reports. Surveying the students a year later in a panel model, the change in citizenship education predicts the change in volunteering. There is a less robust relationship between citizenship education and social trust. The link to outcomes comes through the impact of social capital on student performance. Using the same data, John (2005) shows that changes in the level of social capital affect students' test scores. With the panel, he finds volunteering and trust improve grade performance and examination results, with the exception that social networks of some parents reduced their performance. Thus there is a chain from citizenship education to social capital and then to education outcomes. However, overall the effect sizes are modest and probably this is not the most efficient route to raise education outcomes.

Another example is in crime prevention. Education can be used by government to prevent crime, either directly, through schools and their management, or through forms of instruction intended to reduce crime. Gottfredson *et al.* (2002) carried out a systematic review of the 174 studies in this area that meet the selection criteria. In keeping with the theme of this chapter, it is the instructional component that is for consideration here, though it is hard to disentangle it from other aspects of crime control because most interventions in schools are multi-pronged. The review reports the many programmes designed to establish norms and expectations of behaviour change. These can achieve reasonable effects, with an average of a 9 per cent effect size for use of alcohol and marijuana. The introduction of crime reduction instruction in the curriculum is called Law-Related Education. Out of the 132 effect sizes for the programme reported overall, only 15 showed a significant effect (13 would have been expected by chance). There was some improvement on factual knowledge but not much for other outcomes. There is, however, some room for debate on these findings as small sub-selections of the interventions do seem to do well. Overall, changing classroom and instruction activities has mixed effects across the range of studies. As Gottfredson *et al.* conclude, 'Additional tests of this type of intervention should be conducted to shore up the relatively thin findings for outcomes other than substance use' (2003: 83).

There are relatively few randomised controlled trials in the field. One is by Grossman *et al.* (1997), who study whether a programme called 'Second Step: A Violence Prevention Curriculum' leads to a reduction in aggressive behaviour among elementary school students. The study matched six pairs of schools in the state of Washington, United States, with 790 students in the study. After matching, the researchers randomly allocated schools to treatment and control groups. The curriculum was 30 lessons designed to reduce anger – in effect an anger management course. Student reports by teachers and parents were collected to monitor changes in aggression and pro-social behaviours. There was no change in these reports, however, when controlling for demographic and socio-economic characteristics of the students in a clustered panel regression. The study also measured the changes by direct observations of changes in behaviour, which did change in direction. There was a reduction in physical aggression and an increase in prosocial behaviours that – for aggression – persisted six months afterwards. But one of its measures shows no difference (at least, the observed measure was the one that was generating the inference as it is better than a survey), and the other was barely statistically significant (and based on the more permissive one-tailed rather than two-tailed test), with small effect sizes. Moreover, the summary analysis looking at the changes from baseline to the mean of changes from the second and third measurement periods shows aggression only decreased and pro-social behaviour only increased at borderline statistical significance with a one-tailed test. But a reading of the abstract does not convey these limitations. In addition, it is not a full randomised controlled trial either as it used a matched design rather than full randomisation. It in effect was only randomising 12 schools, but the statistics are reported as if all the students were randomly allocated. A lot depends on the initial matching of the schools.

Another outcome that education can help deliver is a better environment. School-based instruction cannot only influence the students, but also the parents. The idea is that students in general have positive views about the environment, but they may lack concrete ideas about what to do about it, such as saving electricity, doing more recycling and so on. It is possible that students, armed with this information, may influence their families. As ever with intervention, it is hard to use just observational data because it is not possible to control for what effects may cause changes in attitudes and behaviour. To address this problem, Goodwin *et al.* (2010) carried out a school-based randomised controlled trial of 448 primary school students and their families in 27 primary schools located in Vale Royal, North West of England, between January and July 2008. The interventions were two types of class-based instruction on environmental issues, one long and the other short, which were designed to increase environmental awareness. One aspect of the intervention just used for the short treatment involved testing the impact of a video, the other involved homework tasks. The outcomes were measured by surveys of students, which showed no difference after the intervention, partly because of rising environmental awareness of the control group during the intervention. So here is another example of class-based instruction being ineffective.

This review of evidence on citizenship, crime and the environment shows the limitations of education-based information interventions. The results of these studies tend to be mixed, or show weak effects. It is not a strong tool to promote change, perhaps because schools have a range of core functions so extra curricular interventions are never going to get the time and priority when run alongside the functions of teaching and learning. For students, these will be special classes that come across as less important to the teachers, parents and peers.

Conclusions

Information remains a powerful resource, which states and other public authorities have unique access to through their command of large professional bureaucracies dedicated to information collection and scrutiny. In addition, experts and others provide states with a large amount of information to policy-makers free of charge in the hope of influencing public policy. With this resource, states are in a unique position to transmit information expertly and with authority. As a result, people may act on it. States and other public authorities are also able to vary how such information is received and link it with how citizens and other actors make their choices. In such a way, the state can manipulate information for the collective benefit. This is a powerful but understated route to better policy outcomes, which is the position of Thaler and Sunstein, who argue for better choice architectures to influence how citizens respond to public and private organisations and their procedures. Researchers know information willingly received will influence behaviour much more than authoritarian commands.

But in practice, information, whether in campaigns, direct contact, media, education or deliberation, is limited by the salience of social norms and the extent individuals are embedded within their social structures. Typically, individual behaviour is reinforced by the immediate peer group and habits rather than influenced by an external source. In the end, if humans do not want to hear the information or act upon it, they will not change their behaviour as a result of a message. So it is no surprise that many studies show weak effects or that they are temporary and reduce over time. It is also expected that the effects increase when the message is personal and addresses the standpoints of individuals, both in terms of their values and consistent with their habits and routines. So the nudge extension to information provision is able to enhance the power of this tool, and yields some positive results for the kind of pro-social behaviours governments wish to encourage. It can also be used to encourage citizens to provide benefits to their communities, with a more flexible and responsive way of providing services. The broader extension to this tool through discussion and deliberation among citizens has yet to be shown to work, except in a few cases, though it may have the potential to do so, especially when policy is more contentious.

7   Networks and governance

This chapter of the book moves away from the direct tools that can be switched on or off to consider the more complicated, indirect and often softer ones, which are harder to control and partly arise from the unintended actions of the state. For both within and beyond state bureaucracies there are sets of relationships, which in part can be manipulated by the existing tools or fostered directly, which has knock-on consequences for the effectiveness of government. The most powerful of these are the networks that link decision-makers in government to other actors, both inside and outside the state. Inside the state are the bureaus of the central ministries and their agencies, which are replicated at other levels of government like regions and local authorities. Then there is a terrain of decision-making beyond the state in the forms of associations, interest groups, citizen groups and private bodies, such as companies or trusts. Whether inside or outside the state, networks may be thought of as regular relationships between decision-makers, sustained by mutual trust and knowledge, which tend to persist over time. Networks have properties that bestow advantages and costs on different actors, which in turn will affect outcomes outside government. Some of the properties are about the individuals in these networks; others are about the aggregate effects of the networks as the relationships add up to much more than the sum of their parts. This chapter seeks to explore the putative causal relationships that arise from networks.

Linked to networks is governance, which is a broader concept. It describes the wider framework and rules that shape how governments and core decision-makers operate. It forms a set of understandings and constraints on decision-makers. Governance can be a negative force because of the many obstacles to effective policy-making, but it can be used positively as states steer for better manoeuvre in a more complex world, allowing them to use practical knowledge acquired in these networks and to use the opportunities that can emerge in a more open environment. Governance is in part made up of networks, so many of the same arguments about reciprocity apply; but it is more than that as it indicates an overarching structure, which is about the management of the governing system itself.

In spite of the indirect route of positive policy effects, governments around the world have promoted stronger and better functioning networks and better forms of governance, particularly in recent years. In the 1990s, governments and other public authorities sponsored partnerships and funding regimes that mixed private and public money in the name of getting public-sector actors out from their bureaucracies into long-term relationships with other power holders, whether in the private sector, or in the voluntary or third sectors. Latterly, there has been a greater attempt to connect different parts of the public sector together in initiatives, such as Joined Up Governance, which are supposed to embody the spirit of cooperation and to ensure public agencies work together to solve public problems. If the justification of those initiatives is correct, those on the ground should benefit. Whether the agencies actually do join up away from the rhetorical commitment is a critical point. Relationships on the ground may be poor because of long-standing rivalries, the difference in perspectives of agencies with particular tasks, or even the intense hatred that arises from past disputes and conflict of personalities. As ever with networks, there is much promise, but a large question remains over whether they deliver.

A network is a regular link between one actor and another, usually as part of a pattern of relationships among actors, which have a common interest. In public policy a network operates usually across organisations in a locale or in a sector of specialisation, but it can operate within organisations as well, such as between the directorates of a local authority, for example. The unit of analysis can either be the individual or the organisation, or even a faction or bureau within an organisation. In practice, networks in public policy are both individual and organisational, comprised of individuals whose relationships with each other comprise organisational roles. As a result it might be difficult to tie down exactly what a network is.

Given the problems of definition, networks appear as a fuzzy concept and encompass all kinds of human interaction. As a result, networks can appear too amorphous to have much bite when it comes to making a difference to policy outputs and outcomes. But the network idea can be useful in demarcating and understanding a set of relationships across organisations that are useful to achieve policy objectives and often vary in ways that are not necessarily correlated with other determinants of policy outcomes, such as wealth or organisational efficiency.

What aspects of networks are potentially beneficial? One is the character and quality of relationships between actors. This is the idea that a networked relationship can be strong or weak, with the idea that strong ties are better than weak ties (but this can work in different ways, as the chapter shows later on). Frequent ties can be effective means of information transfer, which can be efficient for all sorts of reasons, such as giving useful information over the implementation of public policy, for example details of potential problems or ideas about more effective means for delivering policies, or the necessary information to avoid the duplication of activities or the carrying out of inconsistent ones. The strength of contacts can be measured by frequency, but better is the sense of bonding and expectation of reciprocity within networks, which may be related to frequency of contact, but is much more than that. The claim is that networks are associated with trust, which comes from the investment people and organisations put into networks and the experiences people have of each other as they interact over time. Small acts of cooperation can build up into the expectation that people will co-operate in the future. Trust can emerge from someone liking the person or organisation. Of course, it need not always work as expected, as problems emerge in partnerships, and lack of trust may beget lack of trust. A close network can lead to hatred and distrust, especially if relationships were good in the past but deteriorate because of misunderstandings and self-regarding actions that benefit one party but not the other.

The other aspect of networks that can affect outcomes is the structure of the network. This is the idea that networks have different shapes, such as having a central point through which all or much information may flow, or may be divided into different sub-groups or cliques, or be weakly connected with large numbers of isolated points. It may be the case the networks with central points may overcome coordination problems because of the ability of one or a few actors to be the link points, or it may be the case the networks have efficient links between the different elements, so information transmits efficiently across the network.

There are distinct if complementary ways to understand networks. One account is informal, where the network idea is a metaphor for understanding relationships among policy actors, and is often used in the policy network school of political analysis, concerned with describing the character of rela-tionships within policy sectors, such as education or health (Marsh and Rhodes, 1992). Here the network can be seen as relatively open or closed, with consequent impacts on policy-making, but there is not much discussion of the structure of the network other than these features, one leading to closed decisions controlled by a small elite and producer groups, another more open, with many groups and open access to the media. There is a discussion of the power relationships in this example but with little discussion of the consequences for the quality of policy-making and the outcomes that are produced.

The other way of thinking about networks is through the mapping of the linkages by precise measurement of each contact or relationship, such as whether there is a contact or not, or noting the frequency or quality of con-tacts. It is possible to produce statistics that measure the structure of the net-work by counting the number of contacts, how many there are in relation to the total possible ties (their density), the ease of getting from one part of the network to the other (betweenness) and whether certain actors are at central points and have power because of that. This is sometimes known as formal network analysis or social network analysis (see Scott, 2000 for a review), which is a mixture of mathematics and empirical sociology. The mathematics is about the theoretical foundations and measures using this kind of data, what is called graph theory; the sociology is about most of the applications, such as to friendships, family or employment relationships. The study of political and policy networks is very much an extension to the large literature rather than at its core. Most of the politics and policy applications are largely descriptive or concerned with the political outputs of the networks. The large sociological literature does examine the impact of networks on policy outcomes in health and employment, based on the idea networks are facilitative, helping provide support and useful information, in dense helping networks or through weak ties, which are useful for accessing information in other less proximate networks. This chapter is not directly concerned with these kinds of networks, but they do show the importance of networks and how measuring them in a formal way can reveal how the structure of the network can impact on policy outcomes. The question is whether the robust results from social networks in the wider society at large general-ise to policy networks or whether governing networks are different in character.

Network accounts of politics and policy have been criticised on many grounds. This chapter has already alluded to the difficulties of defining networks. It is often not clear what they measure, as the term network is amorphous in involving contact, friendship, professional allegiance, informa-tion sharing or jointly working together, either one of several or even all of these. Not only is there a problem of definition, but measurement presents difficulties. Many of the standard ways of measuring networks, such as a questionnaire recording contacts between elites or looking at the cross-membership of governing boards, may measure a particular kind of contact, say for meetings or for a particular event, but may not pick up the other aspects of the network that may be as or even more important. These mea-sures may pick up something that is unstable and changes over time rather than the long-term relationship inherent in the network concept. Thus researchers know policy networks change rapidly, which might suggest these relationships are purely functional, needed to get business done rather than being long term and sustaining in time. Then there are some well-known measurement problems with networks, which mean instruments based on respondents recalling their contacts tend to exaggerate the ties, sometimes by a factor of about two, when compared to observational data (Barnard *et al.*, 1980, 1985). As a result, it is not possible to rely on the measures used in most forms of network research. If this is the case, then most of the studies purporting to claim an impact of networks are based on shaky foundations.

The bigger problem with studies of networks is their account of causation. The policy network literature claims networks have a causal impact on out-comes, such as power within networks and the kinds of policies that emerge (Marsh and Rhodes, 1992). This kind of approach has come in for a heavy attack that the networks do not have such an impact (Dowding, 1995). The argument is network structure may reflect power relationships so may not have causal properties at all. This would be consistent with the measurement problems alluded to above – that networks are so changeable is evidence they emerge because of the importance elites and organisational structures place upon them rather than the impact of networks.

Dowding is less critical of formal network analysis, which he considers to provide the potential for understanding the causal effect of networks: 'If the properties of networks are to be clearly identified as causally efficacious then only this type of technique will demonstrate this' (1995: 158). But from working through some examples of the use of this technique, he concludes they either make little progress or tend to assume causal relationships, which are tautological. This results from the same problem – the network is the result of a power relationship determined outside the network rather than having causal properties itself. Overall the contribution of formal network analysis is at best modest, which may be part of the weakness of the method as well as the limited impact of networks themselves. If networks are limited in impact, it may not make much sense governments investing in them. The rest of the chapter will examine whether this statement is true.

As with the other chapters, such as with institutions, there are two elements to understanding how the tool works – one is to understand the causal relationship between the process and the outcomes; the other is the creation of the tool itself, which may involve using other tools in forming stronger networks, which may be difficult to achieve. So with networks the chapter reviews the evidence that links networks to outcomes, how to introduce better networks between organisations and whether changing networks has the desired effect.

Provan and Milward

This section is devoted to one study: Provan and Milward (1995). The extent of space and attention is because it is the most important one – or at least one of most prominent studies in this field. If someone says they are interested in the impact of networks on policy outcomes, then most public-policy researchers will cite it as the seminal study (for example, McGuire and Silvia, 2009: 37). So the chapter needs to do the work justice as well as seeing whether it can bear the weight that is often placed upon it.

The study tests whether networks in mental health affected policy outcomes, what the authors call network effectiveness, in this case client outcomes. The authors start from the assertion of the importance of the structure of networks, similar to the case the chapter makes above, seeking to move beyond seeing networks as aspects of resource dependence, or as a feature of the necessary transactions organisations have to make. They argue that networks may have effects in addition to these organisational properties, which reflect how different organisations coordinate themselves: 'effectiveness must be assessed at the network level, since client well-being depends on the integrated and coordinated actions of many agencies separately providing ... services' (Provan and Milward, 1995: 2). They have a particular concern with the integration of the network, which allows agencies to work together to provide services – in this case mental health – more effectively. The authors show such concerns about network integration appear in policy documents as well as in academic research.

The research method is the comparative case study, where inferences are made from a small number of locations. Provan and Milward seek to utilise the most similar/most different case design, but other than citing Przeworski and Teune (1970) they do not refer to studies that use this method of isolating all the variables bar the one of interest (most similar) or of keeping one variable the same and making all the others different (most different). This is just a comparison of four cities in the United States: Tucson, Albuquerque, Providence and Akron, which were of comparable size so as to have enough of the networks they were searching for, but vary according to both outcomes and networks (this is an approximation to a most similar design). They collected network data in 1991 and 1992 from the heads of the key providers in the cities because of their involvement with severely mentally ill clients. They sought to avoid selection bias by seeking to select agencies that were not well integrated in the network. This is likely because of the way in which informants are recruited to study the network, usually by what is called the snowball, the procedure of selecting participants from key ones and then asking them to nominate others – this could replicate the selection of the most integrated members of the network. In this case, Provan and Milward's decision to include a participant assumes a comparable status in the network. But they excluded some actors who had little or no involvement, then they added others from selecting the interviews, what they call a modified snowball (1995: 6). This led to about 32–36 actors per city who responded. Low response rates are damaging for this kind of study as they tend to exclude those less integrated. This means the study may overstate the integration of the network. They cannot draw comfort from the cases being comparable cities because the response rate will be lower in non-integrated networks, so it is likely they overstate the integration of the network in these places. This weakness is probably not too damaging in this case because it understates the differences so does not damage the ability to make an inference. If anything, this selection bias reduces the chances of making a false positive inference (though this could have affected the results on density – see below). They collected the network data from a questionnaire, administered by an interview, which contained lists of all the actors in the city. The questionnaire asked people to indicate whether their agency was involved with another agency with some regularity. These links were about service delivery. It is from this data that they were able to create measures of the structure of the network.

The outcomes – what they call network effectiveness – were generated by a survey – a 5 per cent random sample of clients who were asked about the quality of life, adjustment, psychopathology (mental illness) and satisfaction. There is a selection problem because on the whole it is the better clients who are likely to participate, so again making the measurement of the outcomes similar to each other in each city, but this does not damage the study in this research design. They collected data from the families and service professionals. The authors pooled the data and compared the results. From the clients they obtained two factors, one on their quality of life, another about their physiological status, which explained 48 per cent of the variance. One factor emerged from the families and case managers, which was a measure of the overall quality of life. These groups' perspectives did not overlap, but the authors were able to pool the results, which did put the cities in an order of network effectiveness. But they could not do this for all the variables, because the case managers put the cities in a different order to the clients and families. As a result they were not able to create a single measure of network effectiveness.

The hypothesis they tested was that network integration – and the co-ordination that flowed from it – would impact on network effectiveness. They used two measures: one is the density of the network, the number of ties over the number of possible ties; the other is network centralisation (which sums up the extent to which people take up central points in the network, such as having more links to others in the network). They found there was no difference between the networks according to service links, that is, density, indicating no impact of cohesiveness – or at least their measure of it – on network effectiveness. They then test network centralisation through the core agency, which does show some differences between the networks with less centralisation in the low-performing network and vice versa, and consistent for the ones in between. From this they claim a linear relationship between centralisation and effectiveness. They supplement this with qualitative data drawn from interviews and observations, finding stability had an impact.

From these modest findings the study has had an impact on the claim that networks influence outcomes. But the foundations for that claim are not secure, in this study at least. For one there are the selection and measurement issues. But the core problem is the study's inference is based on evidence from four cases, which have some similarity, but are not controls in the proper sense of that word. It could be chance the cases have the properties they do in the form of measure of networks and effectiveness, and are in no sense a test of the hypothesis, which would need many more cases to make a valid inference. The findings are presented as if they had scientific backing, but it is not a controlled experiment, nor is it statistically robust. Researchers rely on the interpretation of the data to come up with the insight. The authors accept this limitation when they write, 'we make no presumption, however, that the network and system level variables we considered offer the only possible explanation of effectiveness' (1995: 28), a statement that might be read to say their study does not have any conclusions. The other problem is there is no dynamic element to the study. It does not conclude whether a change in the structure of the networks led to a change in performance, only in four locations the two were associated with each other. It does not show whether clients with good outcomes actually found it easier to form networks because they had fewer problems and caused less conflict. It does not discuss whether there was something unobserved that affected both the outcomes and networks.

In spite of these flaws and the caveats (that the authors admit to), the study is extensively cited. There is now a line of work that it has spawned. The field has expanded to examine the impact of other measures of network structure, but there are few studies looking at outcomes (see Provan *et al.*, 2007, who identify 25, a very small proportion of the total).

Studies continue to appear, but they tend to have flaws. One of the best is Percival (2009), who uses networks to find out if they help people through drug treatment programmes (which veers a little to policy outputs rather than policy outcomes). It starts from the idea that network governance is more efficient than hierarchical forms of administration. The study examines the presence of networks between county police authorities in California, which is part of an implementation of a law requiring treatment rather than prison. The researchers carried out a mail survey of the administrators in each of the 58 counties asking for the names of the key actors, including a lead agency director, probation contact and drug treatment assessment administrator, which were surveyed (a total of 97 surveys were completed, with 53 of the counties represented). The dependent variable in this study is the percentage of clients in each county who successfully completed their drug treatment programme averaged across the second and third years of implementation, 2002–3. They have as explanatory measures certain structural features of the policy-making field, such as specialised teams, drug rehabilitation expertise, policy goal agreement and financial resources. Then there are measures testing the core features of the paper: drug treatment expenditures, client monitoring and frequency of communication (the latter is a question in the survey about the frequency with which the office is notified of a missing treatment, measured on a four-point scale). Only the last of them is a network measure. Then there are some controls in addition to the independent variable. The results show the network variable is significant, as is agreement in the network. In relation to the findings of Chapter 2, there is no impact of public spending. There are some faults with this study, such as the instrument, as the survey could only provide estimates of the network character from one person in 33 per cent of cases. Then there are the small numbers in the regression analysis. The main one is that the network variables are measured in a very simple way. In addition, as with other network studies, it is never discussed whether networks are the result of network effectiveness. Given the weaknesses of the earlier study and its successors, it just cannot be concluded from the existing state of knowledge that the formal structure of networks determines policy outcomes.

The O'Toole and Meier studies

Another influential set of studies testing the impact of networks is by Meier, O'Toole and their collaborators (for example, O'Toole and Meier, 2003b,

2004b; Meier and O'Toole, 2001, 2004, 2005; Hicklin *et al.*, 2007). They offer a multi-factor explanation of the performance of public organisations, where the role of the analysis is to identify data that measure each element to performance and policy outcomes and then to analyse it using regression analysis. Key to their approach is the claim that management matters, a theme that appears more directly in Chapter 4. These authors are particularly interested in the relative influence of managerial choices, in this case whether to invest in inter-organisational networks. They argue that, in a world characterised by a hollowing out of the state due to privatisation and globalisation, networks are increasingly valuable as organisations need to cope with interdependence. Managers need to manage outward as well as downward. What happens is that they use networks to try to control the external environment so as to increase their leverage and avoid problems. They call this buffering, which might allow other personnel in the organisation to focus more directly on their job, thereby improving performance. The other causal mechanism is networks might encourage a different management style, perhaps encouraging more decentralisation, which might be associated with better performance. Third, it may mean managers pick up innovations that get implemented in the schools to their benefit. Finally, networking might encourage the administrative superiors to grant more autonomy to the administrative unit. As a result of networking, performance should go up.

They test for the impact of managerial networking in a statistical model using schools in Texas (the same data they used for studies reported in earlier chapters of this book). There is an elaboration of the model where external and environmental terms are reviewed. Then the authors set out variables to control for the external environment and personnel stability so networking can be seen alongside these. They test this model on data over five years from 1995–99, pooling the respondents and creating 2,535 cases, a response rate of 55 per cent (Meier and O'Toole, 2001). The dependent variable is the percentage of students in each school district who pass state-required, standardised reading, writing and mathematics tests each year. They include series of environmental variables that affect performance, such as poverty, numbers of ethnic minority students and the amount of resources a school has. Their network variable is drawn from the questionnaire and is about how often the respondent is in contact with five sets of people: school board members, local business leaders, other school superintendents, state legislators and the Texas Education Agency. They created a scale from these scores through factor analysis. The model behaves as expected because the networking variable is positive, with a high coefficient, suggesting networks contribute about 4 per cent to student performance. They test various interaction terms in subsequent models by dividing between districts with high and low networking, finding high-networked areas get much more impact from teacher salaries and smaller classes.

The problem with this study is that it does not show the importance of networking as a factor determining performance, merely that high-performing schools have a large amount of networking. They do not have a panel so a change in networking could be associated with a change in performance. In addition, the networking and outcome variables are measured in the same year as the outcomes. This could mean that successful schools might tend to network more, perhaps buoyed up by their success or where managers can afford to network because they are not having to firefight low scores. Finally, in spite of outlining some causal mechanisms, they admit they do not test for them, which means they do not guard against the accusation that the direction of causation is the opposite way round to what they hypothesise.

There is a further study using the same data, but over eight years (Hicklin *et al.*, 2007), which examines whether there are limits to the impact of networking, again using network data from Texas. Essentially, it is the same kind of study, also using pooled data. They obtain a similar estimate for networking as the other papers. They also find a non-linear impact of networking, with a squared term as negative and significant, showing the diminishing impact of networking. The effect disappears when controlling for quality, showing that better quality managers discriminate in their investment in networks.

The final paper along these lines is O'Toole and Meier (2004b), which examines the impact of managerial networking on subgroups, on the grounds that some aspects of networking are negative, because networks seek to benefit the most advantaged clientele. This is an extension of Selznick's (1949) account of networks in the implementation process, which shows that actors in strong networks tend to respond to more powerful interests as illustrated in his case study of the Tennessee Valley River authority. O'Toole and Meier use the Texas school district data, reporting the same estimate of networking of 0.71. The new part of the analysis is the regression on, respectively, the performance of advantaged and disadvantaged students, which behaves as expected – in the main the effect for advantaged students is positive and significant, whereas for the disadvantaged there is in general no impact. The problem is whether this is a causal relationship, as it is likely the managers will have stronger networks in richer areas and it is not possible to control for all aspects of poverty in a regression equation. It is hard to work out how the network ties to business actually have the positive and negative effect the authors suppose. The authors see this as a result of business lobbying, but they do not observe this directly.

Collaborative public management

The next set of studies examines the practice of a cooperative public management and its effects, a stream of work done in the United Kingdom and the United States. Prominent is the work done by Agranoff (2007), who argues that public organisations use a collaborative form of public management to try to achieve common purposes and to add public value. He assumes the benefits arise from the cooperative stance policy-makers bring to networks, rather than a more directive and restrictive mentality that arises from management in hierarchies, which help produce more effective outcomes. Like other studies, the assumption is that networks provide information efficiently. The other assumption is that networks are good for policy development, the exchange of useful ideas and providing venues for solving problems. He writes: 'Multiple actors representing different mandates not only overcome information and resource asymmetries, but create synergistic learning and problem solving that might not have been considered if only single entities had been involved' (2007: 157). Because networks can only work through building consensus they raise the game of policy-making and direct policy-makers to difficult solutions. Agranoff is alert to the costs of networks in terms of the time involved and managers being away from internal management activities. Given the effort needed to build consensus they take up a lot of energy and may lead to a sense of risk aversion among the participants. Actors can use networks to wield power and in the battles organisations can withhold resources rather than provide them. Turf wars can be common too.

The method is different to the others that have been reviewed so far in this chapter. Agranoff studied 14 networks, using interviews with a total of just over 150 professionals to generate findings. This is not a structured case study, but an example of grounded theory where the hypotheses are built from the bottom up. There are a number of objections to this methodology as it cannot test hypotheses in the same way as many of the other studies in this book. There is also acute selection bias because all the networks are successful in some way so it is not possible to compare successful and unsuccessful networks. There is a danger that interviewing managers gets explanations and information that both back up their position and over-emphasise the importance of networks because that is what the managers have been asked about. For there is a well-known interviewer effect whereby respondents tend to empathise with the objectives of a research and give answers that confirm its framework (Boyd and Westfall, 1970). Many of the questions he posed to the respondents are one-sided. Consider this example: 'What processes does your network engage in order to reach agreement and ultimately decisions'. This question assumes the network automatically creates agreement, which is one of the hypotheses of the research study and should not be assumed by the interviewer. Surely the question should offer the possibility of non-agreement so the questioner does not lead along the respondent? The danger of grounded theory is that it can be pushed along by these pressures to produce biased results. The best way to get a good research design is to stand back and think of ways of testing a hypothesis. For qualitative research, it is the way in which it is possible to get leverage from it by being careful how the cases have been selected (King *et al.*, 1994). Given the dismal results of the quantitative studies discussed above, a more open qualitative approach might be able to dig into the networks in rather a better way.

So what does Agranoff conclude? He is rather cagey because he accepts the argument that as networks adapt it is not possible to evaluate them according to a pre-decided standard because they evolve their objectives over time. A lot of the evidence is perceived benefits that the participants observe from their involvement in the network. There is some evidence of tangible outcomes he lists from these interviews. Examples include different kinds of transport uses, improved public access to data and training programmes that vary according to the type of network. It would be fair to say these are outputs rather than outcomes and they seem to be things that are important for the agency. It is not clear that this list justifies the author's assertion that action networks achieve this because success is defined as new initiatives and plans, not their consequences. Then there are the costs of the activities Agranoff conscientiously reports, such as time, exhaustive meetings and withholding resources, though he did not find an example of turf wars as found in other studies. To be fair to the author, he does not allocate benefits to all the networks he studies, but there are quite a lot in his check box, which might reflect the difficulty the study has in distinguishing between beliefs and outcomes. Then he does not use the contrasts between the networks to generate explanations of why networks work. In the end, the book makes an informed defence of networks, with useful insights and good judgements. But it does not get us much further than the quantitative studies.

Collaboration and network governance

The studies cited so far are just a small number of the academic works on networks and governance. Authors are interested in locating the argument in a more general statement about the role of the state, which involves transforming old ways of working to more of an engagement with civil society. Hirst (1994) called this new set of arrangements associative democracy, the way in which the welfare state can rediscover the civic route to public action, which can be a way in which societies solve public problems. Other writers talk about collaborative governance, which is 'A governing arrangement where one or more public agencies directly engage non-state stakeholders in a collective decision-making process that is formal, consensus-oriented, and deliberative and that aims to make or implement public policy or manage public programmes or assets' (Ansell and Gash, 2008: 544). This involves a kind of citizen governance (John, 2009), which can have a more representative basis than traditional forms of representative governance as it seeks out citizens, often in poorer communities. By involving citizens it is claimed that it can improve public-policy outcomes by pooling knowledge and encouraging collective action, as well as by getting the cooperation of those who implement public policies (this links the tool to the institutional and information tools discussed in Chapters 5 and 6, respectively). In spite of a large evidence base that increasing civic and social participation can improve policy outcomes (Halpern, 2004), there is a lack of evidence that shows the link between government efforts to create networks and civic society and policy outcomes. Case studies of local initiatives are indicative

(Brannan, John and Stoker, 2006), but it is very hard to evaluate the consequences of such kinds of operation as well as governance more generally. As Sørensen and Torfing (2009: 240) in a recent review argue, 'The output of governance networks can be extremely difficult to quantify, since it often includes intangible results such as joint problem understandings, common values, future visions, enhanced coordination, cooperative processes'.

Can governments create governance?

The final leg of the network tools argument is to find out to what extent government and other public agencies can create networks and governance. To what extent can the state create better inter-organisational networks? This is the idea that partnerships can be built and better relationships among the networks be forged if governments have the will to do so. This can involve formal changes to rules, say requiring partnerships and networks as part of the conditions for receiving public funding, and removing rights of final decision from public organisations; it might also or instead be about changing policies and the attitudes of public actors working across organisational boundaries, perhaps as part of an attempt to improve the quality of policy-making.

The problem that governments face in creating networks is three-fold. The first is that they are the key actors and it would need a change of culture within government to achieve a change in networking. But government and public agencies have both formal and informal rules or standard operating procedures that mean they tend to do business in the same way no matter what their leaders say or do. There are also informal understandings about how to do things and internal cultures that are even harder to change, but which strongly affect how bureaucrats and politicians behave. The second problem is the organisations and the publics that governments want to connect to also have rules, operating procedures and cultures that may prevent cooperation. The final problem is that requirements and incentives to participate in networks may lead to instrumental behaviour. Participants in networks ensure they achieve measured assessments of organisational performance, but which do not lead to a change in culture and ways of working.

The histories of partnership and networking would seem to bear this out. In England, for example, the Conservative governments of the 1990s made it a requirement for funding that bidders form partnerships. So many did, but largely for instrumental reasons, and much of the same pattern of agencies and local competition carried on as before, with largely a lack of coordination and rivalry between organisations (Fuller *et al.*, 2003). A second example was the attempt by the Labour government to introduce Joined Up Governance, which was an attempt to get over the fragmentation of public services, especially their delivery (see Pollitt, 2003b for a review). The general view is that, in spite of much trumpeting and advocacy, there has been little concrete progress on the ground, such as in local economic development (see Davies, 2009). This is not to say good networks and partnerships do not exist, but it is hard for governments to use this tool with a degree of certainty that changes will take place across the public sector. Then it is hard to know whether the changes that do take place translate into desired policy outcomes.

The best kind of approach is an intelligent management of the networks that does not seek to create partnerships and networks from scratch, imposing cooperation where none exists, but builds on existing structures and practices and encourages good practice (see Kickert *et al.*, 1997). This is a more subtle perspective on the role of governance as advocated by a group of Dutch scholars who regard it as the directed influence of social processes (Klijn and Koppenjan, 2000: 136). Building networks may be part of a more general approach of trying to govern in a non-hierarchical fashion and of responding to the considerable uncertainty of policy-making (Koppenjan and Klijn, 2004). The expectation is that the different approach to governing will create positive feedback, more use of policy networks and improved solutions to public policy problems. Much depends on the quality of leadership in networks (McGuire and Silvia, 2009), which transports the analysis back to the discussions of the impact of public management in Chapter 4. There is a careful balance to be achieved between leadership that commands and forms of governance based on cooperation.

Conclusions

Governing through networks is an attractive corrective to the top-down and regulative tools of government discussed earlier in the book. They appeal to the softer side of government, and the willingness to include actors and work along the grain of society and its social groups. By adjusting, working through cooperative relationships, networks make the best use of the capacity of government to change society. But the very softness of networks and governance may be their undoing – they are very malleable, and hard to define, and manipulated by the very groups society is trying to regulate. The state or public authority is caught in a trap – if it tries too hard it faces resistance; if it relents and tries to rule through governance and networks, it will drift and move away from its preferred course.

Overall, the studies find it hard to assess the impact of networks and governance. It is not possible to trust the results, which is partly an issue of the study design, not necessarily the fault of the tool itself. It is also a hard topic to study rigorously, because it is amorphous and hard to define, so does not create an effective research design, like for an information nudge, as the last chapter shows. But it is still disappointing, given the vast numbers of studies in this area, that few have effective research designs that can evaluate an intervention, such as through in-depth qualitative work.

As the twenty-first century proceeds, these pessimistic conclusions seem to cohere with a more general reaction against networks and governance as important tools of government. In the 1990s and early 2000s such ideas were fashionable and governed academic assessments of the instruments themselves, such as in Salamon's (2002) scheme, called in the 2002 book 'A Guide to the New Governance', which conceptualised the different forms of indirect tools of government. It appeared there was a reinvention of government as it came to discover these new mechanisms. The reality is that governments have been less keen to delegate to networks and to create self-governing partnerships. The academic tide of fashion has turned too. Bell and Hindmoor (2009) provide a powerful book-length statement of the problems with the concept of governance and its practice, arguing that the state remains central in many contexts. This pushes the debate back to the core tools of government. In a similar fashion, Moran (2010b) offers a strong defence of the term government rather than governance as the central topic of enquiry in political science.

8   Conclusions

What is the relative impact of six different kinds of resources governments can use to improve policy outcomes? It may be the case that making this judgement is too hard a task given the large amount of variation across and even within policy sectors, and the differential impact of the resources themselves. The tools themselves are complex and protean, containing different elements, and often evolving to become like other resources of government. It is hard to distinguish the impact of the tools from each other, as many interventions seek to combine the tools of government. Most of all, it is a challenge to separate out the effect of the tool of government from the decision to use it, which arises from the political context, including past policy decisions and performance. But this book is on a quest to find the answer. For the problems social scientists study are always complex: the task is to find a way through to make some generalisations, even if qualified ones. Policy-makers seek to impose some clarity on the way in which they make decisions, which is why the use of one tool of government is unusually prominent even in the most hybrid of interventions. The best evaluations reported in the previous chapters have also sought to separate out the contributions of a particular type of public activity.

Partly to find a way into the problem, the simplifying approach this chapter adopts is to split the task into two steps: the first is about the ease of introducing the tool, the degree to which a particular resource can be applied by the state or other public actor, which is partly about the practicality of getting machinery and processes into place, but is also about the political environment that constrains decision-makers, either through the requirements of institutional rules, the pressure of public opinion for allowing them to act and the weakness of politicians in the face of a traditional bureaucracy. The second is an assessment of the effectiveness of the tools, technical considerations, such as understanding the impact of compulsion, persuasion or networking, for example, but which also may reflect background political constraints and choices as to why a particular tool may have a limited or strong effect in the society at large. Each of the six previous chapters has reviewed empirical studies of these impacts.

To represent the summary, the chapter puts these two dimensions into Table 8.1. The device is a guide to thinking, so is not intended to be an

Table 8.1 The tools of government compared

Resource	Ease of introduction	Effectiveness
Law and regulation	High	Low
Public spending and taxation	Medium	Low
Bureaucracy and management	Medium	Medium
Institutions	Low	High
Information, persuasion and deliberation	High	Medium
Networks and governance	Medium	Low

authoritative assessment. Inevitably it is something of an oversimplification given the variety of impacts and differing conclusions of the studies themselves.

The table has one column for the ease of using the tool and another for the efficiency by which the tool leverages the outcome itself. Each cell has an entry on a three-point scale of low, medium and high.

Law and regulation may be introduced fairly easily, depending on the political system, whether it has a relatively undivided pattern of government or is one where there is a separation of powers and extensive number of veto players (this applies to public finance too). In unitary political systems it is possible to get laws in place very quickly, but in federal and divided ones it might not be so possible for the executive to get its way. But in principle, if there is a will behind executive action, getting a law on the statute book is not a big challenge. But the problem is whether it can be enforced once publicised, and much depends on the acceptability of the law itself, the resources directed to implementing it, whether the law is compelling a form of behaviour or prohibiting it, whether interest groups support it and if the bureaucracy and other public agencies are behind it. Then the population may simply not want to obey it and there is very little a central state or other public authority can do in those circumstances. If obeyed, there is a chance that legal regulation can achieve the desired outcome if the action is clearly identifiable and then can be modified on the basis of legal regulation. Even if a law is obeyed, there might still be negative consequences from passive resistance and lack of internalisation of the norms the law is intending to promote. It would seem as likely that, even if the theory is right, it is possible legal regulation could undermine legitimacy and effectiveness by its tendency to command and control. This may even be the case when the law and regulation aim to be smart and responsive, as they either default to the hierarchical mechanism or legal regulation effectively turns into another instrument more associated with negotiation and provision of information, such as with restorative justice.

Public spending and taxation can be relatively easy to implement, but much depends on the state of public finances and whether there is political support for paying for it. Finance is less effective than might be imagined because it is difficult to get money to the right areas and in the right timescale. The problem is that the impacts are not as high as one might expect because of the difficulty of ensuring that the money has not been wasted and does not get soaked up into the bureaucracy, and in producing policy outputs rather than outcomes on the ground. There may be limits to the extent to which financial incentives will lead to changes in behaviour. Of course money is the precondition for most effective interventions and would be used alongside other tools, but where money is the key to the intervention the costs of using it, especially if applied quickly, might be surprisingly high. It works well if there is an unmet or new need that has not been fully addressed by policy-makers, and taxes work where there is an identifiable group that has an incentive to change behaviour as a result of the change. The overall conclusion for the two classic pillars of the state – law and finance – is that they are reliable forms of public action but tend to disappoint on their promise.

Less direct measures might be able to ensure that governments have the means to implement as well as the direct resources to apply to a problem. Reform of the internal organisation of the bureaucracy, especially in the direction of the new public management, is relatively easy to put into place given the control states have over their internal procedures of administration, and that bureaucrats are under the command of politicians, at least formally. There is good evidence that the reform of the bureaucracy improves the quality of administration and has favourable effects on performance and the delivery of policy. Even though it is hard to show the impact of the new public management, and there are disadvantages from wholesale reform, the best studies show positive effects of particular measures to improve performance though changing incentives, such as from performance-related pay and performance measurement.

Institutional effects are probably the strongest in the book, partly because they alter the rules of the game fundamentally. They also affect the conditions under which citizens and groups cooperate so provide a direct route to improve policy outcomes. But political institutions are hard to introduce, tend to have an impact only in the long term, and their effects may depend on the context in which they are introduced. It is also not clear which institutions are the best to introduce either, whether to concentrate them for accountability and decisiveness or fragment them to allow for the cross-pressure and learning. Nonetheless, institutional reform is a powerful instrument of change that is often underestimated and misunderstood.

Moving to the pair of softer instruments is, first, information, which is an attractive low-cost resource of government, and which is easy to introduce, but where just persuasion alone might not be a cogent reason for individuals and organisations to change their behaviour. But there may be more potential in this set of tools than might at first be thought, as there can be power in well-crafted information signals. The leverage increases when public actors develop the skills to influence the choices of citizens, through nudging them to a preferred course of action. It may also be the case that when citizens get the opportunity to debate public matters and to take decisions into their own hands, they can influence outcomes by making and delivering policies themselves.

Networks and governance are an easier tool for governments to introduce, at least superficially in the form of partnerships and networks between public and private organisations, less so the deeper networks that are core to policy outcomes. The literature makes strong claims about their importance, but the research does not substantiate them. The end result is that there might not be much substance to these networks. Their very fluidity and lack of substance means they find it hard to influence policy and so encourage desired forms of behaviour. They may lack punch and do not change the incentives of powerful actors so much from what they were before. What networks may produce is symbolic policy action without much impact on policy outcomes.

Overall, the evidence for the resources of government is patchy, not pointing to universal efficaciousness of the main things governments do, nor reducing to total pessimism about their effects either. Silver bullets, unsurprisingly, do not exist as there is no tool of government or change process that is both easy to introduce and highly effective. One conclusion to draw is that a good number of the processes over which governments have direct control are just those where the range or impact is more limited, such as finance and law/regulation. The types of impact where government control is indirect are the ones where there are the most gains to be had, which is with the non-standard instruments. So public authorities need to work hard at the things they control the least and leave more alone the tools under their direct command. Governments may need to move away from direct interventions and toward ways of creating virtuous circles of improvement and self-organisation by the newer light-touch interventions.

But it is not that simple. There are usually combinations of activities that need attention. Some factors need to be present in a limited degree: for example, moderate levels of financial intervention and legal control are necessary conditions for effective implementation. Another complication is that countries and sectors may be at very different starting points so need different amounts of provision. The assumption is that most sectors of activity have had some attention, so the question is what more they need. In the case of necessary conditions, it is possible to list out those needed, but only finance has this characteristic (and again not in all cases); all others are choices that can or cannot be added to achieve some change. Another way of looking at the problem of which tools to use is to talk about the different combinations of processes which can be combined to create sufficiency. The development of the tools themselves encourages this perspective, whereby most start with a simple formulation, then adapt to take account of complexity. Thus regulation gets overtaken by responsive regulation and moves closer to network governance; in a similar fashion institutions develop more informal ways of working.

The book's argument, however, is there are fundamental differences between the approaches, and it resists the commonsense claim that all governments have to do is a bit more of everything or to adapt the tools so they resemble each other. This is because of the advantages and logic of essentialism whereby tools lose their distinctiveness and effectiveness if they in effect turn into many elements. The argument the book presents is the tools are an approach to a problem that focuses attention, which has both strengths and weaknesses. Tools that depend on a more top-down approach are hard to use in combination with networks and deliberation. Governments need to choose between using the strong approach of finance, laws and performance management and a softer more indirect approach of changing the information flows between citizens and creating self-sustaining networks of cooperation from institutional reform. Although the evidence points toward the latter, the results are not clear cut, for not all forms of indirect activity have an influence as the critical perspective on networks would seem to indicate, whereas the more top-down approach of hierarchical management does seem to have stronger effects than would be expected from a critique of these methods that appeared in the chapter on law and regulation. In seems that the top-down approach works better within the state, but not so much to people and organisations outside it, such as with law/regulation and public finance. But not all bottom-up approaches work either, as the chapter on networks/governance shows. The key problem for the state or other public authority is to work out the right balance of direction and responsiveness in its management of the tools, which vary with the tools themselves and according to the problems governments face.

One key problem is it is often not possible with the techniques of social science research to make inferences between cause and effect so as to find out when and under what conditions the tools work. The problems of endogeneity and poor measurement dog many studies of this book. The book may be read as a plea for better forms of evaluation, in particular randomised controlled trials, which are a much more robust method of making an inference about the impact of government than other methods. But the book also finds it is difficult to disentangle the different elements at play – even with a well-designed randomised controlled trial. In that sense this book has some of the pessimism of contemporary social science. But it would not be right not to come to a final verdict about which tools to use less and which to use more. For in the end well-designed studies do add to knowledge. So what is the best case that can be made for the right toolkit? What are the recommendations for policy-makers?

The best way to answer these questions is with some easy conclusions first and some more difficult ones later on. The first is that overreliance on the top-down tools of finance and law/regulation is likely to be counterproductive. This is because an overuse of the tool brings out the contradictions with its model of causation. So the overuse of public finance will crowd out other forms of motivation, use up the valuable coffers of the state and have poor value from public policies. This is an overreliance on an economic or financial model of human behaviour. Overuse of the law will lead to loss of legitimacy, resistance from the compliers and a lack of intelligence in the use of the state. The end result is an overreliance on a top-down model of public action, which may lead to the demand for more responsive government, which can be entertained in a more moderate use of the law and regulation. Thus the sparing and economic use of these two tools is an important necessary condition for successful implementation and the achievement of desired policy outcomes.

There is much to say in defence of the third tool of government as there are gains to be had from careful attention to public management and to the incentives of the bureaucrats. There may be more benefits to come in the future from retooling the bureaucracy, such as taking advantage of new technology and creating better e-government (Dunleavy *et al.*, 2006b). There are also gains to be had from effective performance management (Boyne, 2010a). Governments need to think through their delivery chains and to get a level of responsiveness from the bureaucracy. The feedback loop to citizens needs to be in place to create a responsive form of administration. But there is no nirvana to be reached from bureaucratic reform, especially if relied upon too much. So the smart use of the bureaucracy tool is the next recommendation.

In spite of the attractions of a different way of working, the networks paradigm is a very poor choice for investment by governments wanting to improve the delivery of their policies. The evidence is just not there for the effectiveness of this weak tool. Perhaps it suffers from lack of focus and is too malleable in the face of organisational rivalry. The danger is it might increase the bureaucratic tangle and lose the focus of governments keen to implement their policies. So avoiding too much reliance on networks is a sensible piece of advice for policy-makers.

So having knocked the skittles down, what is left? Well, it is the final two, information and institutions. Information is the surprise in the pack, the joker with more power than might have been thought. Who would have thought the power to provide information, thinking about how it affects the choices of governments, and how citizens engage with policy-makers and structure their choices, would have such an impact? But it does, partly because of the way in which individuals can respond to well-crafted information cues. In one sense, many of the other tools of government actually at bottom become informational given difficulties of enforcement and control. The information cue brings together the legitimacy of democratic government and the intelligence in crafting information signals so individuals are nudged to make the right choices. In this way, governments get leverage for not a great deal of cost. At their best these forms of crafted information flows can be moderated and shaped by citizens themselves, who can reflect and debate on the key public issues of the day. It is possible, however, to overstate the impact of this tool as its effect sizes are not high, but policy-makers should use it more cleverly than they do at present.

The final word goes to institutions. If there is a secure finding in the economics literature, then it is that institutions matter in securing the means for citizen cooperation, in facilitating responsive government and in fostering collective action. The problem is that it takes a long time to achieve these results and the guess is that most policy-makers would not want to wait the several decades needed to reap the rewards. There is also the problem that institutional reform is costly, does not gain votes and can easily be messed up. But it is still worth doing and can be a legacy of a government that outlives many of its typical short-term initiatives, such as for job training or local economic development. So the final message of the book is this: if governments want to prioritise where they invest their capacity for improving policy outcomes, they should sharpen their means of communicating information to citizens and engage in institutional reform. When combined with the smarter public management devices, there is a set of powerful tools for governments to use to improve policy outcomes. It requires governments to move away from their classic means of intervention and to use effectively these subtler and smarter resources. In this way, governments may avoid the waste of public resources and overregulation of society of previous decades by acting in ways that facilitate long-term change.

Glossary

Agent One actor in the principal–agent model. The agent is commissioned by the **principal** to provide something. But the agent may wish to shirk the task and can use access to knowledge to prevent the principal from monitoring the agent effectively.

Analysis The process of investigating data in order to test a **hypothesis**.

Asymptotic Where the data have random properties (more precisely: relating to a value that approaches, but never crosses, some set point, often zero).

Before-and-after study An evaluation of a policy that compares outcomes before and after the **intervention** without the aid of a comparison or **control group**.

Behavioural economics A branch of economics that stresses the cognitive influences and limits on human behaviour. By stressing the use of judgement and heuristics, it is thought to depart from the classic rational model of decision-making.

Bias The difference between an estimated effect and its true influence.

Case A unit of **observation**, like an individual, region or country.

Clustered standard errors **Standard errors** that are adjusted to account for the **correlations** between the **errors** of subjects in certain locations or units of study.

Clustering The nesting of units in certain locations or units of study, which may require **clustered standard errors**.

Coefficient A number that multiplies an **independent variable**, translating it into a unit of the **dependent variable**, thereby measuring the impact of an **intervention** or process, often referred to by the term **effect size**.

Cohort study A study that surveys the same individuals over a long time-period – similar to a **panel**.

Consociational A form of democracy that incorporates the elites of divided social groups into a coalition government.

Control (or control variable) A **variable** or measure that influences the values of the **dependent variable** but does not test a core **hypothesis** of the research. Controls need to be included to avoid **biased** or **spurious** findings.

Control group One of the groups randomised as part of a **randomised controlled trial**. The control group does not get the **intervention** so may be used a base from which to compare the impact of the intervention in the **treatment group**.

Corporatism   A form of political decision-making that entrenches the role of trades unions and businesses, characteristic of Scandinavian countries.

Correlation   The degree of association between two **variables**, usually with interval data.

Counterfactual   A piece of information or inference that shows what would have happened in the absence of an **intervention** or event.

Cross-cohort study   Involves the **analysis** of two similar **cohort studies**.

Crowding out   A term that describes the way in which beneficial actions may be driven out by the poor management of incentives. It can refer to private sector investment being crowded out by too large a public sector or where altruistic acts are made unattractive by rewarding them with money.

Curvilinear   A relationship between two **variables** which is not directly proportional. In other words, the relationship is non-linear, and therefore curved.

Data dredging   The practice of trying out different combinations of **variables** and specifications in **regression** analysis so that the **hypothesis** is developed on the basis of observing a **correlation** in the data.

Data reduction   The process of finding a common or underlying **variable** from a set of observed variables. There is a family of techniques, including **factor analysis**.

Deadweight cost   The extent to which the value and impact of a tax are reduced because of its side effects.

Dependent variable   A **variable** that measures what the research seeks to explain.

Determinist   A social science perspective (or person) that assumes that the phenomenon under question is largely or completely influenced by an underlying economic interest or set of social relationships.

Difference-of-difference method   A way of measuring the impact of an **intervention** by taking the difference for the **intervention** or **treatment group** over time, and subtracting the difference of a group that did not receive the **intervention**.

Dummy variable   A **variable** that takes the values of zero and one, and is used in **regression** analysis to assess the impact of an **intervention**.

Effect size   The extent to which the **independent variable** of interest affects the **dependent variable**, usually expressed as a standardised measure. Also a short-hand term to describe the effectiveness of an **intervention**, which may vary between low or high depending on prior expectations.

Endogeneity   When the **independent variable** in a **regression** is not independent but **correlated** with the errors, so that it is not possible to do the **analysis** without **biasing** the results.

Errors   The values in a regression that are not explained by the **variables** and so are assumed to be random.

Estimator A formula or function that provides estimates of a **parameter** from a population.

Experiment A method of research where who or where gets an **intervention** or treatment is randomly different from a **control group**. This includes **natural experiments** and **randomised controlled trials**.

External validity The extent to which research findings may be generalised to other cases.

Factor analysis A form of **data reduction**, whereby **regression** is used to reduce the number of **variables** to a lesser number of factors based on their common variability.

Fixed effects Describes a statistical model where the explanatory **variables** are not assumed to be random. Fixed effects models in panels have additional variables for each unit to control for unobserved heterogeneity.

Gaming Where the organisation arranges its internal procedures to meet a target but without the change in behaviour that the designer of the target intended.

Hawthorne effect The impact of a researcher observing an **intervention** or process, which can be confused with the **intervention** and process itself.

Hyperbolic discounting The preference for a small immediate gain over a larger deferred one.

Hypothesis A statement of the prediction that a social scientist wishes to test.

Impute To estimate a value for **missing cases** using other information in the dataset.

Independent variables Variables measuring what the researcher considers as causes of a phenomenon under consideration; commonly they are tested to see if they predict levels of the **dependent variable**.

Inference Asserting a relationship between two **variables**.

Influence statistics Measures of the impact of a **case** or cases on the estimates provided by a statistical or **regression** model, often carried out by removing one case from the analysis and comparing the results. These measures can be used to find out about the **robustness** of a model and help correct for **bias**.

Instrument A variable that is used in the first stage of a **two-stage least squares regression** which is correlated with the **variable** suspected of **endogeneity** but not the **errors**.

Interaction term An **independent variable** used in **regression analysis** that is created by multiplying two or more of the existing **independent variables**. Interaction terms produce **coefficients** and **standard errors** that estimate the effect of one independent variable moderated by another.

Internal validity The extent to which research findings represent the actual causal relationship.

Interval data Data where the units of measure are on a continuous scale, for example units of income and years of education.

Interrupted time series   A method for finding out whether a population or area that gets an intervention improves when compared to a comparison group. It performs **time series** analysis on the two groups to see if one group's outcomes change at the point of or shortly after the **intervention**.

Intervention   The means by which an agency seeks to change behaviour or outcomes in a population. In an **experiment**, the **treatment group** receives the intervention.

Marginal effect   Change in predicted probability of a **dependent variable** for a unit change in the **independent variable**.

Matching   A technique that seeks to replicate **experiments** when the data are **observational** by selecting a matched sample based on demographic characteristics from the dataset of those who do not experience an **intervention** or condition. It is possible to do **regression** on the sub-sample.

Measurement error   The difference between the actual and measured value.

Meta-analysis   A **systematic review** and estimation of the effects of an **intervention** from a group of studies, which may involve calculating the **effect sizes** and **standard errors**.

Micro data   Data measured at the level of individual respondents, such as by a survey.

Missing cases   Cases that are not present in a dataset because of, for example, gaps in official data or non-responses to a questionnaire. This can reduce the number of observations in a dataset, and may **bias** the results if the cases are not missing at random, meaning some underlying **variable** or variables affect their inclusion. The use of techniques to **impute** the data can overcome the problem.

Model   a) A short-hand to refer to the statistical model that is used to explain a **dependent variable**; or b) a simplified representation of putative relationships in the world, which can be mathematical or informal.

Most-similar/most-different case design   A **qualitative** method of comparison that relies on selecting cases that are either similar or different to each other bar the variable of interest.

Multi-level model   A **regression** model that accounts for the nesting of subjects' observations with larger units, such as individuals in an area. The regression jointly estimates the impact of the **variables** at different levels.

Natural experiment   When one area or group gets a treatment or condition and another does not (by design or accident), but the two are otherwise the same or similar.

Ninety-five per cent test   A short-hand to indicate that a variable is statistically **significant** at an acceptable level of probability.

Nodality   The character of networks that gives them power and capacity, such as being through a central point. One of Hood and Margetts' four **tools of government**.

Observational data   Data collected through observing the subjects of interest rather than from an **experiment** that seeks to manipulate the outcomes.

Observations The values of a variable as measured by the **research instrument**.

One-tailed test A test for a **significant** relationship that assumes the difference between the observed value and the null is in the expected direction. It is regarded as more permissive than the **two-tailed test**.

Opportunity cost The cost of the next-best choice forgone.

Ordinary least squares A form of **regression** where the data are **interval** and follow strict **asymptotic** assumptions.

Outlier An **observation** of a **variable** that is larger than the others, which may affect or **bias** the results.

Panel A dataset where the **cases** or **observations** vary over time as well as over space.

Parameter A number that represents the **hypothesised** relationship.

Performance-related pay A pay scheme that adjusts earnings in relation to measured or assessed performance.

Policy network A description of the long-term relationships that emerge between policy-makers in a sector of activity, such as health or education.

Pooled data Data that combines **observations** across different units, which can form a **panel**.

Political-business cycle The planned association of macro-economic outputs with the timing of elections.

Political culture A stable set of attitudes about politics prevalent in a country or locale.

Principal As in the principal–agent model, the principal wishes to commission a service or activity from an **agent**, but suffers from information asymmetry. The **agent** may wish to shirk but the principal lacks information upon which to monitor the agent effectively.

Qualitative A method of generating inferences and other knowledge by the intensive observation of a small number of **cases**.

Quasi-experiment A research design that is similar to an **experiment** in having a valid comparison group from which to compare the **intervention** but falls short of a **randomised controlled trial** or **natural experiment**.

Random effects Describes a statistical model where the explanatory variables are assumed to be random.

Randomised controlled trial An experiment where the units of **observation** are randomised into two or more groups, with one as the **control group** and the other or others as the **treatment group** or groups.

Reactance Where people see an act of persuasion as a threat.

Regression Summary word for a family of techniques that seek to find out what predicts a **dependent variable** from a series of **independent variables**.

Rent A benefit that interest groups get from lobbying that limits overall welfare.

Rent seeking The process of searching out a **rent**.

Research instrument The technique or process that collects the data for the research to perform **analysis**.

Response rate   The ratio of those who responded to a survey to the number in the **sample**.

Robustness   The health of a statistical model, whether it meets its assumptions.

Robustness checks   Tests designed to detect common violations of a statistical model.

Sample   A selection of **observations** from which is it possible to do **analysis**.

Selection bias   A natural human process whereby some people or units select into an **intervention** and some do not, which means the results may be **biased** when making an inference to the population, possibly leading to an overestimate of the effectiveness of **interventions**.

Significant   A shorthand for statistically significant, that is, that the researcher can be confident with a minimum level of risk (5 per cent) that an **independent variable** affects a **dependent variable** in a **regression**, or there is an association or **correlation** between two variables in a table.

Snowball   A method of recruiting participants in a study by asking contacts to nominate others from their networks. Formally (Goodman, 1961) snowballs have the property of a random sample.

Spatial regression   A form of **regression** that takes account of the **correlation** between places or observations that neighbour each other.

Specification   A shorthand for model specification, the application of a theoretical model to the data, which is important in avoiding **bias**.

Spurious   Where there is not a true relationship between the **dependent** and **independent variables**, but where the data indicate the opposite. Often the relationship is **significant** because of chance or there is another variable that has been omitted from the analysis.

Standard deviation   A measure of the spread of a sample – typically 95 per cent of observations are within two standard deviations either side of the mean. It is the square root of the **variance**.

Standard error   How much a value averaged from several measurements varies from the mean. The standard error is the **standard deviation** divided by the square root of the number of observations.

Stepped-wedge design   Where a random allocation of subjects to the **treatment** and **control groups** is achieved by timing when they get the intervention. In time all subjects get the treatment, but there is still a difference between the groups before this happens, which may be observed.

Systematic review   A structured method of reviewing studies, only including those that meet rigorous criteria (ideally **randomised controlled trials**) and comparing **effect sizes** and the number that are statistically significant. It is similar to **meta-analysis**.

T-value   The estimate or **coefficient** divided by the **standard error**. It measures how many standard errors the coefficient is away from zero or a hypothesised value. Generally, any t-value greater than plus 1.96 or less than minus 1.96 is regarded as **significant**.

Tiebout model   An account of the provision of public goods based on citizens voting with their feet to move to a jurisdiction that offers their preferred combinations of local taxes and services (see Tiebout, 1956).

Time series   A form of **regression** where the **observations** vary over time rather than over space or another dimension.

Tools of government   The different types of resources open to government that can help it achieve its ends. Hood and Margetts classify these as **nodality**, authority, treasure and organisation.

Treatment group   One of the groups randomised as part of a **randomised controlled trial**. The treatment group gets the **intervention** so may be used to compare values of the **control group** so as to evaluate its impact.

Two-stage least squares   A form of **regression** that seeks to correct for **endogeneity** by performing a **regression** on the suspect **independent variable** using an **instrument** and then using the saved scores (which are now not **correlated** with the suspect **independent variable**) to predict the dependent variable in second stage **regression** with all the variables of interest. The short-hand term is two-stage model or regression.

Two-tailed test   A test for significance that makes no assumption about the direction of the relationship.

Utilitarian   A branch of moral philosophy that claims that states should maximise aggregate human welfare.

Variable   A unit of a measurement that varies either over space and/or over time.

Variance   A measure of the spread of a distribution, defined as average squared difference from the mean.

Veto player   Describes a decision-maker who can block a policy (Tsebelis, 2002).

Bibliography

6, P., Fletcher-Morgan, C. and Leyland, K. (2010) 'Making people more responsible: the Blair governments' programme for changing citizens' behaviour', Political Studies 58: 427–49.

Acemoglu, D., Cantoni, D., Johnson, S. and Robinson, J. (2009) 'The consequences of radical reform: the French revolution', National Bureau of Economic Research Working Paper 14831. Online. Available HTTP: http://www.nber.org/papers/w14831, accessed 3 August 2010.

Acemoglu, D., Johnson, S., Querubin, P. and Robinson, J. (2008) 'When does policy reform work? The case of Central Bank independence', National Bureau of Economic Research Working Paper W14033. Online. Available HTTP: http://ssrn.com/abstract=1139349, accessed 26 October 2010.

Aghion, P., Alesina, A. and Trebbi, F. (2004) 'Endogenous political institutions', Quarterly Journal of Economics 119: 565–61.

Agranoff, R. (2007) Managing Within Networks, Washington: Georgetown University Press.

Ahuja, D. and Srinivasan, J. (2009) 'Why controlling climate change is more difficult than stopping stratospheric ozone depletion', Current Science 97: 1531–34.

Albrecht, J. (2006) 'The use of consumption taxes to relaunch green tax reforms', International Review of Law and Economics 26: 88–103.

Alesina, A. (1988) 'Macroeconomics and politics', NBER Macroeconomics Annual 3: 13–62.

Alesina, A. and Summers, L. (1993) 'Central bank independence and macroeconomic performance: some comparative evidence', Journal of Money, Credit and Banking 25: 151–62.

Allwright, S., Paul, G., Greiner, B., Mullally, B., Pursell, L., Kelly, A., Bonner, B., D'Eath, M., McConnell, B., McLaughlin, J., O'Donovan, D., O'Kane, E. and Perry, I. (2005) 'Legislation for smoke-free workplaces and health of bar workers in Ireland: before and after study', British Medical Journal 331: 7525.

Anderson, L. (2001) 'The implications of institutional design for macroeconomic performance: reassessing the claims of consensus democracy', Comparative Political Studies 34: 429–52.

Andersen, M., Dengsøe, N. and Pedersen, A. (2001) An Evaluation of the Impact of Green Taxes in the Nordic Countries, Copenhagen: The Nordic Council of Ministers.

Andrews, R., Boyne, G., and Walker, R. (2006) 'Strategy content and organizational performance: an empirical analysis', Public Administration Review 66: 52–63.

Andrews, R., Boyne, G., Law, J. and Walker, R. (2008) 'Organizational strategy, external regulation and public service performance', Public Administration 86: 185–203.

Ansell, C. and Gash, A. (2008) 'Collaborative governance in theory and practice', Journal of Public Administration Research and Theory 18: 543–71.

Askew, R., John, P. and Liu, H. (2010) 'Experimenting for innovation: testing out design experiments with a drugs policy intervention in Wigan', Policy and Politics, forthcoming.

Atkinson, A. (1999) The Economic Consequences of Rolling Back the Welfare State, Cambridge, Mass.; London: MIT Press.

Atkinson, A. and Morgensen, G. (1993) Welfare and Work Incentives: A North European Perspective, Oxford: Clarendon Press.

Atkinson, A., Burgess. S., Croxson, B., Gregg, P., Propper, C., Slater, H. and Wilson, D. (2009) 'Evaluating the impact of performance-related pay for teachers in England', Labour Economics 16: 251–61.

Aucoin, P. (1995) The New Public Management: Canada in Comparative Perspective, Montreal: Institute for Research on Public Policy.

Ayres, I. and Braithwaite, J. (1992) Responsive Regulation: Transcending the Deregulation Debate, Oxford: Oxford University Press.

Balch, G. (1980) 'The stick, the carrot, and other strategies: a theoretical analysis of governmental intervention', Law and Policy 2: 35–60.

Baldwin, R. and Black, J. (2008) 'Really responsive regulation', Modern Law Review 71: 59–94.

Barankay, I. and Lockwood, B. (2007) 'Decentralization and the productive efficiency of government: evidence from Swiss Cantons', Journal of Public Economics 91: 1197–1218.

Bardach, E. and Kagan, R. (1982) Going by the Book: The Problem of Regulatory Unreasonableness, Philadelphia: Temple University Press.

Barnard, H., Killworth, P. and Sailer, L. (1980) 'Informant accuracy in social network data IV: a comparison of clique-level structure in behavioural and cognitive network data', Social Networks 2: 191–218.

Barnard, H.R., Killworth, P., Kroenenfeld, D. and Sailer, L. (1985), 'The problem of informant accuracy: the validity of retrospective data', Annual Review of Anthropology 13: 495–517.

Barro, R. (1991) 'Economic growth in a cross section of countries', Quarterly Journal of Economics 106: 407–43.

Barry, B. (1975) 'Political accommodation and consociational democracy', British Journal of Political Science 5: 477–505.

Barzelay, M. (2001) The New Public Management: Improving Research and Policy Dialogue, Berkeley, CA: University of California Press.

Becker, G. (1968) 'Crime and punishment: an economic approach', Journal of Political Economy 76: 169–217.

Beetham, D. (1974) Max Weber and the Theory of Modern Politics, London: Allen and Unwin.

Bell, S. and Hindmoor, A. (2009) Rethinking Governance, Cambridge: Cambridge University Press.

Bertelli, A. and John, P. (2010) 'Government checking government: how performance measures expand distributive politics', Journal of Politics 72: 545–58.

Bertelli, A. and Richardson, L. (2008) 'The behavioral impact of drinking and driving laws', Policy Studies Journal 36: 545–69.

Besley, T. and Case, A. (1995) 'Incumbent behavior: vote-seeking, tax-setting, and yardstick competition', American Economic Review 85: 25–45.

Besley, T., Persson, T. and Sturm, D, (2010) 'Political competition, policy and growth: theory and evidence from the United States', Review of Economic Studies 77: 1329–52.

Black, J., and Baldwin, R. (2010) 'Really responsive risk-based regulation', Law and Policy 32: 181–213.

Blackburn, M. (1990) 'Trends in poverty in the United States, 1967–84', Review of Income and Wealth 36: 53–66.

Bloom, H. and Riccio, J. (2005) 'Using place-based random assignment and comparative interrupted time-series analysis to evaluate the jobs-plus employment program for public housing residents', Annals of the American Academy of Political and Social Science 599: 19–51.

Bloom, H., Hill, C. and Riccio, J. (2003) 'Linking program implementation and effectiveness: lessons from a pooled sample of welfare-to-work experiments', Journal of Policy Analysis and Management 22: 551–75.

Bloom, H., Orr, L., Bell, S., Cave, G., Doolittle, F., Lin, W. and Bos, J. (1997) 'The benefits and costs of JTPA Title II-A programs: Key findings from the National Job Training Partnership Act study', Journal of Human Resources 32: 549–76.

Blume, L., Müller, J., Voigt, S. and Wolf, C. (2009) 'The economic effects of constitutions: replicating – and extending – Persson and Tabellini', Public Choice 139: 197–225.

Bohte, J. (2001) 'School bureaucracy and student performance at the local level', Public Administration Review 61: 92–99.

Borzekowski, D. and Robinson, T. (2001) 'The 30-second effect: an experiment revealing the impact of television commercials on food preferences of preschoolers', Journal of the American Dietetic Association 101: 42–46.

Bovenberg, A. and Goulder, L. (1996) 'Optimal environmental taxation in the presence of other taxes: general-equilibrium analyses', American Economic Review 86: 985–1000.

Bovenberg, A. and Mooij, R. de (1994) 'Environmental levies and distortionary taxation', American Economic Review 94: 1085–89.

Boyd, H. and Westfall, R. (1970) 'Interviewer bias once more revisited', Journal of Marketing Research 7: 249–53.

Boyne, G., Farrell, C., Law, J., Powell, M. and Walker, R. (2003) Evaluating Public Management Reforms, Buckingham: Open University Press.

Boyne, G., James, O., John, P. and Petrovsky, N. (2008) 'Executive succession in English local government', Public Money and Management 28: 267–74.

——(2009a) 'Democracy and government performance: holding incumbents accountable in English local governments', Journal of Politics 71: 1–12.

——(2009b) 'Does political change affect senior management turnover? An empirical analysis of top-tier local authorities in England', Public Administration 88: 136–53.

——(2009c) 'When do new agency chief executives make a difference to policies and performance?', paper presented at the 59th Political Studies Association Annual Conference, Manchester, England, April 2009.

——(2009d) 'Democracy as a virtuous circle: performance voting and leadership turnover in English local government', paper presented at the American Political Science Association Annual Conference, Toronto, 4 September 2009.

——(2010a) 'What happens when public management reform actually works? The paradox of performance management in English local government', in Hood, C.,

Margetts, H. and 6, P. (eds), Paradoxes of Modernisation: Unintended Consequences of Public Policy Reforms, Oxford: Oxford University Press.

——(2010b) 'Does public service performance affect top management turnover?', Journal of Public Management Research and Theory 20: 261–69.

——(2010c) 'Top management turnover and organizational performance: a test of a contingency model', Public Administration Review, forthcoming.

Brady, D. (2005) 'The welfare state and relative poverty in rich western democracies, 1967–97', Social Forces 83: 1329–64.

Braithwaite, J. (1985) To Punish or Persuade: Enforcement of Coal Mine Safety, Albany: State University of New York Press.

——(2002) Restorative Justice and Responsive Regulation, Oxford: Oxford University Press.

Braybrooke, D. and Lindblom, C. (1963) A Strategy of Decision, New York: The Free Press.

Brannan, T., John, P. and Stoker, G. (eds) (2006) Re-energising Citizenship: Strategies for Civil Renewal, Basingstoke: Palgrave.

Brennan, A., Rhodes, J. and Tyler, P. (1999) 'The distribution of Single Regeneration Budget Challenge Fund expenditure in relation to local area needs in England', Urban Studies 36: 2069–84.

Brennan, G. and Buchanan, J. (1980) The Power to Tax: Analytical Foundations of a Fiscal Constitution, Cambridge: Cambridge University Press.

Brewer, G. and Selden, S. (2000) 'Why elephants gallop: assessing and predicting organizational performance in federal agencies', Journal of Public Administration Research and Theory 10: 685–712.

Brewer, M., Duncan, A., Shephard, A. and Suárez, M. (2006) 'Did working families' tax credit work? The impact of in-work support on labour supply in Great Britain', Labour Economics 13: 699–720.

Brewer, M., Muriel, A., Phillips, D. and Sibieta, L. (2008) Poverty and Inequality in the UK: 2008, IFS Commentary No. 105, London: Institute for Fiscal Studies.

Bryce, R. Stanley, F. and Garner, B. (1991) 'Randomized controlled trial of antenatal social support to prevent preterm birth', British Journal of Obstetrics and Gynaecology 98: 1001–08.

Bryce, W., Day, R. and Olney, T. (1997) 'Commitment approach to motivating community recycling: New Zealand kerbside trial', Journal of Consumer Affairs 31: 27–52.

Butler, D., Adonis, A. and Travers, T. (1994) Failure in British Government: The Politics of the Poll Tax, Oxford: Oxford University Press.

Cabinet Office (2003) The Magenta Book Guidance Notes for Policy Evaluation and Analysis, London: Cabinet Office. Online. Available HTTP: http://www.nationalschool.gov.uk/policyhub/evaluating_policy/magenta_book/index.asp, accessed 31 July 2010.

Cairney, P. (2009) 'The role of ideas in policy transfer: the case of UK smoking bans since devolution', Journal of European Public Policy 16: 471–88.

Calabresi, G. and Bobbitt, P. (1978) Tragic Choices, New York: W. W. Norton & Co.

Calmfors, L. and Driffill, J. (1988) 'Bargaining structure, corporatism and macroeconomic performance', Economic Policy 3: 13–61.

Carr, J. and Feiock, R. (1999) 'Metropolitan government and economic development', Urban Affairs Review 34: 476–88.

Casper, L., McLanahan, S. and Garfinkel, I. (1994) 'The gender poverty gap: what we can learn from other countries', American Sociological Review 59: 594–605.

Castillo, D. and Saysel, A (2005) 'Simulation of common pool resource field experiments: a behavioral model of collective action', Ecological Economics 55: 420–36.

Castles, F. and Dowrick, S. (1990) 'The impact of government spending on medium-term economic growth in the OECD, 1960–85', Journal of Theoretical Politics 2: 173–204.

Castles, F. and Merrill, V. (1989) 'Towards a general model of public policy outcomes', Journal of Theoretical Politics 1: 177–212.

Chadwick, A. and May, C. (2003) 'Interaction between states and citizens in the age of the internet: "e-government" in the United States, Britain, and the European Union', Governance 16: 271–300.

Cheshire, P. and Magrini, S. (2006) 'Population growth in European cities: weather matters – but only nationally', Regional Studies 40: 23–37.

——(2009) 'Urban growth drivers in a Europe of sticky people and implicit boundaries', Journal of Economic Geography 9: 85–115.

Chetty, R. and Saez, E. (2009) 'Teaching the tax code: earnings responses to an experiment with EITC recipients', NBER Working Paper No. 14836, Cambridge, MA: National Bureau of Economic Research.

Chetty, R., Looney, A. and Kroft, K. (2009) 'Salience and taxation: theory and evidence', American Economic Review 99: 1145–77.

Christopher, K., England, P., Smeeding, T. and Phillips, K. (2002) 'The gender gap in poverty in modern nations: single motherhood, the market, and the state', Sociological Perspectives 45: 219–42.

Chubb, J. and Moe, T. (1990) Politics, Markets, and America's Schools, Washington, D.C.: Brookings Institution.

Cialdini, R. (2001) Influence: Science and Practice, Boston: Allyn and Bacon, 4th ed.

Coggburn, J. and Schneider, S. (2003) 'The relationship between state government performance and state quality of life', International Journal of Public Administration 26: 1337–54.

Cohen, S. and Syme, L. (1985) 'Issues in the study and application of social support' in Cohen, S. and Syme, S. (eds), Social Support and Health, New York: Academic Press.

Cole, D. and Grossman, P. (1999) 'When is command-and-control efficient? Institutions, technology, and the comparative efficiency of alternative regulatory regimes for environmental protection', Wisconsin Law Review, November: 887–938.

Compendium of Health (2003) Statistics Office of Health Economics, 15th ed. Online. Available HTTP: http://www.ohecompendium.org.

Congdon, W., Kling, J. and Mullainathan, S. (2009) 'Behavioral economics and tax policy', National Tax Journal 62: 375–86.

Cornelius, W. and Salehan, I. (2007) 'Does border enforcement deter unauthorized immigration? The case of Mexican migration to the United States of America', Regulation and Governance 1: 139–53.

Cotterill, S., John, P. and Richardson, L. (2010) 'Pledge campaigns to encourage charitable giving: a randomised controlled trial', Political Studies Association Annual Conference, Edinburgh, 29 March – 1 April 2010, Public Administration Specialist Group Panel: Contemporary Challenges to Public Administration – further international comparisons.

Cotterill, S., John, P., Liu, H. and Nomura, H. (2009) 'Mobilizing citizen effort to enhance environmental outcomes: a randomized controlled trial of a door-to-door recycling campaign', Journal of Environmental Management 91: 403–10.

Cotterill, S., Parry, J., Richardson, M. and Mathers, J. (2008) 'Quasi-experimental evaluation of the health impacts of the New Deal for Communities urban regeneration scheme', Critical Public Health 18: 311–32.

Crepaz, M. (1996) 'Consensus vs. majoritarian democracy: political institutions and their impact on macroeconomic performance and industrial disputes', Comparative Political Studies 29: 4–26.

Crick, B. (1964) The Reform of Parliament, London: Weidenfeld and Nicolson.

Cropper, M. and Oates, W. (1992) 'Environmental economics: a survey', Journal of Economic Literature 30: 675–740.

Cukierman, A., Webb, S. and Neyapti, B. (1992) 'Measuring the independence of central banks and its effect on policy outcomes', World Bank Economic Review 6: 353–98.

Cusack T. (1999) 'Social capital, institutional structures and democratic performance: a comparative study of German local governments', European Journal of Political research 35: 1–34.

Davies, J. (2009) 'The limits of joined-up government: toward a political analysis', Public Administration 87: 80–96.

Davies, P. (2004) 'Is evidence-based government possible?', Jerry Lee Lecture 2004, presented at the 4th Annual Campbell Collaboration Colloquium, Washington, D.C., 19 February 2004. Online. Available HTTP: http://www.nationalschool.gov. uk/policyhub/downloads/JerryLeeLecture1202041.pdf, accessed 31 July 2010.

De Vries, M. (2000) 'The rise and fall of decentralization: a comparative analysis of arguments and practices in European countries', European Journal of Political Research 38: 193–224.

Department of the Environment (1994) Assessing the Impact of Urban Policy, London: HMSO.

Department of Health (2008) Tackling Health Inequalities: Ten Years On, London: Department of Health.

Dolinski, D. and Nawrat, R. (1998) '"Fear-Then-Relief" procedure for producing compliance: beware when the danger is over', Journal of Experimental Social Psychology 34: 27–50.

Dorbeck-Jung, B., Vrielink, M., Gosselt, J., van Hoof, J. and de Jong, M. (2010) 'Contested hybridization of regulation: failure of the Dutch regulatory system to protect minors from harmful media', Regulation and Governance 4: 154–74.

Dorling, D., Rigby, J., Wheeler, B., Ballas, D., Thomas, B., Fahmy, E., Gordon, D. and Lupton, R. (2007) Poverty, Wealth and Place in Britain, 1968 to 2005, Bristol: Policy Press.

Dowding, K. (1995) 'Model or metaphor? A critical review of the policy network approach', Political Studies XLIII: 136–58.

Dreher, A. (2006) 'Power to the people? The impact of decentralization on governance', Swiss Institute for Business Cycle Research (KOF) Working Paper No. 121, Dreher, Axel, January 2006. Online. Available HTTP: http://ssrn.com/abstract= 881542, accessed 3 August 2010.

Dror, Y. (1968) Public Policymaking Reexamined, San Francisco: Chandler Publishing Company.

Dunleavy, P. (1994) 'The globalization of public services production: can government be "best in world"?', Public Policy and Administration 9: 36–64.

——(1995) 'Policy disaster: explaining the UK's record', Public Policy and Administration 10: 52–70.

Dunleavy, P., Margetts, H., Bastow, S. and Tinkler, J. (2006a) 'New Public Management is dead – long live digital-era governance', Journal of Public Administration Research and Theory 16: 467–94.

——(2006b) Digital Era Governance: IT Corporations, the State, and E-government, Oxford: Oxford University Press.

Edelman, M. (1964) The Symbolic Uses of Politics, Urbana: University of Illinois Press.

——(1988) Constructing the Political Spectacle, Chicago: University of Chicago Press.

Eijffinger, S. and de Hann, J. (1996) The Political Economy of Central Bank Independence, Special Papers in International Economics No. 19, Princeton University, www.princeton.edu/~ies/IES_Special_Papers/SP19.pdf, accessed 3 August 2010.

Elkan, R., Kendrick, D., Dewey, M., Hewitt, M., Robinson, J., Blair, M., Williams, D. and Brummell, K. (2001) 'Effectiveness of home-based support for older people: systematic review and meta-analysis', British Medical Journal 323: 719–24.

Esping-Anderson, G. (1990) The Three Worlds of Welfare Capitalism, Cambridge: Polity Press; Princeton: Princeton University Press.

Evans, P. (1992) 'The state as problem and solution: predation, embedded autonomy, and adjustment', in Haggard, S. and Kaufman, R. (eds), The Politics of Economic Adjustment, Princeton: Princeton University.

Evans, P. and Rauch, J. (1999) 'Bureaucracy and growth: a cross-national analysis of the effects of "Weberian" state structures on economic growth', American Sociological Review 64: 748–65.

Fan, S., Lin, C. and Treisman, D. (2009) 'Political decentralization and corruption: evidence from around the world', Journal of Public Economics 93: 14–34.

Fernandez, S. (2007) 'What works best when contracting for services? An analysis of contracting performance at the local level in the US', Public Administration 85: 1119–41.

Filmer, D. and Pritchett, L. (1999) 'The impact of public spending on health: does money matter?', Social Science and Medicine 49: 1309–23.

Finkelstein, A. and McKnight, R. (2008) 'What did Medicare do? The initial impact of Medicare on mortality and out of pocket medical spending', Journal of Public Economics 92: 1644–68.

Fishkin, J. (2009) When the People Speak: Deliberative Democracy and Public Consultation, Oxford: Oxford University Press.

Forbes, M. and Lynn, L. (2005) 'How does public management affect government performance? Evidence from international research', Journal of Public Administration Research and Theory 15: 559–84.

Frey, B. (1997) Not Just for the Money: An Economic Theory of Personal Motivation, Cheltenham: Edward Elgar.

Fuller, C., Bennett, R. and Ramsden, M. (2003) 'Organised for inward investment? Development agencies, local government, and firms in the inward investment process', Environment and Planning A 35: 2025–51.

Fullerton, D., Leicester, A. and Smith, S. (2008) Environmental Taxes, London: Institute for Fiscal Studies.

Fung, A. (2004) Empowered Participation: Reinventing Urban Democracy, Princeton: Princeton University Press.

Gains, F. and John, P. (2010) 'What do bureaucrats like doing? A test of the "bureau shaping" hypothesis', Public Administration Review 70: 455–63.

Gains, F., Greasley, S., John, P. and Stoker, G. (2007) 'The impact of political leadership on organizational performance: evidence from English urban government', Local Government Studies 35: 75–94.

Galster, G., Walker, C., Hayes, C., Boxall, P. and Johnson, J. (2004) 'Measuring the impact of Community Development Block Grant spending on urban neighborhoods', Housing Policy Debate 15: 903–34.

Gelardi, A. (1996) 'The influence of tax law changes on the timing of marriages: a two country analysis', National Tax Journal 49: 17–30.

Gerber, A., Green, D. and Larimer, C. (2008) 'Social pressure and voter turnout: evidence from a large-scale field experiment', American Political Science Review 102: 33–48.

Gerber, A., Karlan, D. and Bergan, D. (2009) 'Does the media matter? A field experiment measuring the effect of newspapers on voting behavior and political opinions', American Economic Journal: Applied Economics 1: 35–52.

Glennerster, H. (2002) 'United Kingdom education 1997–2001', Oxford Review of Economic Policy 18: 120–36.

Glewwe, P., Kremer, M. and Moulin, S. (2009) 'Many children left behind? Textbooks and test scores in Kenya', American Economic Journal 1: 112–35.

Glewwe, P., Kremer, M. Moulin, S. and Zitzewitz, E. (2004) 'Retrospective vs. prospective analyses of school inputs: the case of flip charts in Kenya', Journal of Development Economics 74: 251–68.

Goodin, R. and Le Grand, J. (1987) Not Only the Poor: the Middle Classes and the Welfare State, London: Allen & Unwin.

Goodman, L. (1961) 'Snowball sampling', Annals of Mathematical Statistics 32: 148–70.

Goodwin, M., Greasley, S., John, P. and Richardson, L. (2010) 'Can we make environmental citizens? A randomised control trial of the effects of a school-based intervention on the attitudes and knowledge of young people', Environmental Politics, forthcoming.

Greasley, S. and John, P. (2010) 'Does stronger political leadership have a performance payoff? Citizen satisfaction in the reform of sub-central governments in England', Journal of Public Administration Research and Theory, forthcoming.

Greasley, S., John, P. and Wolman, H. (2010) 'Does government performance matter? The effects of local government on urban outcomes in England', Urban Studies, forthcoming.

Green, D. and Gerber, A. (2008) Get Out the Vote: How to Increase Voter Turnout, 2nd ed. Washington, D.C.: Brookings Institution, 2nd ed.

Gottfredson, D., Wilson, D. and Najaka, N. (2002) 'School-based crime prevention', in Sherman, L., Farrington, D., Welsh, B. and MacKenzie, D. (eds), Evidence-based Crime Prevention, London: Routledge.

Grossman, D., Neckerman, H., Koepsell, T., Liu, P., Asher, K., Beland, K., Frey, K. and Rivara, F. (1997) 'Effectiveness of a violence prevention curriculum among children in elementary school: a randomized controlled trial', Journal of the American Medical Association 277: 1605–11.

Gunningham, N. and Grabosky, P. (1998) Smart Regulation: Designing Environmental Policy, Oxford: Clarendon.

Gupta, S., Verhoeven, M. and Tiongson, E. (2002) 'The effectiveness of government
spending on education and health care in developing and transition economies',
European Journal of Political Economy 18: 717–37.

Hall, P. and Gingerich, D. (2009) 'Varieties of capitalism and institutional com-
plementarities in the political economy: an empirical analysis', British Journal of
Political Science 39: 449–82.

Hall, P. and Jones, C. (1999) 'Why do some countries produce so much more output
per worker than others?', Quarterly Journal of Economics 114: 83–116.

Hall, P. and Soskice, D. (2001) Varieties of Capitalism: The Institutional Foundations
of Comparative Advantage, Oxford: Oxford University Press.

Hall, R. (1963) 'The concept of bureaucracy: an empirical assessment', American
Journal of Sociology 69: 32–40.

Halpern, D. (2004) Social Capital, Cambridge: Polity.

Halpern, D., Bates, C., Mulgan, G. and Aldridge, S., with Beales, G. and Heathfield, A.
(2004) Personal Responsibility and Changing Behaviour: The State of Knowledge
and Its Implications for Public Policy, London: Cabinet Office. Online. Available
HTTP: http://www.cabinetoffice.gov.uk/~/media/assets/www.cabinetoffice.gov.uk/
strategy/pr2%20pdf.ashx.

Hansen, K. and Machin, S. (2002) 'Spatial crime patterns and the introduction
of the UK minimum wage', Oxford Bulletin of Economics and Statistics 64:
677–97.

Harford, T. (2005) The Underground Economist, Oxford: Oxford University Press.

Hayashi, Y., Kato, H. and Teodoro, R. (2001) 'A model system for the assessment of
the effects of car and fuel green taxes on CO_2 emission', Transportation Research
Part D 6: 123–39.

Hellowell, M. and Pollock, A. (2009) 'The private financing of NHS hospitals: politics,
policy and practice', Economic Affairs 29: 13–19.

Hendriksen, C., Lund, E. and Stromgard, E. (1984) 'Consequences of assessment and
intervention among elderly people: a three-year randomized controlled trial', British
Medical Journal 289: 1522–24.

Hennessy, P. (1989) Whitehall, London: Secker and Warburg.

Henry, G. and Gordon, C. (2003) 'Driving less for better air: impacts of a public
information campaign', Journal of Policy Analysis and Management 22: 45–63.

Hicken, A., Satyanath, S. and Sergenti, E. (2005) 'Political institutions and economic
performance: the effects of accountability and obstacles to policy change', American
Journal of Political Science 49: 897–907.

Hicklin, A., O' Toole, L. and Meier, K. (2007) 'Serpents in the sand: managerial networking and nonlinear inffiuences on organizational performance', Journal of
Public Management Research and Theory 18: 253–73.

Hills, J. and Stewart, K. (eds) (2005) New Labour, Poverty, Inequality and Exclusion,
Bristol: Policy Press.

Hills, J., Brewer, B., Jenkins, S., Lister, R., Lupton, R., Machin, S., Mills, C., Modood,
T., Rees, T. and Riddell, S. (2010) An Anatomy of Economic Inequality in the
UK, Report of the National Equality Panel, London: LSE/Government Equalities
Office.

Hirst, P. (1994) Associative Democracy: New Forms of Economic and Social
Governance, Cambridge: Polity Press.

Hiscox, M. and Rickard, S. (2002) 'Birds of a different feather? Varieties of capitalism, factor specificity, and interindustry labor movement', unpublished paper.

HM Treasury: (2008) Public Expenditure Statistical Analyses 2008, London: HMSO.

Home Office (1998) Tackling Drugs to Build a Better Britain: The Ten Year Strategy for Tackling Drug Misuse. Online. Available HTTP: http://www.homeoffice.gov.uk/drugs/strategy/index.html.

Hood, C. (1983) The Tools of Government, London: Macmillan.

——(1991) 'A public management for all seasons?', Public Administration 69: 3–19.

——(1995) 'Contemporary public management: a new global paradigm', Public Policy and Administration 10: 104–17.

——(1998) The Art of the State: Culture, Rhetoric, and Public Management, Oxford: Oxford University Press.

——(2006) 'Gaming in targetworld: the targets approach to managing British public services', Public Administration Review 66: 515–21.

——(2007) 'Intellectual obsolescence and intellectual makeovers: reflections on the tools of government after two decades', Governance 20: 127–44.

Hood, C. and Margetts, H. (2007) The Tools of Government in the Digital Age, Basingstoke: Macmillan.

Hood, C., Rothstein, H. and Baldwin, R. (2003) The Government of Risk, Oxford: Oxford University Press.

Hood, C., Scott, C., Jones, G. and Travers, T. (1999) Regulation Inside Government: Waste Watchers, Quality Police and Sleazebusters, Oxford: Oxford University Press.

Howlett, M. (2005) 'What is a policy instrument? Policy tools, policy mixes and policy-implementation styles', in Eliadis, P., Hill, M. and Howlett, M. (eds), Designing Government: From Instruments to Governance, Montreal: McGill-Queens University Press.

Howlett, M. and Ramesh, M. (2003) Studying Public Policy Cycles and Policy Subsystems, Toronto: Oxford University Press, 2nd ed.

Hyman, H. and Sheatsley, P. (1947) 'Some reasons why information campaigns fail', Public Opinion Quarterly 11: 412–23.

Immergut, E. (1992) 'The rules of the game: the logic of health policy-making in France, Switzerland, and Sweden', in Steinmo, S., Thelen, K. and Longstreth, F. (eds), Structuring Politics: Historical Institutionalism in Comparative Analysis, Cambridge: Cambridge University Press.

Imrie, R. and Thomas, H. (1999) 'Assessing urban policy and the Urban Development Corporations', in Imrie, R. and Thomas, H. (eds), British Urban Policy: an Evaluation of the Urban Development Corporations, London: Sage.

Ingraham, P., Joyce, P. and Donahue, A. (2003) Government Performance: Why Management Matters, Baltimore: Johns Hopkins University Press.

Institute for Public Policy Research (2001) Building Better Partnerships: The Final Report of the Commission on Public Private Partnerships, London: IPPR.

Jacob, B. (2005) 'Accountability, incentives and behavior: the impact of high-stakes testing in the Chicago public schools', Journal of Public Economics 89: 761–96.

James, O. (2001) 'Business models and the transfer of businesslike central government agencies', Governance 14: 233–52.

Jamison, D., Breman, J., Measham, A., Alleyne, G., Claeson, M., Evans, D., Jha, P., Mills, A. and Musgrov, P. (eds) (2006) Disease Control Priorities in Developing Countries, New York: Oxford University Press, 2nd ed.

Jäntti, M. and Danziger, S. (2000) 'Poverty in advanced countries', in Atkinson, A. and Bourguignon, F. (eds), Handbook of Income Distribution, Volume 1, Amsterdam: North-Holland.

John, P. (1998) Analysing Public Policy, London: Continuum.

——(1999) 'Ideas and interests; agendas and implementation: an evolutionary explanation of policy change in British local government finance', British Journal of Politics and International Relations, 1: 39–62.

——(2001) Local Governance in Western Europe, London: Sage.

——(2005) 'The contribution of volunteering, trust and networks to educational performance', Policy Studies Journal 33: 635–56.

——(2009) 'Making representative democracy more representative: Can new forms of citizen governance in the UK open up democracy?', Public Administration Review 69: 494–503.

——(2011) Analysing Public Policy, London: Routledge.

John, P. and Brannan, T. (2008) 'How different are telephoning and canvassing? Results from a "Get Out the Vote" field experiment in the UK 2005 General Election', British Journal of Political Science 38: 565–74.

John, P. and Cole, A. (1998) 'Urban regimes and local governance in Britain and France: policy adaption and coordination in Leeds and Lille', Urban Affairs Review 33: 382–404.

John, P. and Johnson, M. (2008) 'Is there still a public service ethos?', in Park, A. Curtice, J., Thomson, K., Phillips, M., Johnson, M. and Clery, E. (eds), British Social Attitudes: The 24th Report, London: Sage.

John, P. and Morris, Z. (2004) 'What are the origins of social capital? Results from a panel survey of young people', British Elections and Parties Review 14: 94–112.

John, P., Ward, H. and Dowding, K. (2004) 'The bidding game: competitive funding regimes and the political targeting of urban programme schemes', British Journal of Political Science 34: 405–28.

John, P., Cotterill, S., Moseley, A., Richardson, L., Smith, G., Stoker, G. and Wales, C. (2011) Nudge, Nudge, Think, Think: Experimenting Our Way to Change Civic Behaviour, London: Bloomsbury Academic, forthcoming.

Jordana, J. and Levi-Faur, D. (2004) 'The politics of regulation in the age of governance', in Jordana, J. and Levi-Faur, D. (eds), The Politics of Regulation: Institutions and Regulatory Reforms for the Age of Governance, Cheltenham: Edward Elgar.

Joshi, N., Ostrom, E., Shivakoti, G. and Lam, W. (2000) 'Institutional opportunities and constraints in the performance of farmer-managed irrigation systems in Nepal', Asia-Pacific Journal of Rural Development 10: 67–92.

Kaestner, R., Korenman, S. and O'Neill, J. (2003) 'Has welfare reform changed teenage behaviors?', Journal of Policy Analysis and Management 22: 225–48.

Kassim, H and Le Galès, P. (2010) 'Exploring governance in a multi-level polity: a policy instruments approach', West European Politics 33: 1–21.

Kaufmann, D., Kraay, A. and Mastruzzi, M. (2007) 'Growth and governance: a reply', Journal of Politics 69: 555–62.

——(2009) Governance Matters VIII: Aggregate and Individual Governance Indicators, 1996–2008, World Bank Policy Research Working Paper No. 4978. Online. Available HTTP: http://ssrn.com/abstract=1424591, accessed 2 August 2010.

Kaufmann, D., Kraay, A. and Zoido-Lobatón, P. (1999) Governance Matters, World Bank Policy Research Working Paper No. 2196. Online. Available HTTP: http://ssrn.com/abstract=188568, accessed 2 August 2010.

Kaushal, N. and Kaestner, R. (2001) 'From welfare to work: has welfare reform worked?', Journal of Policy Analysis and Management 20: 699–719.

Kelman, S. (2005) Unleashing Change: A Study of Organizational Renewal in Government, Washington, D.C.: Brookings Institution.

Kenworthy, L. (1999) 'Do social-welfare policies reduce poverty? A cross-national assessment', Social Forces 77: 1119–39.

Keohane, R. and Ostrom, E. (1995) Local Commons and Global Interdependence: Heterogeneity and Cooperation in Two Domains, London: Sage.

Khaleghian, P. (2004) 'Decentralization and public services: the case of immunization', Social Science and Medicine 59: 163–83.

Khuder, S., Milz, S., Jordan, T., Price, J., Silvestri, K. and Butler, P. (2007) 'The impact of a smoking ban on hospital admissions for coronary heart disease', Preventative Medicine 45: 3–8.

Kickert, W., Klijn, E-H., and Koppenjan, F. (eds) (1997) Managing Complex Networks: Strategies for the Public Sector, London: Sage.

King, G., Keohane, R. and Verba, S. (1994) Designing Social Inquiry: Scientific Inference in Qualitative Research, Princeton: Princeton University Press.

Klapper, J. (1960) The Effects of Mass Communication, New York: The Free Press.

Klijn, E-H. and Koppenjan, J. (2000) 'Public management and policy networks', Public Management Review 2: 135–58.

Koppenjan, J. and Klijn, E-H. (2004) Managing Uncertainties in Networks, London: Routledge.

Kornhauser, W. (1959) The Politics of Mass Society, New York: The Free Press.

Korpi, W. (1985) 'Economic growth and the welfare state: leaky bucket or irrigation system?', European Sociological Review 1: 97–118.

Korpi, W. and Palme, J. (1998) 'The paradox of redistribution and strategies of equality: welfare state institutions, inequality and poverty in the western countries', American Sociological Review 63: 661–87.

Kotter, J. and Lawrence, P. (1974) Mayors in Action: Five Approaches to Urban Governance, New York: John Wiley & Sons.

Kurtz, M. and Schrank, A. (2007) 'Growth and governance: models, measures, and mechanisms', Journal of Politics 69: 538–54.

Ladd, H. (1994) 'Spatially targeted economic development strategies: do they work?', Cityscape 1: 193–218.

Lascoumes, P. and Le Galès, P. (2007) 'Introduction: understanding public policy through its instruments – from the nature of instruments to the sociology of public policy instrumentation', Governance 20: 1–21.

Latimer, J., Dowden, C. and Muise, D. (2005) 'The effectiveness of restorative justice practices: a meta-analysis', Prison Journal 85: 127–44.

Lavy, V. (2009) 'Performance pay and teachers' effort, productivity, and grading ethics', American Economic Review 99: 1979–2021.

Leviner, S. (2008) 'An overview: a new era of tax enforcement – from "big stick" to responsive regulation', Regulation and Governance 2: 360–80.

Levitt, S. (1996) 'The effect of the prison population on crime rates: evidence from prison overcrowding litigation', Quarterly Journal of Economics 111: 319–51.

——(1998) 'Why do increased arrest rates appear to reduce crime: deterrence, incapacitation, or measurement error?', Economic Inquiry 36: 353–72.

Levitt, S. and Dubner, S. (2005) Freakonomics: A Rogue Economist Explores the Hidden Side of Everything, New York: Allen Lane.

——(2009) Superfreakonomics: Global Cooling, Patriotic Prostitutes & Why Suicide Bombers Should Buy Insurance, New York: Allen Lane.

Lewis, A. (1982) The Psychology of Taxation, Oxford: Martin Robertson.

Lijphart, A. (1968) The Politics of Accommodation: Pluralism and Democracy in the Netherlands, Berkeley: University of California Press.

——(1969) 'Consociational democracy', World Politics 21: 207–25.

——(1975) 'Review article: the Northern Ireland problem; cases, theories, and solutions', British Journal of Political Science 5: 83–106.

——(1977) Democracy in Plural Societies: A Comparative Exploration, New Haven: Yale University Press.

——(1984) Democracies: Patterns of Majoritarian and Consensus Government in Twenty-One Countries, New Haven: Yale University Press.

——(1999) Democracies: Patterns of Majoritarian and Consensus Government in Thirty-Six Countries, New Haven: Yale University Press.

Lijphart, A. and Crepaz, L. (1991) 'Corporatism and consensus democracy in eighteen countries: conceptual and empirical linkages', British Journal of Political Science 21: 235–46.

Linder, S. and Peters, B. (1998) 'The study of policy instruments: four schools of thought', in Peters, B. and Nispen, F. (eds), Public Policy Instruments Evaluating the Tools of Public Administration, Cheltenham: Edward Elgar.

Loughlin, M. (1986) Local Government in the Modern State, London: Sweet and Maxwell.

Lyas, J., Shaw, P. and Van Vugt, M. (2004) 'Provision of feedback to promote householders' use of a kerbside recycling scheme – a social dilemma perspective', Journal of Solid Waste Technology 30: 7–18.

Lynn, L., Heinrich, C. and Hill, C. (2000) 'Studying governance and public management: challenges and prospects', Journal of Public Administration Research and Theory 10: 233–61.

——(2001) Improving Governance: A New Logic for Empirical Research, Washington, D.C.: Georgetown University Press.

Majone, G. (1994) 'The rise of the regulatory state in Europe', West European Politics 17: 77–101.

Makinson, J. (2000) Incentives for Change: Rewarding Performance in National Government Networks, London: Public Service Productivity Panel, HM Treasury.

Marsden, D. and Richardson, R. (1992) Motivation and Performance Related Pay in the Public Sector: A Case Study of the Inland Revenue, CEP Discussion Papers from Centre for Economic Performance, LSE. Online. Available HTTP: http://eprints.lse.ac.uk/3647/, accessed 2 August 2010.

Marsh, D. and Rhodes, R. (eds) (1992) Policy Networks in British Government, Oxford: Oxford University Press.

May, S., West, R., Hajek, P., McEwen, A. and McRobbi, H. (2006) 'Randomized controlled trial of a social support ("buddy") intervention for smoking cessation', Patient Education and Counseling 64: 235–41.

McCaffery, E. and Baron, J. (2004) 'Framing and taxation: evaluation of tax policies involving household composition', Journal of Economic Psychology 25: 679–705.

McCombs, M. and Shaw, D. (1972) 'The agenda-setting function of mass media', Public Opinion Quarterly 36: 176–87.

McGuire, M. and Silvia, C. (2009) 'Does leadership in networks matter? Examining the effect of leadership behaviors on managers' perceptions of network effectiveness', Public Performance and Management Review 33: 34–62.

McLellan, T., Hagan, T., Levine, M., Gould, F., Meyers, K., Bencivengo, M. and Durell, J. (1998) 'Supplemental social services improve outcomes in public addiction treatment', Addiction 93: 1489–99.

McNally, S. (2010) 'Evaluating education policies: the evidence from economic research', in Election Analysis 2010, Centre for Economic Performance. Online. Available HTTP: http://cep.lse.ac.uk/pubs/download/CEP_ElectionAnalysis_2010.pdf, accessed 8 August 2010.

McQuail, D. (1979) 'The influence and effects of mass media', in Curran, J. Gurevitch, M. and Woolacott, J. (eds) Mass Communication and Society, Thousand Oaks, CA: Sage.

Meier, K. (1994) The Politics of Sin: Drugs, Alcohol, and Public Policy, New York: M. E. Sharpe.

Meier, K., and O'Toole, L. (2001) 'Managerial strategies and behavior in networks: A model with evidence from U.S. public education', Journal of Public Administration Research and Theory 11: 271–95.

——(2002) 'Public management and organizational performance: the impact of managerial quality', Journal of Policy Analysis and Management 21: 629–43.

——(2004) 'Public management in intergovernmental networks: matching structural and behavioral networks', Journal of Public Administration Research and Theory 14: 469–94.

——(2005) 'Public management and educational performance: the impact of managerial networking', Public Administration Review 7: 45–68.

——(2006) Bureaucracy in a Democratic State: A Governance Perspective, Baltimore: Johns Hopkins University Press.

Meier, K., O'Toole, L., Boyne, G., Walker, R. and Andrews, R. (2010) 'Alignment and results: testing the interaction effects of strategy, structure and environment from Miles and Snow', Administration and Society 42: 160–92.

Meier, K., Polinard, J. and Wrinkle, R. (2000) 'Bureaucracy and organizational performance: causality arguments about public schools', American Journal of Political Science 44: 590–602.

Mendelsohn, H. (1973) 'Some reasons why information campaigns can succeed', Public Opinion Quarterly 37: 50–61.

Miles, R. and Snow, C. (1978) Organizational Strategy, Structure, and Process, New York: McGraw-Hill.

Miron, J. and Zwiebel, J. (1991) 'Alcohol consumption during Prohibition', American Economic Review 81: 242–47.

Moe, T. (1984) 'The new economics of organization', American Journal of Political Science 28: 739–77.

Moehler, D. and Luyimbazi, A. (2008) 'Tune in to governance: an experimental investigation of radio campaigns in Africa', paper presented at Field Experiments in Comparative Politics and Policy, University of Manchester, UK, July 1–2.

Moller, S., Bradley, D., Huber, E., Nielsen, F. and Stephen, J. (2003) 'Determinants of relative poverty in advanced capitalist democracies', American Sociological Review 68: 22–51.

Moran, M. (2003) The Regulatory State in Britain: High Modernism and Hyper-innovation, Oxford: Oxford University Press.

——(2010a) 'Implications of the crisis for regulation of financial markets', paper to the workshop, Public Governance After the Crisis, Friday 28 May 2010, School of Public Policy, University College London.

——(2010b) 'Policy making in an interdependent world', in Hay, C. (ed.), New Directions in Political Science: Responding to the Challenges of an Interdependent World, Basingstoke: Macmillan.

Moynihan, D. and Pandey, S. (2005) 'Testing how management matters in an era of government by performance', Journal of Public Administration Research and Theory 15: 421–39.

Mueller, D. (2000) Constitutional Democracy, Oxford: Oxford University Press.

Murray, C. (1984) Losing Ground: American Social Policy, 1950–1980, New York: Basic Books.

Niemi, R. and Junn, J. (1998) What Makes Students Learn, New Haven: Yale University Press.

Nomura, H., Cotterill, S. and John, P. (2010) 'The use of feedback to enhance environmental outcomes: a randomized controlled trial of a food waste scheme', paper presented at the Political Studies Association Conference, Edinburgh, 29 March – 1 April 2010. For the panel: Experimental Research in Political science: Confronting the Practical, Methodological and Ethical Challenges.

North, D. (1990) Institutions, Institutional Change and Economic Performance, Cambridge: Cambridge University Press.

Nylen, W. (2002) 'Testing the empowerment thesis: the participatory budget in Belo Horizonte and Betrim, Brazil', Comparative Politics 34: 127–45.

Oakley, A., Hickey, D., Rajan, L. and Rigby, A. (1996) 'Social support in pregnancy: does it have long-term effects?', Journal of Reproductive and Infant Psychology 14: 7–22.

Oakley, D. and Tsao, H. (2007) 'Socioeconomic gains and spillover effects of geographically targeted initiatives to combat economic distress: an examination of Chicago's Empowerment Zone', Cities 24: 43–59.

O'Keefe, G. (1985) '"Taking the bite out of crime": Impact of a public information campaign', Communication Research 12: 147–78.

Orr, J., Bloom, H., Bell, S., Doolittle, F. and Lin, W. (1996) Does Training for the Disadvantaged Work? Evidence from the National JTPA Study, Washington, D.C.: Urban Institute.

Osborne, D. and Gaebler, T. (1992) Reinventing Government: How the Entrepreneurial Spirit is Transforming the Public Sector, Reading, MA: Addison-Wesley.

Ostrom, E. (1990) Governing the Commons: The Evolution of Institutions for Collective Action, Cambridge: Cambridge University Press.

——(2010) 'Beyond markets and states: polycentric governance of complex economic systems', American Economic Review 100: 641–72.

Ostrom, E. and Gardner, R. (1993) 'Coping with asymmetries in the commons: self-governing irrigation systems can work', Journal of Economic Perspectives 7: 93–112.

O'Toole, L. and Meier, K. (1999) 'Modeling the impact of public management: implications of structural context', Journal of Public Administration Research and Theory 9: 505–26.

——(2003a) 'Plus ça change: Public management, personnel stability, and organizational performance', Journal of Public Administration Research and Theory 13: 43–64.

——(2003b) 'Public management and educational performance: the impact of managerial networking', Public Administration Review 63: 689–99.

——(2004a) 'Parkinson's Law and the new public management? Contracting determinants and service-quality consequences in public education', Public Administration Review 64: 342–52.

——(2004b) 'Desperately seeking Selznick: cooptation and the dark side of public management in networks', Public Administration Review 64: 681–93.

Pawson, R. and Tilly, N. (1997) Realistic Evaluation, London: Sage.

Percival, G. (2009) 'Exploring the influence of local policy networks on the implementation of drug policy reform: the case of California's Substance Abuse and Crime Prevention Act', Journal of Public Management Research and Theory 9: 795–815.

Perrow, C. (1986) Complex Organizations: A Critical Essay, New York: McGraw-Hill.

Persson, T. and Tabellini, G. (1994) 'Is inequality harmful for growth?', American Economic Review 84: 600–21.

——(2003) The Economic Effects of Constitutions, Cambridge: MIT Press.

——(2004) 'Constitutions and economic policy', Journal of Economic Perspectives 18: 75–98.

Peters, B. and Nispen, F. (eds) (1998) Public Policy Instruments Evaluating the Tools of Public Administration, Cheltenham: Edward Elgar.

Pollitt, C. (2003a) The Essential Public Manager, Maidenhead and Philadelphia: Open University Press/McGraw-Hill.

——(2003b) 'Joined-up government: a review', Political Studies Review 1: 34–49.

Pollitt, C. and Bouckaert, G. (2004) Public Management Reform: A Comparative Analysis, Oxford: Oxford University Press, 2nd ed.

Prendergast, C. (2001) 'Selection and oversight in the public sector, with the Los Angeles police department as an example', NBER Working Paper No. W8664. Online. Available HTTP: http://ssrn.com/abstract=294102, accessed 2 August 2010.

Propper, C., Sutton, M., Whitnall, C. and Windmeijer, F. (2010) 'Incentives and targets in hospital care: evidence from a natural experiment', Journal of Public Economics 94: 318–35.

Pressman, J. and Wildavsky, A. (1973) Implementation. How Great Expectations in Washington are Dashed in Oakland or, Why it's amazing that Federal programs work at all, this being a saga of the Economic Development Administration as told by two sympathetic observers who seek to build morals on a foundation of ruined hopes, Berkeley: University of California Press.

Provan, K. and Milward, H. (1995) 'A preliminary theory of interorganizational network effectiveness: a comparative study of four community mental health systems', Administrative Science Quarterly 40: 1–33.

Provan, K., Fish, A. and Sydow, J. (2007), 'Interorganizational networks at the network level: a review of the empirical literature on whole networks', Journal of Management 33: 479–516.

Przeworski, A. and Teune, H. (1970) The Logic of Comparative Social Inquiry, New York: Wiley-Interscience, John Wiley & Son.

Quinn, J. (1992) Intelligent Enterprise: A Knowledge and Service Based Paradigm for Industry, New York: The Free Press.

Rajkumar, A. and Swaroop, V. (2008) 'Public spending and outcomes: does governance matter?', Journal of Development Economics 86: 96–111.

Rauch, J. (1994) 'Bureaucracy, infrastructure, and economic growth: theory and evidence from U.S. cities during the Progressive era', Department of Economics Discussion Paper No. 94–06, University of California, San Diego, May 1994.
——(1995) 'Bureaucracy, infrastructure, and economic growth: evidence from U.S. cities during the Progressive era', American Economic Review 85: 968–79.
Reams, M. and Ray, B. (1993) 'The effects of three prompting methods on recycling participation rates – a field-study', Journal of Environmental Systems 22: 371–79.
Revelli, F. (2008) 'Performance competition in local media markets', Journal of Public Economics 92: 1585–94.
Rhodes, J., Tyler, P. and Brennan, A. (2005) 'Assessing the effect of area based initiatives on local area outcomes: some thoughts based on the national evaluation of the Single Regeneration Budget in England', Urban Studies 42: 1919–46.
Riddell, W. (2006) The Impact of Education on Economic and Social Outcomes: An Overview of Recent Advances in Economics, School of Policy Studies, Canadian Policy Research Networks Inc. Online. Available HTTP: http://www.cprn.org/doc.cfm?doc=1490&l=en, accessed 26 July 2010.
Riker, W. (1982) Liberalism Against Populism, San Francisco: W. H. Freeman.
Roller, E. (2005) The Performance of Democracies: Political Institutions and Public Policy, Oxford: Oxford University Press.
Rothstein, B. (1998) Just Institutions Matter: The Moral and Political Logic of the Universal Welfare State, Cambridge: Cambridge University Press.
Salamon, L. (ed.) (2002) The Tools of Government: A Guide to the New Governance, Oxford: Oxford University Press.
Salamon, L. and Lund, M. (1989) Beyond Privatization: the Tools of Government Action, Washington, D.C.: The Urban Institute.
Santos, B. (1998) 'Participatory budgeting in Porto Alegre: towards a redistributive democracy', Politics and Society 26: 461–510.
Sartori, G. (1994) Constitutional Engineering: An Inquiry into Structures, Incentives and Outcomes, New York: New York University Press.
Saunders, P. (1986) 'What can we learn from international comparisons of public sector size and economic performance?', European Sociological Review 2: 52–60.
Scott, J. (2000) Social Network Analysis, London: Sage, 2nd ed.
Schick, A. (1996) The Spirit of Reform: Managing the New Zealand State Sector in a Time of Change, Wellington, NZ: State Services Commission and the Treasury.
Schultz, P. (1998) 'Changing behaviour with normative feedback interventions: a field experiment on kerbside recycling', Basic and Applied Psychology 21: 25–36.
Scruggs, L. (1999) 'Institutions and environmental performance in seventeen western democracies', British Journal of Political Science 29: 1–31.
——(2003) Sustaining Abundance; Environmental Performance in Industrial Democracies, Cambridge: Cambridge University Press.
Select Committee on Public Administration (2002) Seventh Report, The Public Service Ethos, London: HMSO.
Selznick, P. (1949) TVA and the Grass Roots: a Study of Politics and Organization, Berkeley: University of California Press.
Shadish, W., Cook, T. and Campbell, D. (2002) Experimental and Quasi-Experimental Designs for Generalized Causal Inference, Boston: Houghton-Mifflin.

Sherman, L., Strang, H., Angel, C., Woods, D., Barnes, S., Bennett, S. and Inkpen, N. (2005) 'Effects of face-to-face restorative justice on victims of crime in four randomized, controlled trials', Journal of Experimental Criminology 1: 367–95.

Sherman, L., Rogan, D., Edwards, T., Whipple, R., Shreve, D., Witcher, D., Trimble, W., The Street Narcotics Unit, Velke, R., Blumberg, M., Beatty, A. and Bridgeforth, C. (1995) 'Deterrent effects of police raids on crack houses: a randomized, controlled experiment', Justice Quarterly 12: 755–81.

Smith, B. (1985) Decentralization: The Territorial Dimension of the State, London: Unwin.

Smith, G. (1999) Area-based Initiatives: The Rationale and Options for Area Targeting, CASE paper number 25, London: LSE/CASE.

——(2009) Democratic Innovations, Cambridge: Cambridge University Press.

Smith, K. and Meier, K. (1994) 'Politics, bureaucrats, and schools', Public Administration Review 54: 551–58.

Snyder, L. (2007) 'Health communication campaigns and their impact on behavior', Journal of Nutrition Education and Behavior 39: 32–40.

Snyder, L., Hamilton, M., Mitchell, E and Kiwanuka, J. (2004) 'A meta-analysis of the effect of mediated health communication campaigns on behavior change in the United States', Journal of Health Communication 9 Suppl. 1: 71–96.

Sørensen, E. and Torfing, J. (eds) (2009) Theories of Democratic Network Governance, Basingstoke: Macmillan.

Soskice, D. (1990) 'Wage determination: the changing role of institutions in advanced industrialized countries', Oxford Review of Economic Policy 6: 36–61.

Stern, N. (2007) The Economics of Climate Change, Cambridge: Cambridge University Press.

Stigler, G. (1971) 'The theory of economic regulation', Bell Journal of Economics and Management Science 2: 3–21.

Stoker, G. (2003) Transforming Local Governance, Basingstoke: Macmillan.

Stone, C. (1989) Regime Politics: Governing Atlanta, 1946–1988, Lawrence: University Press of Kansas.

Stone, D. (2001) Policy Paradox: The Art of Political Decision Making, New York: W. W. Norton, 2nd ed.

Strang, H., and Sherman, L. (2006) 'Restorative justice to reduce victimization', in Walsh, B. and Farrington, D. (eds), Preventing Crime: What Works for Children, Offenders, Victims and Places, Dordrecht, The Netherlands: Springer.

Sunstein, C., Schkade, D. and Kahneman, D. (2000) 'Do people want optimal deterrence?', Journal of Legal Studies 29: 237–98.

Surrey, S. (1973) Pathways to Tax Reform: The Concept of Tax Expenditures, Cambridge, Mass.: Harvard University Press.

Thaler, R. and Benartzi, S. (2004) 'Save more tomorrow: using behavioral economics to increase employee saving', Journal of Political Economy 112: 164–87.

Thaler, R. and Sunstein, C. (2008) Nudge: Improving Decisions About Health, Wealth and Happiness, New Haven: Yale University Press.

Thomson, H., Atkinson, R., Petticrew, M. and Kearns, A. (2006) 'Do urban regeneration programmes improve public health and reduce health inequalities? A synthesis of the evidence from UK policy and practice (1980–2004)', Journal of Epidemiology and Community Health 60: 108–15.

Thorlby, R. and Maybin, J. (eds) (2010) A High-Performing NHS: A Review of Progress 1997–2010, London: King's Fund.

Tiebout, C. (1956) 'A pure theory of local expenditures', Journal of Political Economy 64: 416–24.

Timlett, R. and Williams, I. (2008) 'Public participation and recycling performance in England: a comparison of tools for behaviour change', Resources Conservation and Recycling 52: 622–34.

Tolbert, C. and Mossberger, K. (2006) 'The effects of e-government on trust and confidence in government', Public Administration Review 63: 354–69.

Torgerson, D. and Torgerson, C. (2008) Designing Randomised Trails in Health, Education and the Social Sciences: An Introduction, Basingstoke: Palgrave.

Treisman, D. (2000) 'Decentralization and inflation: commitment, collective action, or continuity', American Political Science Review 94: 837–57.

——(2002) 'Decentralization and the quality of government', unpublished paper, Department of Political Science, UCLA.

——(2007) The Architecture of Government: Rethinking Political Decentralization, Cambridge: Cambridge University Press.

Tsebelis, G. (1995) 'Decision making in political systems: veto players in presidentialism, parliamentarism, multicameralism and multipartyism', British Journal of Political Science 25: 289–325.

——(2002) Veto Players: How Political Institutions Work, Princeton: Princeton University Press.

Tyler, T., Sherman, L., Strang, K., Barnes, G. and Woods, D. (2007) 'Reintegrative shaming, procedural justice, and recidivism: the engagement of offenders' psychological mechanisms in the Canberra RISE drinking-and-driving experiment', Law and Society Review 41: 553–86.

Vogel, D. (1986) National Styles of Regulation: Environmental Policy in Great Britain and the United States, Ithaca, NY: Cornell University Press.

von Hirsch, A., Bottoms, A., Burney, E. and Wikstrom, P-O. (1999) Criminal Deterrence and Sentence Severity: An Analysis of Recent Research, Oxford: Hart Publishing.

Walsh, K. (1995) Public Services and Market Mechanisms: Competition, Contracting and the New Public Management, Basingstoke: Macmillan.

Wanigaratne, S., Davies, P., Pryce, K. and Brotchie, J. (2005) The Effectiveness of Psychological Therapies on Drug Misusing Clients, London: NTA.

Wanless, D., Appleby, J., Harrison, A. and Patel, D. (2007) Our Future Health Secured? A Review of NHS Funding and Performance, London: King's Fund.

Weatherburn, D. and Lind, B. (1997) 'The impact of law enforcement activity on a heroin market', Addiction 92: 557–69.

Weatherhead, E. and Andersen, S. (2006) 'The search for signs of recovery of the ozone layer', Nature 441: 39–45.

Weede, E. (1986) 'Sectoral reallocation, distributional coalitions and the welfare state as determinants of economic growth rates in industrialized democracies', European Journal of Political Research 14: 501–19.

Weingast, B. (1995) 'The economic role of political institutions: market-preserving federalism and economic development', Journal of Law, Economics, & Organization 11: 1–31.

——(2002) 'Rational choice institutionalism', in Katznelson, I. and Milner, H. (eds) Political Science: The State of the Discipline, New York: W. W. Norton.

Weiss, J. and Tschirhart, M. (1994) 'Public information campaigns as policy instruments', Journal of Policy Analysis and Management 13: 82–119.

Welch, S. and Bledsoe, T. (1988) Urban Reform and its Consequences: A Study in Representation, Chicago: University of Chicago Press.

West, D. (2004) 'E-government and the transformation of service delivery and citizen attitudes', Public Administration Review 64: 15–27.

Wilensky, H. (2002) Rich Democracies: Political Economy, Public Policy, and Performance, Berkley and Los Angeles: University of California Press.

Wilkinson, R. (1996) Unhealthy Societies: The Afflictions of Inequality, London: Routledge.

Williamson, O. (1975) Markets and Hierarchies: Analysis and Antitrust Implications, New York: The Free Press.

Wilson, W. (1996) When Work Disappears: The World of the New Urban Poor, New York: Alfred A. Knopf.

Wolf, P. (1993) 'A case survey of bureaucratic effectiveness in U.S. Cabinet Agencies: preliminary results', Journal of Public Administration Research and Theory 3: 161–81.

World Bank (2003) Case Study 2: Porto Alegre, Brazil: Participatory Approaches in Budgeting and Public Expenditure Management, Report Number 27462. Online. Available HTTP: http://www-wds.worldbank.org/external/default/main?pagePK=64193027& piPK=64187937&theSitePK=523679&menuPK=64187510&searchMenuPK= 64187283&theSitePK=523679&entityID=000090341_20031216092121& searchMenuPK=64187283&theSitePK=523679, accessed 25 July 2010.

Yanow, D. (1996) How Does a Policy Mean? Interpreting Policy and Organizational Actions, Washington, D.C.: Georgetown University Press.

Index